LIVES OF
UNFORGETTING

WHAT WE LOSE IN TRANSLATION
WHEN WE READ THE BIBLE

Stant Litore

MORE FROM STANT LITORE

THE ZOMBIE BIBLE

Death Has Come up into Our Windows
What Our Eyes Have Witnessed
Strangers in the Land
No Lasting Burial
I Will Hold My Death Close
By a Slender Thread (forthcoming)

ANSIBLE

Ansible: Season One
Ansible: Season Two
Ansible: Rasha's Letter

OTHER TITLES

The Running of the Tyrannosaurs
The Screaming of the Tyrannosaur
Nyota's Tyrannosaur
Dante's Heart

&

The Dark Need (The Dead Man #20)
with Lee Goldberg, William Rabkin

&

Lives of Unstoppable Hope
Write Characters Your Readers Won't Forget
Write Worlds Your Readers Won't Forget

LIVES OF
UNFORGETTING

WHAT WE LOSE IN TRANSLATION
WHEN WE READ THE BIBLE

AND

A WAY OF READING THE BIBLE
AS A CALL TO ADVENTURE

STANT LITORE

2019

Stant Litore is a pen name for Daniel Fusch.

The English lyrics of *O Holy Night* appearing in the closing chapter of this book are by Adolphe Adam (1847).

Most biblical quotations in the book—unless in Hebrew, Aramaic, Greek, or Latin, or unless translating freely from the original texts—are given in the New Revised Standard Version (NRSV).

Cover design by Roberto Calas.
Cover art by Rustic Vegan on Unsplash.

ISBN: 978-1-7320869-3-7

Contact Stant Litore:
www.stantlitore.com
www.patreon.com/stantlitore
zombiebible@gmail.com
www.facebook.com/stant.litore

CONTENTS

FOREWORD: WHY THIS BOOK?   1

PART 1: "WHAT IS TRUTH?"   15

1. *Aletheia*, or "Unforgetting"   17

PART 2: FIVE THINGS WORTH UNFORGETTING   41

2. *Eshet Chayil:* The Woman of Valor   43

3. *Philoxenia*: The Provision for Refugees   86

4. *Eirene*: The Egalitarian Body of Christ   112

5. *Pisteuo:* Faith is a Verb   133

6. *Parakletoi*: The Advocates   150

PART 3: THE TASK AT HAND: TO BECOME BETTER READERS—OF THE BIBLE, AND EACH OTHER   165

7. To Read Each Other with More Compassion   167

8. To Read the Bible as Children —and as Adventurers   191

PART 4: WHAT GETS IN OUR WAY   227

9. "For The Sake of Your Tradition"   229

10. God Doesn't Condemn LGBTQ+
People (Humans Do)   248

11. Sin is an Activity, not a State of Being   276

12. Our Understanding of Idolatry is Simplistic   292

13. The Trap of "Submission" to Authority   302

14. What "Turning the Other Cheek" Really Means   316

15. Humanity Does Not Rule in "Dominion"
over the Earth   322

16. What "Sparing the Rod" Doesn't Mean   329

17. Conversion through Fear is as Unbiblical
as it is Abusive   331

18. The First-Century Church Didn't Have a Literal Hell   339

19. God's Love Has No Conditions   351

AFTERWORD AND ADVENT:
MAKING THE GOOD STORY A TRUE STORY,
AN UNFORGOTTEN STORY   356

About the Cover

Because people have asked me about the significance of the cover: The photograph is by The Rustic Vegan (www.instagram.com/rustic.vegan); it makes me think of being welcomed to a lovely meal with people who have stories to share that may not be the stories I expect. Thank you for joining me at the table.

If this book moves you, please share it. Good stories, like good meals, deserve to be shared. Buy copies for your friends, your family. You can also write to me at zombiebible@gmail.com and let me know what you thought.

My work on this book—and on my novels, too—has been funded by the generous support of my Patreon members. If you would like to join them, help support my work, and see previews of what I am working on next, you can do that here:

WWW.PATREON.COM/STANTLITORE

May your life always be full of good stories, may your ears always be open to the stories of others, and may you continually unforget that which is most important to your heart.

Stant Litore

for River, Inara, and Círdan, my children

be smart
be brave
be kind

and always do unto others
as you would have them
do unto you

FOREWORD: WHY THIS BOOK?

I WRITE THIS OUT OF LOVE for my readers—who are of many faiths, or none—and out of a passion for ancient languages and a love of the biblical stories that I see so often mangled and misused in our culture, the very stories I've spent my life reading and writing into my own fiction. And I'm writing this because many readers have asked me for it. My hope is that this book will be healing to some and illuminating to others, that it will help peel away destructive ideas and prejudices that have barnacled themselves onto modern Christianity and unearth first- and second-century contexts that help us see and explore biblical passages in a very different light. Like other writers in the long tradition of apologetics—from Francis of Assisi to Dietrich Bonhoeffer, and many others before and since—I am wrestling with how to follow Christ in a broken world and with how to follow Christ in a broken church. Therefore, this book is both a personal exploration of my faith and a plea addressed to those who share it. The plea is: We can be the church that gives sanctuary or the church that kills. May we be the former. And may this book's small acts of recovery and exegesis aid those who yearn for that sanctuary.

The project of making this book is one I have pursued in fear and trembling, knowing well that I am dancing with sacred texts in my hands. I will share a lot of historical and linguistic research along the way—in this, I stand on the shoulders of giants, indebted to many researchers. Among such a crowd of witnesses, I hope I will run the race well.

But this book is not a dry list of dates and dictionary entries. This is not an annotated bibliography, though I will certainly point toward many exciting things to read. And though this book offers a lot of exegesis, it is neither an altar call nor a traditional "bible study." It is an invitation to read our sacred texts more humbly and to read both the Bible and *each other* with more context and compassion. It is a call to approach the Word both "like little children"—with fresh eyes and fresh wonder—and also as adventurers, prepared to take risks and make brave choices as we interpret the texts we have received from the ancients. It is a call to "unforget" passages in our texts that we frequently gloss over, mistranslate, or ignore—but that were important to how the earliest Christians read, experienced, and lived their faith.

So this book is more of a collection of stories—stories about people forgotten, and about ideas forgotten and unforgotten. Stories about who we are or who we might be, those of us who say, "Yes," when a rabbi two thousand years ago says, "Follow me." Stories are messy and imprecise, but they are the tool my Teacher used; the good story—the *euangelion* in Greek—is the origin of the Christian faith; and living this faith consists of emulating a man we first met in a story. Stories are the best tool I have available to me. I hope you will read with openness and compassion. If you have been wounded and hurt by the church, may this book be a balm for your wounds. If you are currently in the church and feel alone, may this book let you know you are not. If you are leading a church, may this book give you food for thought, whether some of it is new to you or a refresher. I offer it to you in love.

THE EVENT: OR, HOW AND WHY I READ THE BIBLE

What drives me to the Bible, time and again, is the story of Jesus, which moves me and changes me and calls me away from comfort or apathy and into adventure. And the invitation to the Event, which is a term philosophers Jacques Derrida and John Caputo use to describe the encounter with the impossible, an unexpected encounter that can shake us to the core. The stories in the Bible, from the parting of the Red Sea to the Resurrection, dramatize the coming of the impossible, the Event that creates previously unforeseen possibilities and opportunities for how we understand not only everything that has yet *to happen* but everything that *has happened.*

First-century, Greek-speaking Christians called this moment a *kairos*, which sometimes gets translated "the right time," "the right season," "the occasion," or "the opportunity." For them, there were three kinds of "time": *chronos, aion,* and *kairos. Chronos* is "clock time," the relentless tick-tock of the day to day, which they associated with Roman time, the time of Empire: the disciplined march of military boots, exacting schedules, and adherence to tradition. Every moment planned and expected. All possibilities anticipated, documented, and known. For the early Christians, *chronos* was a relentless march toward death in a world caged by sin and presided over by corrupt authorities—a world locked and closed, where the only sanctioned and proper interpretation of what your life meant and could be or become ... was Caesar's. An orderly, disciplined, hierarchical world. A constricted and restricted world, an intolerable world, an unjust world. As was said of Adolf Hitler's Germany, in that world the trains always run on time.

But the early Christians also imagined another kind of time—*aion*, eternity, God's time. Time without beginning or end, an eternal present. In *The Consolation of Philosophy*, the theologian Boethius wrote that God exists in just such an eternal present, able to see all of time at once, all pasts and all futures simultaneously. For Boethius, God is able to reach from *aion* into our *chronos*. He is able to touch our inexorable clock-time world with his finger and shatter our expectations and schedules and limitations as easily as a fist might shatter a glass. God's arrival in the world is the unpredictable Event, the impossible that could not be planned for or scheduled. It is a *kairos*, an unexpected moment that stops *chronos*. Frank Kermode, in his book *A Sense of an Ending*, calls *kairos* the "silence between the *tick* and the *tock*." It is when the pendulum stops and you hold your breath, because the timeline you thought you were in—the story you thought you were reading or living—suddenly has the potential to change, right out from under you.

In Peter S. Beagle's fantasy novel *The Last Unicorn*, adventurers are trying to find a doorway to another place, a door that only opens when King Haggard's clock strikes the right time. But King Haggard's clock is broken. The adventurers are confused. How can they open the door if the clock will *never* strike the right time? A talking skull gives them the answer: Any time o' the clock can potentially be "the right time." Any time can be a *kairos,* because the impossible Event, the opening of the invisible door, is not something you put on a calendar. It is something that happens unexpectedly, as a disruption or shattering of *chronos.*

When the *kairos* occurs, it means opportunity— opportunity that is risky and dangerous and requires bravery. Will the adventurers leap through the door in the clock, not knowing exactly where they will land, and possibly arriving to face the menace of the Red Bull, a supernatural monster of sinew and flame? Will the Israelites dare to cross between towering walls of water after God has parted the Red Sea? Will the women facing the empty tomb dare to believe that death has been rolled back and their friend walks and breathes even at that moment in the garden? At the moment of *kairos*, the adventurer is presented with a risky choice. If they seize the opportunity, then potentially the future will be written very differently than they had anticipated. Not only that: the past will be *re*written. Not the facts of the past, but what those facts *mean*. Once the Children of Israel walk through the midst of the sea and enter the desert as a free people, their past lives of slavery and oppression will be understood differently. What their past slavery *means* to their identity will change. The stories they tell of their past will now be told from the perspective of a free people. And in Christian soteriology, the Resurrection is similarly an event that changes both future and past—"redeeming" the past—because if all God's children rise to eternal life, then the death and suffering and loss of the past, which has still happened and is still real, *means* something different than it did before Mary Magdalene saw an empty tomb.

Just like Peter S. Beagle's characters leaping through the clock or the Israelites walking between two parted walls of ocean water, the reader is an adventurer. The reader encounters an impossible Event in the story and has the opportunity (*kairos*) to change how they understand the story and what the story means and what could possibly happen in the story. And as they draw analogies between the story in the book and that other story they are telling themselves about their own life, they have the opportunity to infer and imagine and find new interpretations of what *their* story means. That is the wonder of the Event, when the impossible breaks through the chronological march of time and expectation.

Those of us who follow Christ may call that Event an encounter with the Word of God, the same Word that John the evangelist said was once "made flesh," incarnate in the living person of Jesus of Nazareth. The same Word that the letter to the Hebrews describes as "living and active and sharper than any double-edged sword," sharp enough and shocking enough to cut through the bondage of our traditions and expectations, the prejudices and the habits of our lives, to awaken us to previously unseen possibilities and to call or invite us to action—perhaps to different ways of treating others, or to a new, "more excellent way" of directing our lives (1 Corinthians 12:31).

But because this Event happens inside a story, it can burst upon us regardless of whether or not we believe that God exists. The story can move us, shock us, and call us to action regardless of what we think we know or don't know. That is the function of a story, which acts upon the imagination. This is why both theists and atheists, both Christians and anyone else, can engage with the Bible and find themselves changed by these ancient texts.

I suspect that many people ignore biblical stories and miss the opportunity for *kairos* that is in them. Many religious readers ignore these stories when they read merely for examples to corroborate or elaborate on what they've been taught. Secular readers ignore these stories when they think they must first accept political slogans and agendas that refer back to the stories. To me, this is a tragedy. We are talking about one of our oldest and most diverse treasure-houses of stories, and it is the one such treasure-house that everyone talks about and no one really *experiences*.

These are horror stories and wonder stories, but we've largely forgotten that. A crucifixion is horrific. A child sacrifice is horrific. These stories try to shock us awake and then invite us to ask really tough questions, necessary questions. In my writings over the past decade, I have desired to bring these stories to readers in such a way that they would horrify and amaze us again, *move* us again. I wanted to give readers the encounter with the impossible. For me, biblical texts are not reducible to political slogans or 'life application' self-help messages. I want to take us back out into the heart of the storm on the lake, to that moment when the waves are high and the sky is crushing

7

us down with its dark weight, God is asleep, and we are hanging on to the gunwale for dear life, learning who and what we are. In *The Zombie Bible*, I have tried to do that through fiction. In this book, I want to do it through exegesis and eisegesis, through demonstrating the kind of reading adventures that can help us encounter the impossible Event when we delve into these ancient texts.

EXEGESIS AND EISEGESIS: IS ASLAN A TAME LION?

The problem is that we read the Bible—and many other texts, too—in ways that permit us to avoid being adventurers. To avoid the invitation to adventure is to skip the encounter with the unexpected or the impossible, to read comfortably without having to make dangerous choices in interpreting what we read, without having to really consider or choose between the possibilities the story might present to us. That is, we read in ways that allow us to skip the *kairos*, the opportunity. We take wild, impossible texts—like those in the Bible—and we read them tamely.

Often we do this because we are reading either *only* exegetically or *only* eisegetically. These two Greek words describe two complementary methods for interpreting a text. Exegesis is reading something *out* of a text, as when we dig deeply into the language and place the text in its historical and cultural context. Eisegesis is when we read something *into* a text, as when we import our own contemporary situation and concerns into a text. For example, let's suppose we're reading J.R.R. Tolkien's *The Lord of the Rings* together. Reading *The Lord of the Rings* exegetically, we might analyze how the hobbits' culture works, how that culture gets expressed or challenged over the course of the book, and what values the hobbits hold dear. Reading *The Lord of the Rings* eisegetically instead, we might choose to hold up Frodo and Sam as heroic, "everyman" role models for the values *we* hold dear.

There are consequences when we limit ourselves to one method of reading or the other.

If we only do *exegesis* and bring nothing of ourselves into the text, the text becomes merely an inert relic of the past, the object of a merely academic ritual—rather than a story that might enthrall or harrow us or move us to tears.

On the other hand, if we only do *eisegesis* and we go into the text looking for something to confirm or clarify our own situation or our received tradition, then the text becomes merely a mirror, a reflection we hold up, unknowingly gazing at an image of ourselves. Rather than a story of the unexpected that might shock, upset, or change us, the text becomes an imitation or expression of the story about ourselves that we have already written. We see our own prejudices and concerns mirrored endlessly in the text. Like Boromir adventuring in Lothlorien in *The Lord of the Rings*, what we find there is something we took in with us.

This happens often when we read the Bible. In many religious communities today, especially within evangelical traditions, we have prized eisegetical reading—for example, life application studies and the finding of "object lessons" in the Bible. We have prioritized eisegesis to such a degree that we no longer encounter the stories and the texts in the Bible as unexpected or shocking. We go in looking for evidence of traditions, prejudices, and beliefs that we already hold; we no longer go into the text fresh and asking questions, approaching the Word "like a little child" (Luke 18:17). We use the Bible as a prop to hold up church doctrine—rather than encountering the living Word who once drove moneychangers out of a place of worship, flipping over all the furniture and the expectations and commerce that temple had become packed with. We have made the Word our slave rather than our deliverer. In many popular contemporary Christian study bibles, each passage has its precise and officially sanctioned interpretation, carefully footnoted at the bottom of the page, and the reader is continually assured that nothing unexpected will happen. Everything in the text has its place. Everything is disciplined. Everything can be explained. Nothing you will encounter is inconsistent with the doctrines passed down to you by your elders. The trains run on time, and Aslan is understood to be a "tame lion." (In *The Lion, The Witch, and the Wardrobe*, the children who visit Narnia keep asking if Aslan, the great lion whom Narnian citizens revere, is "safe." The Narnians reply, "Of course he isn't safe. He isn't a tame lion." He might do the unexpected. He might ask impossible choices of you, might ask you to do what appears impossible to you.) We have insisted, as a culture, that the Bible be a tame, safe text—whether we are Christian theists using the Bible as our sacred text or whether we are atheists rejecting, avoiding, or satirizing it. In either case, we have accepted that the Bible is to be evaluated and responded to according to its effectiveness as a disciplined, authoritative, *chronos*-bound text, a sort of spiritual manual, handbook, or reference guide—a fixed, static object. For religious readers, that often means treating the Bible as a text we check everything against, the way we have been taught to use a dictionary or an encyclopedia, a place we go to "look things up." Many atheists treat the Bible in the same way, with the difference that they may regard the Bible as a flawed or inaccurate or even counterfactual encyclopedia, and therefore not an encyclopedia it would be prudent to look things up in. But what if we looked to the Bible not as a place to find definitions and check our tradition, but instead as an opportunity (a *kairos*) to challenge, question, and investigate our definitions and our received tradition? What we so rarely do is encounter the Bible as a library of evocative stories, of texts that shock us with the impossible and invite difficult choices.

Remember that *chronos*—clock-time, in which every-thing is planned and scheduled and anticipated, the time that helps the Roman soldiers march in step—is the relentless march toward death. *Kairos* is the impossible, the resurrection, the reversal or inversion, the opportunity, the unplanned, the encounter with the living and active Word. It is an encounter that comes upon us like a thief in the night, and no one—unless perhaps the Father—knows the hour and the day, the page or the verse, when it might happen. It is the moment when readers become adventurers again rather than mere recipients, "doers" and not just "hearers," the moment when they have to make choices.

Whether a reader is religious or secular, the hope of adventure is the same. The possibility of the impossible, the arrival of the Event, the chance to ask new questions we've never thought of before—that is what I yearn for when I read. It is especially what I yearn for when I open the Bible, trembling and alert while I read. Here is a vast library of stories compiled in three languages, across three continents, and over many centuries, a library of rhetorical arguments and psalms and love poems and narratives and personal letters that might present any number of challenges to what I think I know both about the text (*exegesis*) and about myself and my culture (*eisegesis*).

I believe we have swung very far in the direction of *eisegesis* in our culture, reading our own traditions and concerns into the text; for this reason, I will offer a lot of *exegesis* in this book. I want to conduct some linguistic archaeology, digging up and excavating fascinating ideas embedded in the texts of the Bible in the original languages the Bible was written in, ideas that were once very important to people but that are now frequently forgotten, misunderstood (because of the differences between our cultural context and the cultural contexts in which those ideas were born), mistranslated, or neglected. These ideas are now "hidden in plain sight," right there in the text. Ideas that are worth *un*forgetting. This is important to do because each of our encounters with these ideas that are hidden in plain sight can shock us, stir us, trouble us, or change us. Each one can offer a chance of *kairos*. At each, if we are willing to accept the adventure and the risks that go with it, the text—and for Christian readers, the living and active Word—might cut through our tradition, our prejudices, our expectations and we might discover something we had previously thought *impossible*.

That is the adventure before us.

Turn the page.

PART 1: "WHAT IS TRUTH?"

1. *Aletheia*, or "Unforgetting"

What This Chapter is About

In languages descended from or heavily influenced by Latin, it is possible to bludgeon people with truths, because in Latin, a truth is a *thing*. But this is less possible in Koine Greek. In the Koine Greek of the New Testament, truth is an *activity*, not a blunt object.

"I am the Way, and the Unforgetting, and the Life."

Jesus

LET ME TELL YOU A STORY. It's an ancient Greek story, so you can expect that it will be entertaining and extravagantly absurd at the same time. After all, these are the same people who told stories about young women getting impregnated by golden rain from the sky or pissing off a god and getting punished with uncontrollable lust for the local prize bull—so Greek stories tend to be both wildly imaginative and completely bonkers. This story is a little more tame than many, and also more sad. But it's one that, at one time, everyone in the Greco-Roman world knew. It's a story about what happens when you die.

DRINKING FROM THE WATERS OF LETHE

The Greeks loved life and health and vitality. Borrowing (or robbing, when possible) from the Egyptians, they created vast medical institutions. They created the Olympic Games and frequently celebrated athletic achievements above military, academic, or domestic ones. There is an old story about Philip of Macedon (the father of Alexander the Great) that the day his son was born, he was away at war. Three messengers rushed up to him, one after the other. The first told him his army had been victorious. He nodded stoically in response. The second told him his wife had given birth to a son. Philip hardly blinked. But the third...ah, the third told him that his prize chariot team had won the race at the Olympic Games. And Philip was so overjoyed at the news that he threw a festival at once.

In fact, the ancient Greeks were so in love with physical beauty and health and with the sheer joy of *being alive* that in their language, the word for "beautiful" and the word for "good" were the same word: *kalos*. To the Greeks, to be beautiful is also to be good, noble, and righteous; to be ugly is to be bad, evil, malformed in spirit and soul. That is the dark side of the Greek love of health and beauty. If you were unhealthy, clearly you had offended the gods. If you were unwell but also wealthy, you might offer an appropriate sacrifice to the god you had offended, to atone, or else to the god of healing, to beg his overriding favor. You might hire doctors or surgeons. But, if you were *not* wealthy and you lived with a physical or mental illness, or in pain, or you weren't conventionally pretty, then you were also out of luck in that culture. That world had little place for you.

Two other side effects of this fascination with health and vitality above all else were a privileging of the active life over the contemplative life (*we* might revere ancient philosophers, but their own generation tended to see them as scoundrels, layabouts, troublemakers, and corrupters of youth—and in one famous case, a philosopher was forced to drink poison just to remove that nuisance from the community) and a grim view of the afterlife. The Romans' *carpe diem* is really a Greek sentiment translated into Latin: Seize the day while you have it.

Once you die, the afterlife is not a paradise but a place of cold and shadow and thirst. The shades of the newly dead drink from the water of the river Lethe (the Greek word for "forgetting") and once they swallow that water, they forget all that ever mattered to them in life—who they were, who they loved and who loved them, what they feared and hoped for and regretted. We get the English word "lethargic"—which means apathetic, sluggish, drained of energy and life—from the name of that river. Having drunk its water, the dead walk onward into Hades' realm, restless, silent, alone though they walk in a great crowd, thirsting always for they know not what. In the *Odyssey,* Odysseus needs answers from the dead, so he goes to a doorway to Hades, performs a sacrifice, and fills a trench with hot blood from the slaughtered animal. The dead smell the blood, and they come fluttering up from the dark realm like so many bats, restless, desperate, thirsting for the thing they had forgotten but can now smell: *life*.

There's another story about this, one almost as old. A bride and a groom are separated on their wedding day by the bride's sudden death. Orpheus, the groom, is heartbroken. But he is also the first singer in the whole world, and *music* is still so new and surprising that at the sound of his melodies, trees march down mountain slopes to get closer to the song, and rivers change their course to get near enough to hear it better. Lovesick young Orpheus goes down to the underworld, bribing its guardians—including the ferryman and the three-headed dog—and confronts the king and queen of the afterlife. "I want Eurydice back," he says. They say, "Tough." Then he plays them music and sings them a song, a love song, a grief song, a song about the tragedy of death and of lives cut short too soon. And it is the first song ever heard in Hades' kingdom. The silent dead look up. Maybe they cry in a brief flash of memory. Moved, the lord and lady of the underworld tell Orpheus that Eurydice's shade will follow him back to the world that knows sunlight, but there is a catch. He must not look back over his shoulder until he reaches the land of the living. He must trust that the silent ghost of his bride is following.

Well, it's obvious how that story ends. He makes it almost all the way back, but with each step he grows more terrified that he has been cheated. At last, grieving Orpheus glances back. And for just an instant, he sees Eurydice. He sees *memory* flood back into her eyes: the memory of who she is, and who they briefly were together, and what it means to be alive. And then—

Then she is gone.

And no song of Orpheus's and no wailing or tears can change it.

Well, the Greeks rarely told *happy* stories.

The point of this one is that for the Greeks, death was the place of forgetting. And immortality wasn't something you received in the afterlife; your immortality was your fame, your glory, the living remembering you. You mattered as long as your name survived unforgotten after your death. Now, *Lethe* wasn't always all bad, not for all the poets, because life is full of suffering and pain, too, and the Greeks liked the idea of being able to forget pain. When Odysseus's son visits Sparta and the men tell stories, weeping, of Troy and of all their friends who died on foreign soil, Helen brings them *nepenthe*, a drug they can drink that will make them forget their grief for an evening—a foretaste of Lethe.

So oblivion did have its attractions, but mostly it terrified. The poets describe the passage into Hades' realm as harrowing and full of horror. But death itself wasn't what was scary. *Lethe* was scary.

Forgetting—and being forgotten—that was the terror, the true horror that haunts Greek stories. It is that fear that drives Achilles to choose a short, brutal life over a long one in exchange for his name being remembered for all time. It is that nightmare that sends the ghosts screeching up from beneath the earth to speak with Odysseus, craving life and remembrance. It is that dread that sends Orpheus into the underworld—not the sorrow that he has lost one he loves, but his horror that she has forgotten him and their time together. That time together is now like a dream, something only he has experienced and only he remembers—something, as the days pass, that he can't be sure was actually real.

DRINKING FROM LIVING WATER

First-century Christians in Greek-speaking communities also told a story about thirst and about *lethe*. It was a different story. In it, a traveling rabbi gives sermons and shows up at wedding parties to transform water into fine wine (and really *fine* wine, none of that end-of-the-night nonsense). And one day, he visits a foreign town and sits himself down by a well, because all of that walking tires you out something awful. After his students have gone into town to purchase provisions, a middle-aged woman comes out to draw water from the well. Now the rabbi Jesus asks her for a drink; walking is thirsty work. She stops and gives him a hard look. She is a Samaritan; she is descended from intermarriages between various local tribes and survivor Hebrews who fled to the hills to escape being dragged away captive by a conquering army centuries before. When the descendants of those captives returned, there was fierce strife between her people and theirs. They do not like each other. She reminds the rabbi of that, rather pointedly. How dare *he* ask *her* for a drink? Your people, she reminds him, walk all over my people, and now you expect me to take care of you?

And the rabbi Jesus, with his often quirky sense of humor, grins back and says that if she knew the gift God has for her, and who is speaking with her right now, she would ask *him* for water instead, and he would give her living water so that she would never thirst again.

The verbal sparring continues. Taken aback, the woman of Samaria says, "Give me this water, so I don't have to go down to the well every day." Jesus says: Tell you what, go get your husband, and you can both come down and drink.

"I have no husband," she says.

Jesus nods. "That is right. You have had five husbands, and the one you're with now isn't your husband. Without concealment [*alēthes*] you have spoken."

Hearing intimate facts of her life told to her by a stranger in her land, the woman takes Jesus to be a prophet. But he is not a prophet of *her* people, so she challenges him: Your people say to worship in Jerusalem, mine say to worship on this mountain. Which of us is right?

He gives her a remarkable answer:

> Woman, believe me, the hour is coming when you will worship the Father neither on this mountain nor in Jerusalem. ... The hour is coming, and is now here, when the revealed worshipers [or "unconcealed worshippers": *alēthinoi proskynētai*] will worship the Father in spirit and unforgetting [*alētheia*], for the Father seeks such as these to worship him. God is spirit, and those who worship him must worship in spirit and unforgetting [*alētheia*].

JOHN 4:21, 23-24

Later, when others in her village ask her why she is listening to this foreign prophet, the woman tells them that he spoke to her unconcealingly: "He told me all the things

I have ever done." And many in that village heed the traveling rabbi, believing now that a third way of worshipping God has been revealed to them—neither on the mountain nor in the Temple, but *en pneumati kai alētheia*—in spirit (or with every breath; *pneuma* in Greek is both "breath" and "spirit") and in unforgetting.

That word—*aletheia*—usually gets translated "truth" in English. It means "unconcealment" or "unforgetting."

LETHE AND *ALETHE*: TRUTH IN GREEK

Much of this book will be about things that are hidden and need to be unhidden—matters that are hidden in plain sight in our texts (concealed beneath the weight either of English translation or of our cultural prejudices that influence how we read and how we interpret what we read). So it is especially important to me that we start this adventure together with the Greek word for truth, which is not the word for "fact" but instead the word for unhiding and unforgetting.

Truth in Greek is *a-lethe* or un-Lethe. For the first-century Christians who wrote the gospels and a thick packet of letters to each other, the *euangelion* or the gospel (the "very excellent news") is the *aletheia* or un-Lethe, the unconcealment. Their idea is that we have been living in such a way that not only has God been concealed from us but we have been concealed from each other. Rather than drink continually from *lethe*, forgetting our God and our neighbor, we might drink the living water of *alethe* and unforget all that we have forgotten and unconceal all that has been concealed from us. For the early Christians, this discovery or recovery conveys "tidings of great joy"— because we find that we are the beloved, adopted children of God (see Chapter 4), delivered and given refuge (see Chapter 3) and offered an unexpected seat at the table of heaven.

I know this unpacking of the Greek word we gloss as "truth" will be new to many readers, but this isn't new research or even new theology. It's been almost a century since Martin Heidegger first examined the etymology and usage of Greek *alethe/aletheia*. In his analysis of Plato's allegory of the cave, *Platons Lehre von der Wahrheit*, Heidegger concludes:

> At first truth meant what was wrested from a concealment. Truth, then, is just such a perpetual wresting-away in this manner of uncovering.
>
> MARTIN HEIDEGGER

In languages descended from or heavily influenced by Latin, it is possible to bludgeon people with truths, because in Latin, 'truth' is a *thing*. But this is less possible in Koine Greek. In the Koine Greek of the New Testament, truth is an *activity*, not a blunt object. It's the undoing of *lethe* (forgetting, covering, concealing). It's literally *a-lethe*, un-lethe.

The Greeks feared being forgotten; the early Christians taught that they were God's unforgotten children, remembered and loved by a God who is *kardiognōsta pantōn,* "heartknowing of all" (Acts 1:24), who knows every hair on every person's head (Luke 12:7), and who calls every star in the sky by name (Psalm 147:4). Such complete love,

25

they said, "casts out all fear" (1 John 4:18). To receive the good news that we are so known and so loved fills the heart with joy—with *agallíasis* (Acts 2:46), a word that literally means a spring gushing up and overflowing. Like the living water Jesus told the Samaritan woman about, living water overflowing the heart and quenching the heart's deep thirst.

In early Christian ethics, to forget who we are in relation to God and each other is to thirst again and to fall back into slavery to our fears. Paul warns against this "falling back" in his letter to the Christians in Rome:

> For all who are led by the Spirit of God are children of God. For you did not receive a spirit of slavery to fall back into fear, but you have received a spirit of adoption. When we cry, "Abba! Father!" it is that very Spirit bearing witness with our spirit that we are children of God, and if children, then heirs, heirs of God and joint heirs with Christ.

ROMANS 8:14-17

Do not forget who you are! he cries to them, like Orpheus to Eurydice at that last fatal moment before she is gone. Once we drink the waters of *lethe* and forget, even though we walk this earth and eat and breathe and mate, we walk as the restless, forgetful dead. So thirsty that we will listen to false promises, to lies about who we are and what defines us. So thirsty, perhaps, that we'll put on a white KKK hood or a MAGA hat. So thirsty that we'll spend our lives acquiring status or possessions, believing these will give us value or satiety. So thirsty that we try to use or consume others as objects to fill the void within us.

Drinking *lethe*, we forget what gives us value. Not knowing who you are makes it easy (even desirable) to accept others' lies about who you are, to live in a "spirit of slavery," with your identity as a beloved child of God concealed—even from yourself—and with *others'* identities as beloved children of God, as your siblings in one family, concealed from you.

It is the undoing of this concealment that is *aletheia*, *un*forgetting. More than just remembering or "recalling" a thing to mind, *aletheia* is continual—the daily act of holding a promise present in your mind and heart, of letting that promise drive all that you do, the ongoing activity of un-*Lethe*'ing your heart. When Jesus says, in John 8:32, that "the truth will make you free" (*hē alētheia eleutherōsei hymas*), he is referring to that continual activity of unforgetting. When Paul counsels Timothy not to swerve from the truth (2 Timothy 2:14-19), in Greek he is not asking his colleague to hold fast to an intellectual opinion he has in his head; rather, he is saying, *Keep unforgetting the promise. Keep unforgetting who loves you as a son, and how much he loves you.* And that isn't a one-time activity but something that is ongoing, every hour, something to be actively doing all the time. The walk of faith involves resurrecting your heart, day by day, hour by hour, from the dry underworld of forgetfulness where life is expressed only in hues of gray, where consciousness persists without the constant awareness of joy and love.

When someone young and in love slips a love letter inside their clothing to keep it near their heart and to feel the paper against their skin, that is an unforgetting: an ongoing, constant unforgetting of the new love and joy, and of the promise for the future that the letter embodies. That is *aletheia*. For Christians, too, this *aletheia* is to be achieved by a love story or love message—by an *euangelion*, a gospel—a "good story" of who loves us, what has been done for us, and how we might live, loving each other.

When Jesus says "I am the Truth" in John 14:6, he is not saying 'I am the Fact' or 'I am a List of Things for You to Believe.' In the Greek text, he is saying "I am the Unforgetting": *I am the incarnation of the Unforgetting of God and his promises; I am literally God's Unforgetting of you, in my birth and in my death and resurrection. I am the unconcealing and unforgetting of God; I am the opposite of Lethe because I am not the water of forgetting but the water of life, the water that fills you so you need not thirst; I am the Resurrection and the Life.*

In the Greek New Testament, rather than 'believe in the truth,' you strive all the time to unforget promises, and you hold dear and trust the one who gave you the promise. Where most of our culture's conversation about belief is transactional in nature (accept this premise and sign on the dotted line), the original text is entirely relational (trust someone and hold their promise constantly before you). We'll talk about that a lot more in Chapter 5. For now: How different might our society be, if more communities of faith today experienced truth not as a list of intellectual positions or beliefs, but as the ongoing *aletheia* (unforgetting) of promises made, the unforgetting of relationships with God and with other human beings, whom God loves?

That gorgeous word *aletheia* doesn't have a precise equivalent in modern English; we compromise by continuing to translate it "truth." William Tyndale and, later, the translation committee who produced the Authorized Version commissioned by King James I settled on our word *troth* or *truth*, which at the time meant "a promise" in English. That meaning still exists today in our word *betrothed*—one who is promised to another—or in the archaic phrase "to pledge our troth." Truth (a promise) is something you pledge to another or something pledged to you, to which you hold fast. We have kept the word over the centuries in our Bible because that word has become sacred to us.

But English has changed over the centuries. When we hear the word *truth* now, we no longer hear a "promise"— in much the same way that when we read the word *charity* in the King James Bible, we no longer hear "unconditional love." These words have shifted over time. And now we are readers living on the opposite side of the Enlightenment and the Age of Reason. By us, truth is often regarded as a synonym for a fact, something that can be verified or that we must believe *has* been verified. *Veritas* is the Latin word for truth—that which can be verified. When Roman writers such as Cicero or Marcus Aurelius write of *veritas*, they write of that which many people see at once and can attest to. "Fact" is another Latin word—it comes from the participle *factum est*: "it happened."

In the book of John, when Jesus is brought to trial, he talks with the Roman procurator about truth, and Pontius Pilate has no idea what he's talking about. "What is truth?" Pilate asks at last in exasperation, because his cultural and linguistic vocabulary leaves him ill-equipped to "get" it— much as our own leaves *us* ill-equipped to "get" it. This same confusion between *truth* and *fact* causes us a lot of trouble in our own culture. In our time, some religious communities and institutions can easily come to see themselves as bastions and guardians of *facts*—and of facts that are alternative to the facts taught outside their walls.

The Greek word for truth implies a responsibility for those who receive it. If truth is the activity of unconcealment, that implies that something, or someone, is continually being concealed from us—or, more precisely, that we are continually permitting things to remain concealed from us. That we are permitting God to be concealed from us, and permitting our neighbors—in all their pain and all their humanity—to be concealed from us. To be forgotten by us, continually, from hour to hour, from day to day, from century to century. *Aletheia*—truth—is literally the undoing of that.

TRANSLATION AS COMPROMISE

> For what was originally expressed in Hebrew does not have exactly the same sense when translated into another language. Not only this book, but even the Law itself, the Prophecies, and the rest of the books differ not a little when read in the original.
>
> ECCLESIASTICUS (THE PROLOGUE)

Before we continue, let's step back for a moment and talk about translation. I've made no secret of my conviction that a lot of meaning gets lost—or rediscovered—in the act of translation between languages and between cultures. And that is worth talking about.

Translation is a beautiful and tragic act of ongoing compromise. Think of language as a technology. Different languages are capable of expressing activities and relationships differently and have the equipment (vocabulary) for expressing different concepts. We're continually adding to or modifying our language in order to adapt it to our need to express new activities or concepts, or to express them differently. You can think of how a language expresses activities and relationships as grammar, and how it expresses concepts as vocabulary.

Now, the simpler the grammar and the more concrete the vocabulary used in a statement, the easier it is to translate reliably. For example, in the sentence *"I sit in a chair,"* both the grammar and the vocabulary appear to be simple, and this may be a relatively easy sentence to translate between languages.

You can still run into some difficulty, though, even in this case, because of differing contexts. If the culture whose language you're translating this into doesn't *have* chairs, then you're probably either going to substitute in something that is kind of close ("I sit on a cushion"), or you're going to leave the word untranslated, footnote it, and potentially introduce it into that language's vocabulary as a new word.

Matters might get more complex if in one of the cultures (either the one that wrote the statement originally or the one you're translating the statement into), only certain people would sit in the chair in this situation. Maybe, based on status, someone would be required to stand and would never sit in that chair. So depending on who is speaking, "I sit in a chair" might imply an act of assuming authority, an act of protest, or a statement of egalitarianism, or any of a number of things. So in translating the simple statement "I sit in a chair" from one language to the other, you might have to find some way to convey that difference in social context, which partly determines the significance of that sentence.

However, in many other cases, you'll be able to translate "I sit in a chair" fairly well between languages.

But. If the grammar is more complex, or if the vocabulary is more abstract, that's when things get tougher.

What Happens with Grammar

For example, ancient Greek has several verb tenses that convey continuous action. The sense of the original sentence might be that I am always and continuously sitting in that chair; it isn't a defined, one-time activity. Like Pa Kettle's chair in the old black and white *Ma and Pa Kettle* films from the 1950s, this chair may be where I am and it's where I stay. How do you convey that fully in a language that doesn't have tenses conveying continuous activity, without taking a paragraph to do it?

Or maybe it isn't tense that creates a challenge; maybe it's voice. Ancient Greek has a middle voice that we don't have in English. In Greek, that's conveyed just by putting a different ending on a verb. In this case, the meaning may have been: I sit myself in this chair; I seat myself; no one else put me here, I put myself here; I am very deliberately sitting myself in this chair. There is some nuance there that gets lost when the sentence is translated simply as "I sit in a chair" or "I'm sitting in a chair" in English.

Now, this might not be a big deal when we're talking about sitting in a chair. But suppose you're translating a sacred text, and you're working with a sentence like, oh, let's say "I repent." So maybe in English that becomes "I am repenting." Or "I repent." Or "I keep repenting." But in each of these cases, the English suggests either a finite activity that is happening now but will either be over in a moment or (in the case of "I keep repenting") a finite activity that will have to be repeated. It's a transactional activity: it happens, then it's done. Unless you repeat it. But maybe in the original language, the verb tense suggests an ongoing activity that you are continually engaged in— an ongoing process, a continuous transformation rather than a one-time or iterable transaction.

In this way, you could actually arrive at a translation that's faithful in a technical sense, but that conveys to some readers the opposite of what appears to have been intended in the source text, because you went from saying that you are engaged in an ongoing, continual process of repentance to saying that you are either doing a one-time momentary act of repentance or you're repeating a series of one-time, transactional acts of repentance.

English doesn't have as many tenses and voices as some languages do. It used to have less. (Like I said, we add as we need to!) For example, English didn't originally have a future tense, and still doesn't have one in a technical sense. For the Anglo-Saxons, the future was uncertain. You couldn't say definite things about the future; you could only say what you intend, what you desire or "will" to happen, or what the gods "will" to happen. And if you will it strongly enough and the gods are not against you, maybe it will happen, just so.

So you would say, "I will to build a boat" or "It is my will that I build a boat." Or you might say, "I will to fight him"/ "It is my will that I fight him." And because that's way too many words and takes too long, we shorten it to: "I will build a boat" and "I will fight him." But what we're technically saying is that it's my desire to build a boat tomorrow, it's my will that this happen, or it's God's will, or it's someone's will that a thing happen after this present moment, … because English grammar doesn't include an actual future tense.

Similarly, we don't have a tense for expressing continuous action, so we shove in a bunch of other words (a participle, a helping verb, maybe an adverb) to try to make up for it. Maybe we write something like "I am repenting" or "I am always repenting" or "I am continuously repenting." Maybe that helps convey that it's a process, maybe not. English requires extra effort to express continuing processes; our linguistic Anglo-Saxon ancestors preferred for things to just be done, or not done.

Other examples:

There is a plural "you" in Greek that always refers to a group or community, never to an individual. Because modern English lacks a plural "you" (except in certain regions, such as the deep South, where you can convey this idea by saying *all y'all*), we can easily misread a statement that was about a community experience as being about a personal experience, or misread an instruction to a community as an instruction to an individual.

In Koine Greek, just like in modern Spanish, language is very gendered; if you are speaking to a group of women but there are one or two men present, you could address them as *adelphoi* (brothers), and any mixed group would get masculine pronouns, because that's how Greek grammar works. The literal word-for-word "brothers" in English doesn't accurately translate *adelphoi*. It's why some modern translations of the New Testament amend this to "brothers and sisters," recognizing that the speaker or writer is often addressing a mixed group, or that the letter is intended to be read to a group that is not just populated by men.

"Brothers and sisters" introduces problems of its own: It appears to exclude people who are outside that binary, and it establishes an artificial priority of brothers over sisters (men first, then women). What do we do in English with the grammatical accident of the gendering of the Greek word? It's clumsy to render *adelphoi* literally in English. "Kin," "relations," or "my community" might be truer to the intent of *adelphoi*, but in our culture those options don't sound as personal and close-knit as "brothers." Maybe you can go with "friends"; that's the solution that the Quakers came up with. No matter what choice of word or phrase you make, translating *adelphoi* into English is an act of compromise.

What Happens with Vocabulary

The other thing that happens: The more concrete a concept, the easier to translate; the more abstract, the more difficult. This is because the more abstract the concept, the less likely that there's an equivalent in the language you're translating into. Lots of languages have chairs, hammers, houses (though not all; some might have a tent or temporary shelter, which is rather a different thing than a house), and knives. But what if the concept is

35

more abstract, like peace, justice, freedom, truth, or the American way? How does that translate?

Maybe you want to translate this sentence from your ancient sacred text into English: "We sit in peace."

In English, that sentence likely conveys that we are sitting quietly, calmly, without any conflict. That's because English "peace" is an opposite to "conflict" in our language and in our way of thinking. We ask the dead to "rest in peace." We ask people for some "peace and quiet." We say that someone who died in their sleep "died peacefully," without struggle or suffering. We talk about "war and peace." Our word "peace" comes from the Latin *pax*; think of the Pax Romana, the imperial order and security maintained within the boundaries of the Roman Empire. It's an order that provides calm for most by suppressing the dissidence of some—a *pax* that does not tolerate or permit conflict.

But now maybe you're translating from ancient Greek, where the word is *eirene*, and this word doesn't mean the absence of conflict. It's a word derived from *eiro*, "to bind" or "to weave," and it suggests people woven together in community. It's not that conflict is absent or suppressed; it's dealt with lovingly, and reconciliation has been achieved. The community is now sitting (continuously) together in that reconciled state; they are woven together ("in love," according to the ideal proposed in the New Testament) so that each person's contribution is recognized and each person has justice; each person's needs are met. They are sitting together continuously in the trust that should a conflict arise, it will not be suppressed but discussed lovingly, and reconciliation will be reached. That's *eirene*.

But how do you translate that? "We are sitting continuously in the trust that conflicts will be mediated and reconciled, that no one in the community will be suppressed, and that we are all in this together"?

"We sit in peace" doesn't necessarily convey that in English. In fact, for many readers, it may convey exactly the opposite. It may lead people to idealize a situation where conflict is avoided and where problems are hushed and shoved swiftly under the rug so as not to "disturb the peace."

But you don't "disturb" *eirene*. You either weave it, or you unweave it. Your every action either weaves or unweaves community. When we translate *eirene* in the New Testament, we are translating it between two very different cultural and literary contexts. (We will explore *eirene* again, more deeply, in Chapter 4.)

Or what about *mishpat*, the Hebrew word we find all over the place in the Old Testament? There is no English equivalent, so depending on context, the translator has to choose: Maybe "judgment," or "justice," or "pardon," or "charity." But in ancient Hebrew, these weren't separable concepts. You couldn't separate justice and charity, or judgment and pardon, because the concept you had in mind was that each member of the community gets what befits their actions, meets their needs, and what makes the community whole, together. That's *mishpat*.

But in English, when we write "judgment," we don't mean all of that. And when we write "charity," we don't mean all of that. We give charity "at the office," and that signature we write on the donation check is not really *mishpat*.

Similarly, the difficulty of translating *aletheia*.

We human beings are trying to communicate complex and abstract ideas using a flawed (though marvelous) technology that we have developed for this purpose: language. But because languages differ (and because each language is constantly developing further and changing over time), translation is both art and science: How do you convey something that's swiftly understood in one language but for which another language has no concept? It's so worth doing—but it is always an interpretive compromise. Walter Benjamin, in his essay *The Task of the Translator*, suggests that sometimes the most faithful translation is actually the least faithful: that is, if you can find a way to convey the tone and the concept and the voice of the original text, that could be more important than conveying the actual words. On the other hand, this also means that each such dynamic translation is an interpretive act: a translator's best guess at the tone, context, concept, and voice.

Or maybe you stick to the literal word-for-word and try, to the extent possible, to remove the translator's voice and interpretive stance. But then you have an artifact that may have been bleached of much of its meaning and passion, and *it* may not be very faithful to the original either.

So you keep trying to arrive at another, more faithful translation. The work is never done. The work is always worth doing and is always a compromise—in the translator's judgment, the best compromise available to them at the time.

The good news is that *our* language is always changing, and we are always finding ways to do things with English that we couldn't before. Many of our best translators are incredibly creative, and our translations of culturally crucial texts open new opportunities to develop our language. The King James Bible introduced many new words and concepts into English that we just didn't have before, because sometimes the beautiful compromise the translators reached was to make up a new word or borrow one from somewhere else, the same way our generation has done with "mouse" and "tweet" and others.

I wish more teams of biblical translators today were allowed to be bolder or more creative, to take risks and discover the unexpected—as Emily Wilson did in the first English translation of the *Odyssey* by a woman, challenging choices that centuries of translators have made; or as Anne Carson did in *If Not, Winter*, allowing Sappho's fragments to be represented on the page *as* fragments rather than trying to give the illusion of complete poems; or as Marcia Falk did in her translation of "The Song of Songs" from the Old Testament not as a single poem but as a collection of love lyrics with varied voices. (Falk's scholarship has influenced the past twenty years of translations of the "Song of Songs," so that many of her choices and discoveries are now replicated inside of Bibles appearing on the backs of church pews.) I think translation committees will often be locked into a beautiful and tragic compromise between the desire to serve and preserve our tradition and the desire to explore and understand the text. Nevertheless, I hope we will get bolder, more creative, more *adventurous* Bible translations in the decades to come.

Language matters. Nuance does get either lost or discovered in translation. And sometimes, nuance doesn't just mean "an interesting detail." Sometimes it means "the entire point." That can be simultaneously a terrible discovery (when we look at our past and at the ways our tradition has been hijacked to permit and justify injustices and atrocities) and an exciting discovery (when we look at our future, at new possibilities for reading, learning, loving, faithing, and acting as the hands and feet of God in a turbulent world).

This is something we need to be able to explore and talk about, because our sacred texts in translation shape the lives of many people. They are referred to in our politics. Verses and vocabulary are snatched out of context to justify contemporary cultural prejudices, specific exercises of power, and policies and acts of violence against our neighbor. The ongoing compromise of translation, far from being just an academic enjoyment, has a real impact on real lives.

It isn't the trivial things that get lost or discovered in translation. But that doesn't have to be scary. It can be exciting. It means that an ancient text—especially a sacred text—always has new things for us to discover. For those who share my faith tradition, it means that "the Word is living and active and sharper than a double-edged sword," that it can still cut through the carefully-arranged furniture of our lives and our culture, tip the comfortable things we think we know upside down, and call us to new faith and to new lives. That is an exciting thing! That is good news.

In the chapters ahead, we'll look at five concepts from the Bible that are not easily translated into English. —Yet these five are so worth unforgetting. Turn the page, and come with me on this adventure. We have much unconcealing to do together.

PART 2: FIVE THINGS WORTH UNFORGETTING

2. *ESHET CHAYIL:* THE WOMAN OF VALOR

WHAT THIS CHAPTER IS ABOUT

Early Christianity in Europe may well have been a feminist movement. This history is frequently obscured by the distance in time and cultural context; by the choices later historians made to exclude names, stories, and accounts that had been important to earlier writers; by choices made while translating the Bible into English; and by the uses to which biblical texts are put today. Today, a number of biblical verses get surgically removed from their context and appropriated to justify the subjugation of women; some of our translations have resulted in passages that are misused to convey the *opposite* of what they likely conveyed to their original listeners and readers. Probably all of us have seen verses weaponized for such a purpose, to preach about women being silent in church or submitting to their husbands. And just as probably, few of us have ever read the Old Testament ideal of the "woman of valor" or the New Testament ideal of the "battle-ready" woman. When you translate radical or subversive texts into the language of Empire, you eventually get Imperial texts. In this chapter, we will take a close look at what has been lost. There are powerful, nearly forgotten stories of our sisters who came before us, and these stories are worth unforgetting.

"I commend to you our sister Phoebe, a deacon of the church at Cenchreae, so that you may welcome her in the Lord as is fitting for the saints, and help her in whatever she may require from you, for she has been a benefactor of many and of myself as well. Greet Prisca and Aquila, who work with me in Christ Jesus, and who risked their necks for my life, to whom not only *I* give thanks, but also all the churches of the Gentiles. Greet also the church in their house. Greet Andronicus and Junia, my relatives who were in prison with me; they are prominent among the apostles, and they were in Christ before I was."

PAUL

MISOGYNY WALKS AROUND wearing religion's clothes, and this is a great frustration to me because our holy texts are *packed* with stories of relentless, brave, daring women whose lives we conveniently overlook, whose stories we either fail to tell at all or tell very badly. And because I love their stories, and because this is a book about what (and who) gets overlooked in traditional translations and interpretations of the Bible, I want to open this chapter with a shout-out to the bold women of the Bible; may they be unforgotten. My admiration to Rizpah, who guarded the bodies of her children from wild animals and carrion beasts all night, defying the king and his soldiers; to Deborah, a middle-aged prophet who settled the court cases no one else could and led armies against an invading force; to Jael, who drove a tent peg through a dude's head; to Mary, who fled to another country to keep her baby from being killed and then later after returning raised her child in a small town where everyone thought she was a "slut"—and raised him so well that the world still reveres his name (and hers) to this day; to Vashti of Persia, who was commanded by the king to show up naked and wearing only her crown to "display her beauty" for the entertainment of his guests—and who told the king, "No"; to Mary Magdalene, who endured the disbelief of many when she told of what she saw, but who didn't disbelieve herself; to Judith, who seduced an invading general in order to get close enough to chop off his head; to a woman whose name we don't remember, who stood on the wall of a starving city and killed the tyrant Abimelech by chucking a brick down at his head; to Miriam, the first of the prophets of the Children of Israel after their departure from Egypt, singing on the shores of the Red Sea moments after seeing her people's enemies crushed under falling water; to Huldah, who commanded such respect that when the lost sacred texts were discovered, the priests handed them over to her and said, "Please interpret these for us, Huldah"; to Dorcas the healer, who refused to leave those dying of fever, no matter the contagion; to the Queen of Sheba, who traveled a continent to meet people of learning and establish trade deals for her nation; to Joanna and Susanna, who funded Jesus's ministry and had a great deal to do with the early disciples not starving on the road; to Prisca, Mary, Apphia, Julia, Phoebe, Junia, Chloe, Euodia, Syntyche, Tryphena, Tryphosa, and others, apostles and leaders of the early church; to Mary sister of Martha who studied with a rabbi, and to Martha sister of Mary who did the dishes and cooked so she could; to the unnamed, brave woman who suffered continual bleeding and a life of being outcast and untouchable by her community and who yet found the courage to seek out a miracle worker and commit what her community would treat as an unforgivable act: to touch him; to Anna, who spent nearly a century prophesying in the Temple; to Shiprah and Puah, both just and cunning (who may have been either individual midwives or, as rabbinical scholars have suggested, sisterhoods of midwives), who refused to slay Hebrew infants and who, when questioned by Pharoah, used the monarch's own racial bigotry to deceive him: "We tried to carry out your command, O Pharoah, but the Hebrew women are such animals," they reported blithely, "that they squat and give birth before we can even get there!"; to Jochebed, who sent her baby down a river in a basket rather than let him be found by genocidal soldiers; to Abigail, who prevented a massacre; to Dinah, who got blamed for one; to Hadassah (Esther), who stopped a genocide from happening on two continents; to Tamar, who found an unusual, daring, and quite horrifying solution to her father Judah's neglect in leaving her unprovided for and starving; to the witch at Endor, visited in the night by a king who had sworn to exterminate everyone like her, yet so moved by their common humanity that she cared for him and fed him after he fainted with terror and exhaustion at a vision; to Delilah, who outwitted and captured her people's greatest foe; to Mahlah, Noa, Hoglah, Milcah, and Tirzah, who marched up to Moses in the desert and said, "We don't have a brother, and we want to inherit our father's property"; to the *eshet chayil* (the "woman of valor" who "stretches out her hands to the needy") who fed Elijah when he staggered, exhausted and starving, to her doorstep, though she had only a single cake of bread left in the house; to the Shulammite, who loved a foreign king, survived prejudice and brutality, and chose love over fear, even against all the terror-pressure of past trauma; to Bathsheba, so often remembered as a victim of either rape or seduction, so often reduced in our retellings to a momentary plot device, but whose actual story lasted decades and who successfully maneuvered her only son to the throne; to Naomi, who lost so much to famine and tragedy, yet found joy again; to Ruth, who immigrated to a land hostile to her people, yet stayed and kept her mother-in-law and herself fed and alive, daily risking rape or worse in the fields where young men followed the vulnerable, "exotic" immigrant gleaners at a near distance; to Lydia of Thyatira, the businesswoman who funded Paul's missionary work in Macedonia because a story he told once lit her heart on fire; and to so many, many others who lived such stories.

UNFORGETTING THE WOMAN OF VALOR IN THE BIBLE

We've frequently forgotten or neglected the tales of these women. Yet their stories are right there in our Bible, as if hidden in plain sight. They are a remainder that has been left out of our traditional interpretations, these stories that fill the Bible but that we have neglected to read or attend to. The names and stories of these women are among the things in this book that I wish for us to *un*forget—that we *must* unforget, if we are to take, rather than avoid, the adventure of reading the Bible.

Today we read the Bible in English, a language deeply influenced by Latin, and we read it in translations informed by an interpretive tradition dating back to the long centuries when the Bible was available to Europe primarily through the Vulgate, a late fourth-century Latin translation. But the Bible was not written in Latin by Romans. It is a library of texts (66 books in Protestant Bibles, 73 books in Catholic Bibles, 81 in Greek Orthodox Bibles) in Hebrew, Aramaic, and Greek. These are languages that operate very differently from Latin—or English. And these texts were set down within cultures that faced different tensions from our own. Reading the Bible at a distance of 2,000 years, we emphasize different things than the Bible's first readers would have. Some things we leave out of our tradition altogether—like that list of valorous women.

There is another obstacle, too, besides the gaps between languages and cultures, and it has to do with the relationship between the Bible and power. Many sections of the Bible were written originally by people who had little power in their societies. Paul wrote letters under house arrest; some of the Psalms were written by a people living in captivity; Nehemiah wrote his account of the restoration of Jerusalem while continually on the brink of civil war; Jeremiah's prophetic texts only survived because scribes made too many copies for all of them to be burned; and a few scholars think the letter to the Hebrews may have been written by a woman in the early church. (The possibility intrigues me; Hebrews is the only New Testament letter that does not name any authors. But the use of a masculine grammatical ending in one verse makes the case for female authorship difficult, though not impossible.)

Because we ourselves live in a place and a time where the Bible has become an authorized and sacred text recognized by a majority of American citizens and honored in government rituals (as when public officials are sworn into office with one hand resting on a Bible), and where biblical verses are quoted regularly in political speeches, it is easy for us to read the Bible today as if it was written by and for those in power, or as a text that can be used to authorize the views of those in power in *our* society. Treating the Bible as a foundational cultural text, we read into it what we expect to find: our own cultural prejudices and values. Thus some biblical passages have been translated or interpreted in ways that permit their weaponization against our most marginalized citizens, in ways that are anachronistic and would even have been offensive to the communities to which the texts were initially written. When you translate radical or subversive texts into the language of Empire, you eventually get Imperial texts.

For example, let's look closely at two biblical passages that have been put to the purpose of subjugating women and validating rigid gender hierarchy. We'll look at how these passages—one written in Hebrew in the Old Testament, one in Greek in the New Testament—have been mangled and misunderstood in English, and at what we might find in the original texts. Then, I'll share some stories of the early church—overlooked stories, nearly forgotten stories, stories that challenge things we think we know both about our past and our present.

The Proverbs 31 Woman

The first of these two passages is Proverbs 31, from a Hebrew wisdom text. Proverbs 31 has been treated as one basis for defining "family values" in some Christian communities in the U.S. In most Christian translations of Proverbs 31, men are told to praise and admire "the virtuous woman" (or, in a few versions, the "capable woman" or the "capable wife"). But the Hebrew *eshet chayil* does not mean "virtuous woman." It means "woman of valor." (Jewish translations into English get this right.)

We get "virtuous" because the translation committee commissioned by King James I four centuries ago translated *eshet chayil* in that way, and because that Authorized Version became our sacred text, future committees have dutifully followed suit. In the seventeenth century, the word "virtuous" made somewhat more sense; the Victorians hadn't yet gotten their hands on the word (and wouldn't for another 250 years) and at the time, "virtuous" still suggested the Italian *virtù*, meaning manliness, purposeful action, and bravery—not moral purity or goodness. *Vir* is Latin for "man," and we get from it not only the English word *virtue* but also *virility*. The "virtuous woman" in Proverbs 31 is the very same woman whom the King James translation tells us is clothed "in strength and honor," like a warrior (Proverbs 31:25).

However, the Hebrew *eshet chayil* doesn't suggest manliness or masculinity. It suggests *valor*. The woman of Proverbs 31 is brave, persistent, audacious, resourceful, and ready for anything. In that chapter, we find her running a business. We find her planning for the future, charting a course toward her dreams. A more apt translation of *eshet chayil* into contemporary English may well be "a daring woman." Or at least, we could adopt the Jewish translation and go with "valorous woman"; it is far more accurate.

What I want us to notice is the wide gap between the "daring," bold woman and the "virtuous," well-behaved woman. This gap persists in our modern Bibles for two reasons. First, the fact that the meanings of many words have shifted dramatically over the past four hundred years, so that words that meant one thing to the readers of King James' 1611 Authorized Version often convey something completely different to us now. Second, we bring with us into the Bible, eisegetically, a bias from our own culture and our religious tradition, an expectation that in those pages we will find meek, submissive women—and instructions for women to be subservient beings. In reality, little of that is in the text. That's in *us*; we bring it with us when we translate or read the book. We insert it because we expect it. And once it's there, it gets used within our religious communities to justify and reinforce a subjugation and marginalization of women that may be faithful to the nineteenth-century Victorian ideal of "the angel in the house" but that is unbiblical and anachronistic.

I wish to remind my fellow Christians: you and I, we did not become Christians to learn from the Victorians or to run our households in the Victorian way. That's not why we're here.

The Battle-Ready Women of the New Testament

Here's a second example, one that is misused in much the same way as Proverbs 31, as justification for the subjugation of women. We often find Ephesians 5:22 quoted for this purpose, and we usually read the verse in translation as "Wives, submit to your husbands." But the Greek sentence begins a verse earlier and continues well past 5:22, and in Koine Greek, it reads more like this:

> Set yourselves in support of one another out of reverence for Christ: wives, for your husbands... husbands, love your wives... *etc.*

There are several problems with how we use this passage. The first problem is that we start quoting it midsentence, and so we lose sight of the fact that in any case we couldn't talk about wives submitting to husbands without also talking about husbands submitting to wives.

The second problem is that the word we keep translating "submit" here (*hupotassemenoi*) does not mean "obey." In fact, our modern "submit" doesn't even mean what "submit" meant in English when the word was selected by King James's translators. When the scholars involved in the 1611 translation used the word "submit," they were drawing from Latin *sub* + *mittere,* meaning to "send oneself out under"—like an officer under a command, to get a mission accomplished. (In fact, we get the English word "mission" from the same Latin verb.) Similarly, the Greek *hupo* + *tassomenoi,* means to set or deploy yourselves in military formation under a command.

A more accurate paraphrase of the line about wives might be something like one of these:

> "Wives, support your husbands."

"Wives, deploy yourselves in support of your husbands."

"Wives, arrange yourselves for battle for your husbands."

Or less literally but perhaps more faithfully to both the biblical ideal of the *eshet chayil* and to the larger context of this passage:

"Wives, go to battle for your husbands."

"Wives, defend your husbands."

The word being translated here is a combination of the verb *-tasso* with the prefix *hupo-*. What we miss right away in English is that this verb was a military term for arranging soldiers in ordered formation to confront an enemy. In fact, if you were to look up the verb in Strong's concordance (it's #5021), you would find the following explication:

"/*tasso* (place in position, post) was commonly used in ancient military language for designating/appointing /commissioning a specific status…"

"*tasso* was primarily a military term meaning 'to draw up in order, arrange in place, assign, appoint, order…"

What we're talking about is not an ancient Greek word for abstract obedience but a concrete metaphor of military support. The grammar is important, too. The ending of the word *hupotassemenoi* tells us we're in the middle voice. "Arrange *yourselves* under." "Deploy *yourselves* under." This is important, because as we will see in this chapter, the women of the early church were called to lives of vigorous activity, not passive subservience.

Now, you *could* interpret this verb that appears in Ephesians 5:21 as "place yourselves under your husband" and you might be *technically* correct. That could prompt you to look, as past translators have, for something in English that means "be subject to." But if we do that, we lose the context of *hupotassemenoi,* which is about forming up for battle—a battle in which husbands and wives are expected to deploy and station themselves in support of each other. Reading the verse glibly, we find it too easy to read into this passage confirmation of the norms of our own culture, rather than paying close attention to the context in which the verse appears. That context will give us clues that could provoke us to make bolder interpretive choices as we read this letter.

This reference to *hupotassamenoi* is embedded within a passage that provides an extended military metaphor for how each member of a first-century Ephesian community can be continually, spiritually battle-ready. The advice for husbands, wives, and others builds toward the closing argument of the letter:

> Finally, be strong in the Lord and in the strength of his might. Put on the whole armor of God, that you may be able to stand against the schemes of the devil. For we do not wrestle against flesh and blood, but against the rulers, against the authorities, against the cosmic powers over this present darkness, against the spiritual forces of evil in the heavenly places. Therefore take up the whole armor of God, that you may be able to withstand in the evil day, and having done all, to stand firm..."
>
> EPHESIANS 6:10-13

The passage goes on from there to describe the armor of God in detail, in which each piece of armor metaphorically represents a particular skill or attribute that the early Christian must "put on." For example, the belt of truth (because it is *unforgetting who we are* that holds all the armor to our body), the breastplate of righteousness (because a loving and godly *justice* and not our own *self-rightness* is what must protect us), the sandals of preparedness of the gospel (because it is *to live and share the good story* that we stride forward) etc. Whether the early Christian is male, female, or child, or whether master or servant (all are addressed in the preceding lines, in Ephesians 5:21-6:9), all are invited by the author to put on the full armor of God and deploy themselves together, fully armored and fully ready, as one community, against a spiritual enemy that is imagined as "the powers over this present darkness, the spiritual forces of evil in the heavenly places." It is specifically in this context that the writer of Ephesians is using military verbs like *tasso* ("deploy"/"set in formation").

In the gender-segregated Greek communities of first-century Asia Minor, there is no *need* for anyone to tell wives to obey their husbands; marital obedience is already a basic expectation in that culture. What the writers of the New Testament are proposing is an alternative to the hierarchical structure with which everyone is already familiar. They are calling for radically interdependent relationships in which parties who are not equal in their communities nonetheless yield to and honor each other. Husbands who in Greek cities have significant legal authority and material power over their spouses are being asked to love their wives (in Ephesians 5), and to *listen* to them "with understanding," treating them as "fellow heirs" in God's house (in 1 Peter 3).

And if you read the lines that *precede* the "deploy yourselves in support" passage (Ephesians 5:1-20), you will discover that the larger context is a letter providing advice to an *ekklesia* seeking to liberate itself from the "bondage" of the "unwise" hierarchies, traditions, and ways of living that have confined their people in the past. *Ekklesia* literally means "those called out" or called away from their tradition and their culture. Those called to live in a radically new way, "not as unwise people but as wise," joyous in their newfound freedom and fellowship ("singing and making melody...and giving thanks"), even though "the days are evil" (Ephesians 5:15-20).

Focused on support and interdependency, Ephesians was written to challenge hierarchy, not support it, and to propose a radical egalitarianism in human relationships. Missing that context, we have taken one piece out of a Greek sentence and have adopted it as a standalone aphorism to hang a doctrine on—specifically a doctrine regarding women's roles in [the household / the church / society – take your pick]. And we have missed entirely the point the original writer appears to have been making, which has to do with the need to live as a community in which all members are actively supporting each other, each member ready to step in wherever the other is vulnerable. (For another example of that idea, see 1 Corinthians 7:12-16, in which unbelieving spouses, particularly husbands, are described as vulnerable, still in bondage to old sins and old ways of thinking, half asleep, like soldiers blundering into enemy fire. Believing wives are encouraged in that passage to deploy themselves in support of those husbands: "Wife, for all you know, you might deliver your husband. Husband, for all you know, you might deliver your wife."

The first-century *ekklesia* is invited to operate in concert (*homothumadon*, "of one mind") like a Greek phalanx or a Roman battle square. Soldiers in the Roman army fought as a cohesive unit, not as individual warriors. Each soldier wields a blade in one hand and, with the other, shields the soldier to their left. It is a military ethos reliant on interdependency. That is what Ephesians is about—not hierarchy and obedience, but the disciplined and alert support that Christians are called to provide each other. *Hupotassemenoi* is actually a remarkable word to use in this first-century Greek text because military metaphors were usually reserved for men. In Ephesians, however, people of all genders are invited to equip themselves with the "full armor of God" and deploy themselves within a battle-ready unit in support of each other. The early Christians described themselves as under threat from both spiritual adversaries and from oppressive earthly governments. To live—and to live "in a manner worthy of their calling," carrying out their mission—they need to behave as a community with the same solidarity, unity of purpose, and mutual support that they could witness in the Empire's legions. All members of a community under threat are expected by the epistolary writers to operate as a unit and to be well prepared to support each other in battle—to support unbelieving spouses, to represent Christ and the community before an oppressive state, and to testify to the hope that they have—regardless of their gender, class, or position. Such military metaphors are woven throughout the language of the early church; in fact, the Greek word that we translate "sin" in the New Testament is also a military term: *hamartia*, which is what happens when the spearman misses the mark or when one of the soldiers in the line lunges forward but fails to strike their target, leaving that soldier and the soldier next to him momentarily vulnerable and open to attack.

When we pluck out one verse by itself and use it as rhetorical backing for a gender hierarchy that is traditional in *our* culture, we risk committing two errors. First, we're missing the forest for the trees. It is as if we have grabbed up one branch and commenced beating women with it, while the writer of Ephesians stands to one side shouting, *"Wait! What are you doing?! Stop that! Put that down! Look at the forest! Put the branch down, quit beating on your sister, and look at the whole forest! It's important!"* And second, we may be advocating a message that, in spirit, is opposite to the message the epistle was written to convey. That is, we're enforcing culturally traditional divisions using a verse isolated from a letter that advocated a radical interdependency. In other words, that forest we're missing…is a forest we still need to see, badly, in our own time. That's something to think about.

UNFORGETTING THE WOMAN OF VALOR IN THE EARLY CHURCH

There is a nearly forgotten history of women's ministry and apostleship in early Christianity that we badly need to recall, and we also need to understand how that history was forgotten. The story of that forgetting is pertinent to our own time—and to how we interpret the sacred texts we have inherited. For example, many of the New Testament verses on chastity that are taken by teachers of American "purity culture" as justification for the subordination of women were very likely intended in the first and second century to have the opposite effect. Chastity and virginity were prized in the early Christian churches partly as a way to free people up to preach and work in the community outside the home. Roman law after Augustus required young men and women to wed and bed and produce healthy Roman babies. Augustus Caesar's *Lex Julia* penalized the unmarried with much higher taxes—and incentivized both getting married and getting frequently knocked up. However, for women there were two exemptions from the tax penalty, one for registered and professional prostitutes and one for priestesses. Rome had this idea that priestesses needed to be virgins—so priestesses weren't expected to marry.

Now, in most Roman religions, it was very hard to become a priestess, and the number of priestesses were few. But in early Christian doctrine, every single Christian was a priest of God, and the members of the church collectively were the "bride of Christ." Thus, any Christian could claim the marriage exemption. A young man could travel *agamos* ("unwedded") like Paul. A young woman could declare herself a holy virgin, and rather than devote her life to raising a good Roman family, she could teach, she could preach, she could run a business (as many Christian women did—just look to Lydia of Thyatira for a quick, biblical example). She could join a sisterhood of holy "widows." Some of these sisterhoods were evidently communities of religious scholars—secluded but corresponding with each other by letter—or of anchoresses; there were "desert mothers" (*amma*) as well as desert fathers (*abba*) in the early church. But many other communities of "widows" were active and engaged in education, social work, and philanthropic work in their communities, gathering funds for the poor and organizing care for the homeless and the orphan.

Still others traveled as apostles. As Marg Mowczko has pointed out, it is highly probable that the "sister woman" Paul mentions in his first letter to Corinth referred to a female coworker on an apostolic mission:

> Do we not have the right to be accompanied by a sister woman [*adelphē gunē*], as do the other apostles and the brothers of the Lord and Cephas?
>
> 1 CORINTHIANS 9:5

In many English Bibles, you will see *adelphē gunē* translated as "believing wife," but it literally means either "sister woman" or "sister wife"—and rendering it "wife" is an odd choice because Paul himself was *agamos* (unwedded). Clement of Alexandria, writing in the second century, understands *adelphē gunē* to mean female coworker; he mentions that the apostles "took women with them, not as wives, but as sisters, that they might be their co-ministers in dealing with women in their homes." The Greek word Clement uses for these women is *sundiakonoi*, co-deacons. (In first and second-century letters, a *diakonos* is different from a deacon in a modern church; the term usually refers to an evangelist or minister with a sacred commission.) Clement describes how essential the sister women were to missionary work when visiting those cities in which men and women were more segregated—cities where male apostles could not visit and share the gospel in women's spaces without arousing scandal. In fact, the very *arrival* of these traveling, teaching, multiple-gender apostolic teams in segregated communities must have itself provoked quite an upset to the local patriarchy and its gender expectations!

It would be difficult to *over*state this impact—or the implications of Clement's second-century account of how Christianity spread through the Greek and Roman world. In the first-century Greek home, the women's rooms were in the back; it was here, in secret, that early Christians met, prayed together, held religious services, and shared the good story. These were spaces that only women could grant access to. The spread of Christianity didn't only happen *in* women's spaces but *because* of them and *by means* of them. The fact that letters between churches were often penned by literate men and that our histories of the church were chronicled by men makes it easier for us to miss the women apostles—unless we are paying close attention. Unless we notice that Paul's letters are addressed to many women apostles and that he continually sends his greetings to the churches that meet in women's houses—and that he greets the women who lead those churches. Consider how Paul concludes his letter to the churches in Rome:

> "I commend to you our sister Phoebe, a deacon of the church at Cenchreae, so that you may welcome her in the Lord as is fitting for the saints, and help her in whatever she may require from you, for she has been a benefactor of many and of myself as well. Greet Prisca and Aquila, who work with me in Christ Jesus, and who risked their necks

for my life, to whom not only *I* give thanks, but also all the churches of the Gentiles. Greet also the church in their house…Greet Mary, who has worked very hard among you. Greet Andronicus and Junia, my relatives who were in prison with me; they are prominent among the apostles, and they were in Christ before I was…Greet those workers in the Lord, Tryphaena and Tryphosa…Greet Rufus, chosen in the Lord; and greet his mother—a mother to me also…Greet Philologus, Julia, Nereus and his sister, and Olympas, and all the saints who are with them."

ROMANS 16

For more on Clement's testimony and other ancient writings that attest to the sister women, I recommend Marg Mowczko's article on the sister women:

https://margmowczko.com/believing-wives-female-co-workers-of-the-apostles/

And also see Mowczko's article on Sister Apphia, who was one of the three *synergoi* ("coworkers") and "fellow soldiers in Christ" to whom the letter to Philemon was addressed:

https://margmowczko.com/apphia

Paul gets a "bad rep" for his teachings on women in the church in the New Testament, but Marg Mowczko argues that this is largely because of the use that much later readers and teachers have made of Paul:

In light of the many women Paul mentioned warmly, though briefly, it is difficult to see how Paul could have been misunderstood as someone who disliked women and who deliberately curtailed, suppressed, and even prohibited their ministry. The reason for this misunderstanding is that a couple of verses in his letters have been magnified and emphasized, while other verses about women have been minimized or ignored. Paul's instructions in 1 Corinthians 14:34-35 and 1 Timothy 2:12 had local and limited applications.

MARG MOWCZKO

As evidence, Mowczko cites not only some of the examples I have shared above but many others from the New Testament that we have traditionally neglected or glossed over (because they do not fit what we expect to read), such as Paul's appointment of Lydia as the first convert in Philippi and thus probably as the pastor gathering the church in that city; the fact that Paul wrote the letter 1 Corinthians in response to correspondence with a woman Chloe, likely a leader he wrote letters to and received letters from; Paul's mention of women prophesying and praying aloud in 1 Corinthians 11:5, which contradicts the way we typically apply his advice elsewhere about silence in church; Paul's greetings to two female leaders in the church (Prisca and Aquila) in the very same letter (2 Timothy 4:19) that gets quoted as doctrinal support for barring women from pastoring and teaching— the same two "who risked their necks" for his life (Romans 16:3-4); and the deep respect with which Paul greets Junia, "prominent among the apostles," who was "in Christ before I was" (Romans 16:7).

Paul's letter to the Romans closes with an official recommendation for Phoebe, a *diakonos* of another church, who evidently arrived with the letter and was most likely charged with delivering it to the elders in that church. Patrick Gray, in *Opening Paul's Letters*, explains:

> Paul's coworkers who delivered his letters did not drop them in the mailbox and then go on their way but, rather, would likely have read them aloud to the recipients and been available to explain the significance of the references they contained.
>
> PATRICK GRAY

Therefore, it is likely that Phoebe was the first person to read aloud, interpret, and teach the book of Romans.

Paul was an ex-Pharisee and a man who spent much of his adult life traveling in parts of the world where men and women were segregated. I suspect Paul struggled often with how to live the radical egalitarianism he professed. But it is at least clear that Paul traveled with, taught alongside, endured prison with, appointed, respected, and learned from (in Junia's case) women apostles and leaders. The use that our culture has made of Paul's writings (to subdue or silence women) is simplistic and a disservice both to the dead—to Paul and his female *synergoi* ("coworkers")—and to ourselves.

When the early church shared stories of their founder Jesus, these stories upset gender expectations throughout the Mediterranean world. The gospels included tales of women like Mary and Martha—two sisters, one of whom grants Jesus and the disciples space in her house to study, another of whom sits down as a disciple herself by Jesus's feet to learn, just as the men do. When Martha tries to rebuke Mary, Jesus defends his student: "Mary has chosen the better part, which will not be taken away from her" (Luke 10:42). Another Mary—Mary Magdalene—is the first to encounter the risen Christ, the first to share the good news; in the Easter story, for one morning, all of Christianity on earth consists of Mary Magdalene. The early churches also told the story that on Pentecost, when the first Christians were filled with the Holy Spirit, men and women were worshipping in the upper room together:

> When they had entered the city, they went to the room upstairs where they were staying... All these were constantly devoting themselves to prayer, together with certain women, including Mary the mother of Jesus, as well as his brothers. ... When the day of Pentecost had come, they were all together in one place. And suddenly from heaven there came a sound like the rush of a violent wind, and it filled the entire house where they were sitting. Divided tongues, as of fire, appeared among them, and a tongue rested on each of them. All of them were filled with the Holy Spirit and began to speak in other languages, as the Spirit gave them ability.
>
> ACTS 1:13-14, 2:1-4

In the Pentecost story, they are "all together" in the upper room, men and women, filled with the Holy Spirit. They leave the room to prophesy and teach in many languages, and those who hear demand to know if they are drunk or mad. Some, pilgrims from far countries, want to know how it is that they hear these apostles speaking in *their* language. In response, Peter quotes the prophet Joel, explaining specifically that both men and women will bring humanity visions and teachings from God during the last days of the earth:

In the last days it will be, God declares,
that I will pour out my Spirit upon all flesh,
    and your sons and your daughters shall prophesy,
and your young men shall see visions,
    and your old men shall dream dreams.
Even upon my slaves, both men and women,
    in those days I will pour out my Spirit;
        and they shall prophesy.

ACTS 2:17-18

It is easy for us to miss this, but in the first centuries of our era, this would have *shaken* readers. It would have alarmed them or moved them. The first evangelists and the first apostles, who went out into the world to talk about eternal life and a new way to live as co-heirs with Jesus in the family of God—included "both men and women."

If you are a woman in the church reading this whose heart is called to an active life or to leadership, may this give you courage. You are not some aberration of modern society, as others will insist. What follows is a list of names honored and trusted by the writers of the New Testament. These are your sisters.

Lydia of Thyatira
Apphia
Prisca
Mary
Julia
Phoebe
Junia
Chloe
Claudia
Euodia

Syntyche
Tryphena
Tryphosa
Persis
Nympha
Damaris of Athens
Dorcas of Joppa
The "elder," a "woman appointed by God" in 2 John

The list of women ministers gets even longer once you venture outside the New Testament into second and third century apostolic writings. Even those texts (more frequent in later centuries) written by Christian men in criticism of women who prophesied, who preached as apostles, or who adopted gender-neutral clothing and coiffure, by their very existence testify to the normalcy of women leaders in the early church.

Where to Learn More

If you would like to read more about the women apostles and ministers of the early church, here are some resources:

Burrus, Virginia. *Chastity As Autonomy: Women in the Stories of Apocryphal Acts.* Edwin Mellen Press, 1987.

Fiorenza, Elisabeth Schussler. *In Memory of Her: A Feminist Theological Reconstruction of Christian Origins.* The Crossroad Publishing Company, 1983.

Jensen, Anne. *God's Self-Confident Daughters: Early Christianity and the Liberation of Women.* Westminster John Knox, 1996.

Mar, Alex. "Rebel Virgins and Desert Mothers." *Atlas Oscura.*
www.atlasobscura.com/articles/the-rebel-virgins-and-desert-mothers-who-have-been-written-out-of-christianitys-early-history.

Mowczko, Marg. "Exploring the Biblical Theology of Christian Egalitarianism." www.margmowczko.com/

Torjesen, Karen. *When Women Were Priests: Women's Leadership in the Early Church and the Scandal of Their Subordination in the Rise of Christianity.* Harper, 1995.

How and Why It Changed

The prevalence of women in ministry was one reason that during the times of emperors Nero, Domitian, Trajan, and particularly Diocletian, Christianity was so hated by the Roman government. It wasn't just that Christianity was nominally monotheistic (so that converts stopped sacrificing to their ancestral deities); it was the growing numbers of women who were teaching and leading and bursting into activity in their communities. To men in power in Rome, this would have appeared unsettling and even threatening. In Rome (as throughout the Mediterranean world during those centuries), control of women's bodies was tied to the stability of the *domus* or house—both the individual house or family, and the larger house of the state. The well-behaved wife was a visible sign of the stability of the home, and well-behaved and securely wedded, childbearing women were a sign of the stability of the state. A Roman man who could not "control his wife" could not be trusted to be stable or successful in any other matter, and a Roman province that could not control its women was assumed to be weak, undisciplined, immoral, and vulnerable. When Christian women refrained from marriage, and founded and taught in religious orders—when their bodies were not under the legal control of any man—their autonomy was interpreted as evidence that the Roman house was weak. This is why persecutions of Christianity frequently coincided with times of economic turmoil. It was at times when the state was disordered and at risk that the Roman emperors cracked down on Christianity—and especially on Christian women. If they could just get Roman women under control, perhaps they could get the state back under control, too.

Emperor Diocletian draws my particular ire. Diocletian's Rome was in distress; goods that had once cost a single coin (a *denarius*) skyrocketed to a hundred, and then to a thousand, prompting the hurried legislation of an "Edict on Maximum Prices," which imposed a death penalty on those who broke it but which was nevertheless largely ignored. The economy became so chaotic that some districts ceased selling goods altogether and resorted to barter or black market. Everything was falling apart. Amid this economic and political crisis, religious orders in which women operated autonomously and without regard to class or caste—in Chapter 3, we'll look at one Roman governor's shock at finding two women who were domestic slaves serving as leaders in the church—were a clear sign to Diocletian of how "out of control" the state was. And Diocletian reacted violently to reassert the state's control. His attempt to exterminate Christianity in the Roman Empire in the year 303 was conducted in large part as an attack on Christian women. He revoked the state's recognition of Christianity as a legal religion and had priests, bishops, and deacons arrested. In many provinces of the Empire, ministers who were women and who refused to sacrifice to Roman deities were imprisoned and raped by order of local magistrates, or forced to register as prostitutes (and then raped), as in the cases of Irene of Thessalonica, Tecusa and her order of seven holy virgins, and others. Their autonomy was deleted, their bodies brought forcibly under the control of the state. In *Die Frau im romischen Christenprozess*, Friedrich Augar documents at least thirteen separate accounts attesting to the judicial rape of Christian women that he deems historically reliable. These women became *servae poenae* (penal slaves), their legal status reduced to property of the state; Diocletian's persecution was a state-ordered enslavement of women who were engaged in Christian ministry.

Early Christian writers lament this loss. Responding to smaller-scale persecutions prior to Diocletian, Tertullian accuses the Roman judges of delivering Christian women to a *leno* instead of a *leo*—that is, to a brothel-keeper instead of a lion. Hippolytus mourns that women accused of Christian ministry were subjected to "public rape" and torture, and Cyprian suggests that those who were sentenced to death were more fortunate because they could no longer be threatened "with rapes and brothels." And the fourth-century historian Eusebius writes of the persecutions enacted under Diocletian's edict with a startling immediacy, chronicling events that happened during his own lifetime:

> I saw with my own eyes the places of worship thrown down from top to bottom, to the very foundations, the inspired holy Scriptures committed to the flames in the middle of the public squares, and the pastors of the churches hiding disgracefully in one place or another.... The spectacle of what happened after this beggars description: in every town great numbers were locked up, and everywhere the gaols built long before for homicides and grave-robbers were crowded with bishops, presbyters and deacons, readers and exorcists, so that now there was no room in them for those convicted of crimes. ... Women were tied by one foot and hoisted high in the air, head downwards, their bodies completely naked without a morsel of clothing, presenting thus the most shameful, brutal, and inhuman of all spectacles to everyone watching. Others again were tied to trees and stumps and died horribly; for with the aid of machinery they drew together the very stoutest boughs, fastened one of the martyr's legs to each, and then let the boughs fly back to their normal position; thus they managed to tear apart the limbs of their victims in a moment.

EUSEBIUS

This Roman spectacle of horrors served a political purpose. Like the *ludi Romani*, the games in which gladiators at times surrendered their lives, penal executions were a show. By subtracting women's autonomy over their lives and their own bodies in the most humiliating, painful, public, and visible ways possible, Roman magistrates hoped to deter other women from following their sisters' footsteps. What was at stake in these verdicts was not merely the stripping away of "purity" as our modern culture would understand it, but the stripping away of agency and autonomy—the malice of enslaving women who had preached a gospel of liberation.

After Diocletian's persecutions, women were much more marginalized in ministry—in part because many Christian women who had been leaders in the church no longer existed, or lived as penal slaves in Roman brothels, and in part because of the actions of Diocletian's successor. Constantine's Edict of Milan in 313—ten years after Diocletian's atrocities—granted Christianity the Emperor's protection and secured bishops, priests, and deacons immunity from such persecutions, but Constantine's patronage of Christianity and his adoption of the new faith as a state religion did not restore women to ministry. Quite the opposite. Increasingly, the church ceases to become a community that meets in women's private areas of the house—a community that exists in part because of and for women—and becomes instead a community that meets in public spaces (spaces regulated and presided over by Roman men). Deacons and bishops begin to pen letters urging women into more secluded or silent roles, arguing in effect that the church no longer needed women's permission, apostleship, or leadership in order to exist. The implication was that since the church no longer needed women, women were no longer needed in the church—except in carefully defined, controlled, and traditionally *Roman* roles.

Constantine also undertook an aggressive centralizing of the disparate church communities. He wanted to organize the hundreds of churches under one creed, using one canon of texts, and presided over by one patriarchal hierarchy that would merge church and state officials. One of the outcomes of this adoption of the church by the state was that not only did women remain marginalized in church leadership; they were also increasingly anonymized or absented from church histories and hagiographies. Diocletian erased women physically from leadership; Constantine's reforms began a process whereby in time, the *memory* of them was erased, too. Living in a time when so many things can be Googled, it may be difficult for some of us to appreciate how swiftly memory can be unwritten or rewritten.

In *God's Self-Confident Daughters*, Anne Jensen examines the first four church histories (those of Eusebius, Socrates, Sozomen, and Theodoret) and demonstrates that the later the text, the fewer women are mentioned in it (the count drops precipitously with each successive text after Eusebius), and the more likely it is that those women who *are* mentioned in the history are left unnamed. Jensen uses the example of an anonymous woman from the affluent class in Edessa who, by insisting on being included in a planned execution, averted a massacre. Eusebius' account offers a lot of detail and context about this heroic woman who saved hundreds of people; each successive text over the next two centuries offers less and less information about her, until this heroine is barely more than a footnote, buried under the tales of the lives of male colleagues who did and risked less. Also, the later the text, the more likely it is that women in leadership, when mentioned at all, are described in connection with heresy. The earliest Christian historiographers mentioned male and female teachers and prophets, but did not regard women in ministry as likely heretics, but simply as a part of the Christian tradition. In *later* histories, anonymous women are noted in the text primarily to comment on heresy (to which women are presumed to be more susceptible by later authors).

Karen Torjesen opens her book *When Women Were Priests* by describing the (possibly ancient) vandalism of a mosaic depicting four Christian women, one of them a bishop:

> Under a high arch in a Roman basilica dedicated to two women saints, Prudentiana and Praxedis, is a mosaic depicting four female figures: the two saints, Mary, and a fourth woman whose hair is veiled and whose head is surrounded by a square halo—an artistic technique indicating that the person was still living at the time the mosaic was made. The four faces gaze serenely out from a glistening gold background. The faces of Mary and the two saints are easily recognizable. But the identity of the fourth is less apparent. A carefully lettered inscription identifies the face on the far left as Theodora Episcopa, which means Bishop Theodora. The masculine form for bishop in Latin is *episcopus*; the feminine form is *episcopa*. The mosaic's visual evidence and the inscription's grammatical evidence point out unmistakably that Bishop Theodora was a woman. But the *a* on Theodora has been partially effaced by scratches across the glass tiles of the mosaic, leading to the disturbing conclusion that attempts were made to deface the feminine ending, perhaps even in antiquity.
>
> KAREN TORJESEN

By the early fifth century, 112 years after Diocletian tore women violently out of the ministry and 102 years after Constantine began the centralization of the ministry as a patriarchal and state institution, many churches had become so transformed into bastions of patriarchy, and women's teaching (whether inside or outside of the church) had become so identified with "heresy," that incidents such as the death of Hypatia of Alexandria had become possible. Hypatia was a learned pagan philosopher and a woman, and she was brutally murdered by a lynch mob of Christian men in the year 415. To me, Diocletian's persecutions and Hypatia's murder provide tragic bookends to the story of the late-antiquity marginalization of women in a religious movement that had begun centuries earlier with their liberation.

But it was not so in the beginning.

TWO MODERN PATHOLOGIES THAT BETRAY OUR HERITAGE

There are two modern pathologies in U.S. society today that have infected our churches, and in whose vigorous defense biblical verses are frequently plucked out of context. Yet these two pathologies each offer a deep betrayal and offense to the origins of Christianity. I hope the context I have shared in this chapter will make it clear why I urge Christians especially to get on the front lines of battling these two social ills, which are most often labeled "purity culture" and "rape culture."

Purity Culture

By *purity culture*, I mean the movement over the past few decades, sponsored by some evangelical denominations in

America, to secure and ensure the "purity" of Christian youth and particularly of Christian teen girls. This culture is expressed through rituals that emphasize male ownership of young women and that express teens' virginity as a necessary corollary to that ownership. Rituals include the wearing of purity rings, the making of purity vows (in which a young woman vows to her father that she will keep her virginity until marriage or a father pledges to keep his daughters virgin and pure), and the holding of purity balls (formal father-daughter dance events to celebrate virginity pledges). And this culture is expressed through rhetoric that ties the value of young women not to their intrinsic humanity but to their physical virginity; young women are taught that once they have had premarital sex, they are equivalent to "a chewed-up piece of gum," that no one will want them, and they have passed from a pure and desirable state to a physically, morally, and spiritually filthy state.

Purity culture makes women into transactional objects, handed securely from father to husband, whereas chastity was important to the early church because it *freed* young men and women from a transactional economy of the Roman *domus* or the Greek *oikos*. (That Greek word for "house" is the same word that our English "economy" comes from. *Oikonomia* means the affairs of the household). We forget how radical a figure Jesus was in the ancient Mediterranean cultures, how radical he might still be to our culture today. He taught about separation from the transactional economy of the world; in the kingdom of heaven there is no economy. The kingdom of heaven is where a person sells all that they have in order to buy the field where its one treasure can be found. The kingdom of heaven is where a shepherd abandons ninety-nine sheep to go look for one that is lost. The kingdom of heaven has no economic sense. It is the arrival of the unforeseen, unearned gift—the gift of grace, the gift of unconditional love.

A woman in the early church might leave home and town and go traveling with other apostles, on fire with the story she has heard and desiring to share it with women in other communities far away. She wishes to share the grace, the gift, the freedom she has herself found. Her chastity becomes the means by which she can travel to do so, the means by which she might pass from one house to another without obligations to a husband who might restrict her or confine her or limit her action. God calls her to *limitless* action, and therefore, her body must be autonomous, owned by no other human being. The first and second-century Christian woman removes herself from the economy of marriage and state, declares that her body is no object of transaction but a "living temple" where she might serve her God unmolested, and a vehicle to carry her where she must go. This is a profound Christian liberty—the same liberty Jesus calls his disciples to when he tells them to leave behind mother and father, or to let the dead bury their dead, or to abandon all the economy of the world and leave that field unplowed and that house unbuilt. Pick up and go. Leave all behind. In the clothes you now wear, with whatever you have right now in your pockets, walk out there and get God's work done in the world. In the fourteenth century, the English mystic Margery Kempe walked down to a boat and said she needed to sail it to Israel. "Why?" the boatman asked, aghast. "God needs me to," she said. Her countrymen called her Mad Margery, but the early Christians might have understood her. Paul writes often of the madness—the holy "foolishness"—of those who follow God, measuring nothing in their lives according to the economy of the world, reckless in their desire to share the gift of grace.

For both men and women in early Christianity, *chastity* did not mean bodies kept pure and under control; it meant *autonomy* and the freedom to consecrate one's own body to a holy purpose, to be "battle ready," to do God's work in the world. Liberated from the demands of the household and the need to bear and raise children for the Roman state, young Christians could preach, teach, serve their communities selflessly, devote themselves to prayer, or travel as missionaries. Paul, in his first letter to Corinth, speaks of married Christians as being restricted in action, bound to the affairs of the Roman *domus*:

> I want you to be free from anxieties. The unmarried man is anxious about the affairs of the Lord, how to please the Lord; but the married man is anxious about the affairs of the world, how to please his wife, and his interests are divided. And the unmarried women and the virgin are anxious about the affairs of the Lord, so that they might be holy in body and spirit; but the married woman is anxious about the affairs of the world, how to please her husband.

ROMANS 7:32-34

We often hear Paul quoted as saying that it is better to marry than to burn (1 Corinthians 7:9), but his larger message in the first letter to Corinth is that it is better to remain single than to marry. ("Better to marry than to burn" is an unfortunate translation, by the way; the Greek means to burn in passion, not to burn in hell, which is what some have taken the passage to mean). And the reason it is better to be single is because, unbound by the affairs of the household (and by extension, many duties to the Roman state—such as the duty to bear healthy Roman children), one can do God's work in the world, wherever in the world God sends you.

In the early church, the two—chastity and active work in the community on one side, and marriage on the other—were seen as alternate paths for a Christian's life to take. When we lack the context in which Paul is writing, we emphasize very different things in the passage than his original readers would have. For Paul, celibacy undertaken by free choice was a *charisma*, a gift of the Holy Spirit—one of those many gifts given by God so that his people might work vigorously for the advancement of the faith, the succor of their neighbors, and the education and edification of the church.

First-century Christians were called to lives of active involvement in their communities as the agents of God, his "hands and feet," serving collectively as the body through which God operated in the world. The first-century ideal of chastity was intended to expand the agency of young men and women, whereas modern purity culture so often seeks to contract and limit agency. Purity culture is a *violation* of the Christian tradition of chastity. What we have done in this culture is taken the implement of freedom and liberty and reforged it into chains. We have taken what in the first century was a declaration of autonomy—a radical declaration that could get those who

79

made it tortured or killed by paternal authorities who saw
them as rebels—and we have turned it into a transaction, a
sale of the woman's body to her father and later to her
husband.

Rape Culture

A second pathology of our society that has infected our
churches is rape culture, and by *rape culture*, I mean a set of
attitudes that treat sexual assault as something "to be
expected" or that trivialize assault. In "rape culture,"
survivors are frequently treated as culpable for having been
assaulted, rather than men as culpable for having assaulted
them. This culture is enforced by a judicial system that
rarely convicts rapists and that issues light verdicts after
convictions. This culture is maintained when young men
are taught to pressure women for sex, while young women
are taught to avoid being raped. Rape culture is expressed
by rhetoric such as "boys will be boys" and "she must
have been asking for it," and by the questions that
survivors get asked after a rape by law enforcement, by
ministers, by friends and family: What were you wearing?
Were you drinking? Did you lead him on? Rape culture
dismisses men's responsibility, refrains from holding men
accountable, and places the full responsibility for assault
on the shoulders of women who have been assaulted. And
this culture is upheld when churches teach very selectively
from biblical passages about rape.

There is a bitter irony when rape culture exists in the
church. As we have seen, in late-antiquity Rome, a
woman's chastity was seen as an act of rebellion, and rape

(forcibly removing women's chastity and therefore autonomy) was a weapon used by government officials against the early church. When you read stories of early Christian women martyrs who refused to give up their virginity, that is the context. When Thecla, in the second-century text "The Acts of Paul and Thecla," repeatedly escapes attempts at rape in order to continue traveling and preaching (where the rapists are hired by someone who had wanted Thecla to marry their son and took spiteful exception to her vow of chastity, or by a village magistrate who sees in Thecla's teaching on chastity a threat to the unit of the Roman family and consequently to the social order), the context is that rape was a weapon employed by local or imperial authorities to limit the spread of this subversive new religion.

Diocletian's government especially used rape to gut the early church, to attack many of its leaders and to rip out its heart. That was seventeen centuries ago. But those wounds still remain, no matter whether we have forgotten the Roman blade that cut into the Body of Christ. Those wounds still bleed each time a woman entering the ministry is told by her male peers that women should be silent in church. They bleed each time a woman says, "I was raped" and Christians respond to her either with outright dismissal or by casting the blame back on her, by telling her she should not have dressed immodestly or had that drink.

Within communities of faith, we need to talk about this.

Because this rape culture is not acceptable. And it is not Christ. And it needs to end. Misogyny and rape were the weapons used *against* the early church; permitting or excusing misogyny and rape today, in our own time, is a bitter betrayal both of our ancestors in the faith and of our brothers, sisters, and others in our communities today.

The Bible is packed with cautionary accounts (which we risk overlooking) of women who say, "This man in power raped me" or "He tried to rape me," and whose voices are then summarily dismissed or denied by other powerful men, often with disastrous results. In Genesis 34, Dinah is raped by the prince of a local city, and her father's response amounts to: *Well, it is what it is, you just have to make the best of it.* Two of her brothers listen, at least, though their solution is to go slaughter the rapist's town.

In 2 Samuel 13, Tamar is raped by her half-brother Amnon, and when the king learns of it, he shrugs. His refusal to hold Amnon accountable eventually leads to a civil war.

In Daniel 13 (which is included in the canonical text in Catholic, Greek, and Slavonic Bibles), two town leaders stalk Susanna until they find her alone in her bath, where they molest her and try to blackmail her into bed. When she screams, they run, and they retaliate then by trying to have her sentenced to death for adultery. Until a prophet steps in, everyone is prepared to believe the two men over Susanna.

But as a teen, I didn't often hear those stories. The biblical "assault" story I heard with frequency was the story of Joseph and Potiphar's wife from Genesis 39—the only story of "fake rape" accusation in the entire Bible. This story has at times been reframed for teenage boys as a cautionary tale that pretty women might lie about good Christian boys and get them thrown in prison. Which completely misses the point of the story, which is about the abuse of power.

Potiphar's wife is a woman of property and wealth, and Joseph is a slave in her household. She and her husband literally own Joseph. She tries to use him as a sex slave. He refuses, and to get rid of him, she tells her husband that Joseph tried to rape her. That's a story about power over others as sex objects. It's a dynamic that repeats itself in our own culture in the form of the irrational fear that black men will assault white women, a fear that when invoked, often gets black men and children killed. But we don't often talk about that. We don't talk about the point of the story of Potiphar's wife. Instead, we turn it into something that it isn't.

Every other story in the Bible that addresses this issue hits the same note: the refusal of communities to hold powerful men accountable for the rape of women who are in more vulnerable positions; the quick dismissal of these women's voices as either probably lying or as not a big enough deal to do anything about; the often lethal consequences to these women, who may be mutilated or sentenced or killed, like Susanna or the Levite's concubine in Judges 19; and the disastrous outcomes for communities that refuse to hold powerful men accountable for assault.

A first-century rabbi and his students would have known these stories. So in his Sermon on the Mount, the Rabbi Jesus talks to people about lust.

He doesn't tell people, "boys will be boys."

He doesn't tell young women, "don't wear such short, slutty skirts."

Instead, he says, "Boys, if you really can't keep yourself from grabbing a woman, it would be better for you to chop off your hand. And if you really, really can't keep yourself from stalking her, it would be better for you to gouge out your eye. In fact, whatever part of your body is causing you to sin, just chop the thing off. That's better than the alternative. At least then, you wouldn't be harming God, yourself, *and* her; you'd only be harming yourself—and only your body, rather than your soul."

That is a paraphrase of Jesus's teachings on lust in the Sermon on the Mount in Matthew 5. (Of course, I caution against taking his instructions to "remove members" of the body literally, as legend says at least one saint did. The point of the sermon isn't self-mutilation but self-responsibility.)

That's why I find it troubling when our culture's default assumption is that a woman who accuses a man in power of rape or assault, a woman who has everything to lose by doing so, is lying and was probably "asking for it," anyway. That's neither intellectually nor biblically sound. Why aren't we all yelling, like Daniel, "Are you such fools? Have you condemned a daughter of our people without first considering her account?"

We get to hear about Potiphar's wife and the dangers of lying women, but why don't we learn about Dinah or Susanna? Why is the message we convey "Don't dress provocatively, girls," instead of "Boys, you can exercise some *egkrateia* (self-control)"? If we are to live as Jesus taught us, then we must live as fellow heirs of the gift of life. And we must scrap the notion that women bear the responsibility for rape, its consequences, or its prevention. Even the way we talk about this has to change. We say "women are raped" or "she was raped" in the passive voice, as if denying the existence and culpability of the rapist. When we say instead "A man raped her" or "Some men rape women," we stop playing the game of deferring responsibility. We need to stop telling schoolchildren to wear longer skirts. We need to stop 'slut shaming.' We need to start teaching boys *egkrateia* (self-control), because to do anything less is literally sin (*hamartia,* "falling short") of what Jesus taught us to do. There is no equivocation on this point in the Sermon on the Mount. Jesus places the full responsibility for handling men's lust on men. He says: If you truly can't behave as God would have you behave, take extreme measures to make sure you do, because God just doesn't accept "boys just can't help themselves" as an excuse.

So, my fellow Christian men, we need to get on this. Just as we need to pluck the weed of purity culture out of our faith, we need to yank the weed of rape culture out, too. And burn it. And never let it grow again.

3. *PHILOXENIA*: THE PROVISION FOR REFUGEES

WHAT THIS CHAPTER IS ABOUT

My heart breaks at the vocal support from some religious communities for bans on refugees and for walling out the *xenoi*: the "others," the "aliens," the "immigrants." We have forgotten that early Christians defined themselves as the *xenoi*, as refugees given refuge in God's house and called to extend *philoxenia* ("love for the stranger") to all others who are unhomed.

"They confessed that they were strangers and foreigners on the earth, for people who speak in this way make it clear that they are seeking a homeland … they desire a better country, that is, a heavenly one.

"…Do not forget to love and provide for strangers, for some have hosted angels and this was hidden from them."

THE LETTER TO THE HEBREWS

IMAGINE THAT YOU LIVE in Asia Minor 2,800 years ago. You speak Greek, but you can't read or write it. Oh, your ancestors could, centuries ago. They kept elaborate records. They had an alphabet. Maybe they established vast trade networks across the Mediterranean. Maybe they sent youths to compete in *taurokathapsia* in the arenas of Minoan Crete, where young people danced and vaulted naked over the backs of long-horned bulls. They were remarkable, your ancestors. No one today can do what they did. Your grandparents have told you their stories, as their grandparents told them. There is an oral tradition about the heroes and civilizations of the distant past. You know the stories of the thousand ships that sailed against Troy, and of the wooden horse Odysseus built. You know about Theseus venturing into the labyrinthine palace of the king of Crete, and of the Scythian nomads, warrior women on horseback, who invaded these lands long ago. You know of Mycenae and its splendor.

When those civilizations collapsed, the peoples of the Aegean Sea lost the technology of writing. Their trading networks became more temporary, contingent, and ever-shifting. Even when they picked up a new system of writing at last from (probably) the Phoenicians centuries later and began writing down the stories of Troy and Mycenae and Ithaca, they remained scattered, loosely connected, competing peoples. There was no more Minoan civilization; Mycenae now was near mythical. They didn't think of themselves yet as Hellenes. In Homer, there is no word for a unitary Greek people; they thought of themselves as many different peoples.

What haunts and intrigues me are the intervening centuries, the centuries without writing, when highly trained rhapsodes recited the tales not only of heroic warrior ancestors but also of great palaces presided over by women like Penelope or Arete, palaces containing wealth and spectacle barely imaginable to the listening audiences.

Now imagine if much of our own world collapsed in the near future, perhaps under the pressure of climate change (which some historians believe was a factor in doing in the Mycenaeans.) Suppose our descendants lost stable contact and trade with each other and lost the technology of writing. Suppose there were no "Americans" anymore, and for seven hundred years, every city and its environs became its own culture with its unique dialects of English, Spanish, and other languages. The cities fight, establish trade or see trade crumble, raid each other, get overpopulated and send out colonizers to other regions. Trained storytellers stand in the square or at the bar or at the pulpit reciting aloud the stories of past legendary people, Washington and Lincoln and Martin Luther King Jr. and all their exploits. They tell stories of women who wove spells out of arcane numerical symbols to send boats across the sky to the deserts of the moon, and of how an angry god smacked one of these Challenger boats out of the air, furious at its intrusion. They'll tell stories of the freeing of slaves and stories of people whose spirit left their body to talk to thousands of other people at once through tiny mirrors they carried in their pockets. They'll tell stories of wars fought over oceans by impossibly united tribes that launched fleets of a thousand ships, and of fleets that sailed the night sky and not only the waves.

And then one day, some people on another continent will create a system of writing again. Perhaps in Nigeria or Brazil. Vast new empires awaken on other continents. Through piracy or trade, a writing system makes its way to the shores of North America, and someone or someones, between the years 2800 and 3100, writes down a few epics, perhaps the *Lincolniad* (a story of warfare between kindred and the liberation of slaves) and the *Apolliad* (an odyssey across a star-filled sea to find the moon, with the explorers threatened by hungry space monsters, either aided or hindered by seductive and brilliant mathwitches, and harassed by the fury of an angry moon god). Audiences *ooh* and *aaahh* at these stories of a legendary past of incredible splendor. And the *Lincolniad* and the *Apolliad* become foundational cultural texts of new civilizations, read and translated and studied for thousands of years.

If you can imagine that, you may have an inkling what it was like at the end of the Greek Dark Ages to sit on the hillsides of Asia Minor listening to recitations of the *Iliad* and the *Odyssey*.

"I AM A STRANGER IN A STRANGE LAND"

In Greece, the lasting impact of these "dark ages"—this awareness of the fragility of life, when you didn't know when another tribe would burn your village, when locusts would devour your crops and leave you to starve, or when plague would take your children from you—was the persistent knowledge ancient peoples had of their interdependence on each other. This knowledge went bone-deep. You felt it in the beat of your heart and in your marrow, the moment you stepped out your door into an unkind world. If not for "the kindness of strangers," you might not make it home again.

That's one of the things that the *Odyssey* is all about—the risks and necessity of trusting a strange host and the risks and necessity of receiving a stranger, of not turning strangers away. The giant Cyclops, the witch Circe, and others in the story prove to be dangerous and lawless hosts who don't recognize the traveler's right to hospitality and succor. The Cyclops eats his visitors for dinner, and Circe transforms travelers into animals by magic. Other hosts fulfill the *letter* of the tradition by inviting homeless wanderers into their houses and offering them gifts, but violate the *spirit* of the tradition—like the Lotus Eaters, who extend gifts that entrap and drug the wanderers rather than empower them in their search for home. On the other hand, in the *Odyssey* there are dangerous guests, too. There are the suitors, devouring the resources of Ithaca, and there is Odysseus himself, who often proves a perilous guest. But throughout, both the risks and the rewards of welcoming others into your home are cast against the backdrop of conventions and codes of behavior that everyone knows about, even if they violate them. Those wanderers who are farthest from home or without a home are watched over especially by Zeus, protector of strangers, and violence offered against them earns Zeus's reproach and thunder. Compassion toward the stranger must ultimately trump caution. In the dark ages that produced the oral tradition from which the *Odyssey* came, provision and protection extended toward strangers was what rendered civilization possible. The offer of shelter to the stranger is a recognition that in this unstable world we might all be strangers and travelers together, all subject to unexpected circumstances. Those of us who are opening our home today may need a home opened to *us* tomorrow.

Emily Wilson describes the ethics of the *Odyssey* in the introduction to her new translation:

> There is a stranger outside your house. He is old, ragged, and dirty. He is tired. He has been wandering, homeless, for a long time, perhaps many years. Invite him inside. You do not know his name. He may be a thief. He may be a murderer. He may be a god. He may remind you of your husband, your father, or yourself. Do not ask questions. Wait. Let him sit on a comfortable chair and warm himself beside your fire. Bring him some food, the best you have, and a cup of wine. Let him eat and drink until he is satisfied. Be patient. When he is finished, he will tell you his story. Listen carefully. It may not be as you expect.
>
> EMILY WILSON

The encounter with the stranger can be a *kairos*, an opportunity for adventure. That is also true of an encounter with a strange text; in her introduction, Wilson is concerned that as translators and readers, we have become so set in our traditional reading of the *Odyssey* that we have neglected much of the adventure of reading and interpretation to which the epic poem invites us. Yet encountering the unforeseen and unexpected—and being open to that encounter—is the very adventure that the *Odyssey* is all about.

Whenever—in life or fiction—we encounter the stranger, the unexpected, the unforeseen, we can respond either with *xenophobia* (fear of the stranger) or *philoxenia* (love of the stranger). If *xenophobia,* then we reject the adventure of getting to know that stranger. We might slam our door shut. We might throw up a wall. We might attempt to kill, cage, or drive the stranger out. If we respond instead with *philoxenia*, we may invite the stranger inside, like Odysseus welcomed into the shepherd's hut when he arrives on Ithaca or like the unexpected dwarves welcomed into Bilbo's home in *The Hobbit*. Feed them, hear their story and their music, and answer the call to adventure—which is not only a call to go steal a treasure from a dragon beneath the Lonely Mountain, but is also a call to community with those we didn't know a day ago. In any case, shelter them—because you also will one day need shelter.

Even as the Greek-speaking peoples carried this ideal of *philoxenia* out of their dark ages, so too, the ancient Hebrews conceived of themselves as strangers who had traveled across a strange land and who therefore were called by God to shelter strangers themselves. Consider this passage:

> When a stranger resides with you in your land, you shall not oppress the stranger. The stranger who resides with you shall be to you as the citizen among you; you shall love the stranger as yourself, for you were strangers in the land of Egypt: I am the Lord your God.
>
> LEVITICUS 19:33-34

For you were strangers in the land of Egypt: you know what it is like to be immigrants. You know what it is like to flee oppression. And you know what it is like to come into a new land as strangers in it. Therefore, the Lord your God tells you: Love the stranger as yourself. Love them as you would your own citizens.

The levitical law institutes the ancient festival of Sukkot for the Hebrews as a reminder of this facet of their identity and of their responsibilities to each other and to God. At Sukkot, all the settled people of Israel, both the "homeborn" and "the stranger who resides with you," are urged to leave their homesteads and their towns and dwell in temporary booths and shelters in the countryside for a week—so that they will never forget their time in the wilderness, nor forget that they are all sojourners together on God's earth. This is also what Deuteronomy 6 instructs the Hebrews to unforget—when they lie down and when they wake up, when they walk down the road. It is the memory they are told to bind on their foreheads and write on their doorposts: their identity as refugees and delivered slaves, brought across a wilderness and granted refuge. By recalling that identity both at Sukkot and in the practice of their daily lives, they would be less likely to live lives of pride, the ostentatious lives of "self-made" people who, secure in their houses, would fail to see others' children starving in the streets outside. In the book of Jeremiah, the "weeping prophet" finds such lives abhorrent; he accuses his people of forgetting their history and therefore also their covenant with God, of baking cakes for the goddess Astarte in their homes and stocking houses full of bread while others' children sit famished in the street outside. These are not the lives of People of the Covenant, Jeremiah insists; this is not the way of people who live in daily awareness that their homes may be temporary, of people who know that they were once refugees.

Just as it was for the Greeks, cruelty toward the stranger is a terrible offense in ancient Hebrew ethics. In fact, this is the key refrain throughout the book of Genesis, a book about nomads in search of a home. When

Jacob lives in Laban's country, he is swindled by his host. When Abraham's servant goes to another land to find a spouse for Isaac, the matchmaking criteria he bases his decision on is simply: Which young woman, seeing him and his camel near dead of thirst at the well, will offer him water and a place to rest the night? Who will treat the stranger with kindness and provision? That is how the servant will know that he has found the right wife for his master's son.

When Abraham travels through Canaan and Egypt, there are repeated stories in which he stays in a new place and begins to shiver with terror that the people in that country "do not fear God." Abraham frets that if these people do not fear God, they may mistreat strangers, steal from them, oppress or enslave them, even kill them. Driven by this fear, Abraham chooses to pretend that his wife is actually his sister, so that if the people of the land desire her, they will not find it necessary to kill him when they seize her. Abraham is rebuked by his hosts for his cowardice and deceit, but the stories illustrate just how deep that traveler's fear was, and how important the code of provision for the stranger was to that culture. So much so that, when the Hebrews are eventually treated as a cheap labor force by the Pharaoh of Egypt, the story of their mistreatment and their exodus to search for a new home becomes one of the defining stories of what it *means* to be Hebrew: *You shall love the stranger as yourself, for you were strangers in the land of Egypt.*

There is also the story of Sodom. This is a story that we have often chosen, in our culture, to interpret as somehow being about gay people. For the ancient Hebrews, the story was about failing to shelter the stranger; the men of Sodom treat the stranger and the most vulnerable members of society with violence and rape. The prophet Ezekiel interprets the story in this way:

> This was the guilt of your sister Sodom: she and her daughters had pride, excess of food, and prosperous ease, but did not aid the poor and needy.
>
> EZEKIEL 16:49

Jesus reads the story in this way, too. When his disciples travel across the land, he warns them that not all towns will receive strangers kindly:

> If anyone will not welcome you or listen to your words, shake off the dust from your feet as you leave that house or town. Truly I tell you, it will be more tolerable for the land of Sodom and Gomorrah on the day of judgment than for that town.
>
> MATTHEW 10:14-15

In Genesis, when God visits Abraham and warns him that Sodom is to be destroyed, he, too, gives the reason for it:

> I must go down and see whether they have done altogether according to the outcry that has come to me.
>
> GENESIS 18:21

The word translated "outcry" here is *tseaqah*, and it means a cry of distress. It literally means a woman's scream, but in the Bible it is also used figuratively in cases where people who are vulnerable are suffering violence. It is the word used in Exodus when the Hebrew laborers in Egypt are oppressed and their children are thrown into the river or slain with the sword. It is the word used in 1 Samuel when the people of Israel are defeated in war and the Ark of the Covenant is taken from them, when they cry out in profound abandonment and fear that God may no longer reside with or protect them.

Throughout the Bible, when Sodom is mentioned, it is in the context of a society that is "proud" and does the "abominable thing" of offering violence to those who are vulnerable (Ezekiel 16:50). It is *that* sin that gets dramatized in the story of Sodom's destruction (Genesis 19). In the story, two angels in disguise visit Sodom. At night, men of the city gather outside Lot's house where the two angels are staying. The men are drunk, and they desire to rape the strangers and rob them. Lot has offered the strangers shelter because Lot is a man who "fears God," and once a stranger eats food at his table, his greatest responsibility within that culture is to shelter that stranger, no matter what happens. Horribly, Lot's last resort is to offer his own daughters to the crowd in place of his guests; the original readers of Genesis would have understood that horror to be a lesser crime than permitting violence to a guest who has sought and received your protection. Whether Greek or Mesopotamian, obligations to a guest are sacred. Everyone at some point must venture outside the home; a threat to those who lack the security of a home violates the one code that permits any form of civilization to exist. In Genesis, it is for that violation that Sodom is burned out of the world.

WRESTLING WITH THE WORD: *PHILOXENIA* AND *XENOPHOBIA* IN THE OLD TESTAMENT

I'll tell you another story. In Genesis 32, two strangers meet on a riverbank in the ancient world. One is a terrified patriarch fleeing southward with his family. He has a furious father-in-law miles behind and a vengeful brother miles ahead. The other is an unnamed man who wrestles with him all night:

> Jacob was left alone; and a man wrestled with him until daybreak. When the man saw that he did not prevail against Jacob, he struck hm on the hip socket; and Jacob's hip was put out of joint as he wrestled with him. Then he said, "Let me go, for the day is breaking." But Jacob said, "I will not let you go, unless you bless me." So he said to him, "What is your name?" And he said, "Jacob." Then the man said, "You shall no longer be called Jacob, but Israel, for you have striven with God and with humans, and have prevailed." Then Jacob asked him, "Please tell me your name." But he said, "Why is it that you ask my name?" And there he blessed him. So Jacob called the place Peniel, saying, "For I have seen God face to face, and yet my life is preserved." The sun rose upon him as he passed Peniel, limping because of his hip.
>
> GENESIS 32:24:31

Israel, whose descendants become both the subject matter and the chroniclers of the Bible, is both a name and a sentence: "He wrestles with God." Who are the children of Israel?—They are those who wrestle with God in the dark. Unable to see God's face clearly. Uncertain of their

97

footing or of the outcome, yet determined to wrest a blessing out of an encounter with their deity. Many stories in the Old Testament repeat the pattern of this early story: a messenger or a message comes in the dark, and the people who receive it must wrestle and struggle with it. Like Jacob, we cannot overcome or conquer or subdue the divine messenger or message, and the encounter changes us. Wounds us, marks us. We might walk afterward with a limp. The encounter may mark us in other ways too. It might rename us, change what we think of as core to *who we are*. The message might draw us away into the wilderness, might wrench us free of all our certainties and leave us struggling and striving in the dark. We may find ourselves "alone," having become strange even to ourselves.

But if that struggle with the message or messenger from God provides a *kairos*, an opportunity, to rename and redefine ourselves, it also provides an opportunity to draw nearer to others, too. As the story in Genesis continues, the wounded patriarch meets at last with his estranged brother Esau. When he had left Esau before, he left as *Jacob*, the swindler, the grasper, who thieved from his brother both his birthright and his paternal blessing. Now the patriarch returns home as *Israel*, the wrestler, the adventurer—one who walks boldly through the dark to seize opportunity, and does not hide from either the possibilities or the necessities of the moment. Jacob left with things that were not his; Israel returns, driving flocks before him as generous and reconciliatory gifts for his brother. Wounded by that encounter in the night, he returns home as a mender of wounds.

Just as Israel wrestles with the God he encounters as a stranger in the dark, readers are invited to wrestle with the strange and living Word of God. It is in this wrestling, this striving for understanding and for a blessing, that both the pleasures and the anxieties of reading the Bible are to be found. As Roland Barthes suggests in *Le Plaisir du Texte (The Pleasure of the Text)* and C.S. Lewis in *An Experiment in Criticism*, there is joy in wrestling meaning out of a story that might mean many things. For Barthes and Lewis, as for generations of Jewish readers of the Bible, the pleasure of the text is to be found in the dance, in the push and pull of interpretation, in the unexpected encounter, in wrestling with the winged apparition in the dark. Remember that the "living and active Word" of God comes to us always as a stranger, as "a thief in the night." And Jesus, as both a first-century rabbi and the incarnate Word, acts as a teacher to his disciples not by reinforcing ancient precepts, nor by giving them all the answers, but by shocking them with disturbing questions and with evocative and troubling stories that invite his listeners to ask difficult questions, to make difficult choices. We are called to engage with the Word as freshly as children and as boldly as adventurers far from home.

Like the children of Israel and like the rabbi Jesus, we must be readier to engage with and not merely dismiss the Old Testament's discontinuities. Unwillingness to wrestle with the text in all of its possibilities and contradictions is born out of some modern traditions within Christianity that see *eisegesis* (looking for a story about us reflected in the text, at the risk of reshaping the text to fit us) as more critical to our experience as readers and as children of God

99

than *exegesis* (pulling the story of the past out from the text, at the risk of finding *ourselves* reshaped by the text). When we are willing to read exegetically and not only eisegetically, we can choose to find the contradictions and varying perspectives within the Bible to be part of the joy and pleasure of the text. We can treat the Bible's difficulties and paradoxes as an invitation to adventure— (to an encounter with a strange God, an encounter that might leave us changed and "strange" too), rather than as a threat to the reader or to our tradition. We can choose to find it exciting when this library of strange and ancient texts recorded by ancient peoples invites to undertake many interpretive adventures. (I will talk more about this in Chapter 8.)

One of these adventures has to do with the question, "How do we treat the stranger?" The ancient Hebrews wrestled with this. We see this wrestling documented over centuries of time across the Old Testament. From book to book across the Bible, we witness a tug of war between xenophobia on the one hand (often connected to the levitical edict to keep one's tribe pure and uncontaminated by foreign influences) and on the other hand, the requirement to shelter the stranger.

So, on the one hand, in the book of Judges, you have a series of illustrative tales about the threats that strangers bring to your land and your people. They may invade you, as Sisera does. They may overwhelm and enslave you, as the Midianites do. They may seduce you, as Delilah does. Similarly, in the book of Ezra, we read of a priest commanding the people to divorce foreign wives. In 1 Samuel, we read of a prophet commanding genocide.

On the other hand, in the book of Ruth you have the tale of a foreign woman being offered violence in Israel, and the godly are those who intervene and offer her shelter; Ruth is the stranger in the land, but her name may have meant "companion." In Ruth, the immigrant is your companion who is to be sheltered and who has much to offer your people. Ruth brings Boaz love and Naomi laughter. In the Bible, her descendants include King David and Jesus.

In the books of Daniel and Esther, we read tales of Hebrews who are strangers and captives in others' lands and who suffer injustice and oppression. And throughout the Psalms, the poet (often identified as David) speaks as a political refugee living in exile among strangers and pleading for defense and deliverance from his enemies: "You are my Rock and my Refuge," David sings to God, in psalm after psalm, often in the most tender terms:

> Yet it was you who took me from the womb;
> you kept me safe on my mother's breast.
> On you I was cast from my birth,
> and since my mother bore me you have been my God.
>
> But you, O Lord, do not be far away!
> O my help, come quickly to my aid!
>
> For he did not despise or abhor
> the affliction of the afflicted;
> he did not hide his face from me,
> but heard when I cried to him.

PSALM 22:9, 22:19, 22:24

And in *The Song of Songs*, we have a hauntingly beautiful erotic love poem (or possibly, as Marcia Falk suggests, an arrangement of poems) in which love conquers all, and the love between a Hebrew ruler and a foreign immigrant prevails. In the *Song*, the Hebrew people and their officials treat the Shulammite woman violently, beating her and raping her:

> Making their rounds in the city
> the sentinels found me;
> they beat me, they wounded me,
> they took away my veil,
> those sentinels of the walls.
>
> SONGS 5:7

Afterward, as though fearing rejection, the Shulammite hardly dares to see her lover, and instead she urges the Hebrew women to find him, to speak to him on her behalf, and to let him know that she is still "faint with love" for him (Songs 5:8). When the Hebrew women demand to know why they should seek him for her, she launches into a long poem describing her lover's physical beauty and his gentleness of speech and defending her love for a man of their tribe:

> …His appearance is like Lebanon,
> choice as the cedars.
> His speech is most sweet,
> and he is altogether desirable.
> This is my beloved and this is my friend,
> O daughters of Jerusalem.
>
> SONGS 5:15-16

When she and her lover are reunited, he assures her that he finds her lovely and beautiful and desires no less to be with her; to him, she is "my dove, my perfect one, my only one" (Songs 6:9). Nothing that has happened to her has changed that. Her own song of love for him is equally tender: "I am my beloved's and my beloved is mine" (Songs 6:3). The language of the poem becomes progressively more erotic and sensual, until in her joy the Shulammite cries out to her beloved:

> I am my beloved's,
> and his desire is for me.
> Come, my beloved,
> let us go forth into the fields,
> and lodge in the villages;
> let us go out early to the vineyards,
> and see whether the vines have budded,
> whether the grape blossoms have opened
> and the pomegranates are in bloom.
> There I will give you my love.
>
> SONGS 7:10-12

At last, we reach one of the closing choruses of the *Song of Songs*:

> Set me as a seal upon your heart,
> as a seal upon your arm;
> for love is strong as death,
> passion fierce as the grave;
> its flashes are flashes of fire,
> a raging flame.
> Many waters cannot quench love,
> neither can floods drown it.

If one offered for love
all the wealth of one's house,
it would be utterly scorned.

SONGS 8:6-7

This is an especially remarkable love poem if you consider that in ancient Mesopotamian cultures, the loss of a woman's virginity rendered her unmarriageable—in an age that regarded women as property items, it destroyed her market value. But to the young man in *The Song of Songs*, the "song more excellent than any other," her rape has no impact on her value, because her value is that of a person, not that of a commodity to be owned—and because there is no economy in love. There is no market. A king could offer "all the wealth of his house" in exchange for love, and he would only be mocked—because neither love nor your lover are commodities to be bought.

I could spend my entire life writing happily about *The Song of Songs*. Along with the fragments of Sappho and the Descent of Inanna, it is one of the most tender ancient love poems I have ever read. And it is maybe the Old Testament's most beautiful expression of love being an activity that recognizes no "strangers," only human "companions" to shelter, love, defend, and share life with.

Like the two lovers in the poem who must decide, each and together, what the Shulammite's rape means to them, the reader must, too. The reader has to make choices about how to interpret what happens in the texts they read. The reader enters into a relationship with the text, one that will be threatened, one that will be defined and redefined by each successive encounter with the text. The reader is an active participant in the adventure, not a passive recipient—a wrestler with God; after all, the apostle James calls upon those who hear the Word to be "doers of the word, not hearers only" (James 1:22):

> For if any are hearers of the word and not doers, they are like those who look at themselves in a mirror; for they look at themselves and, on going away, immediately forget what they were like. But those who look into the perfect law, the law of liberty, and persevere, being not hearers who forget but doers who act—they will be blessed in their doing.

JAMES 1:23-24

For James, we are not to read the Bible like people gazing into a mirror, seeing only a momentary reflection of ourselves, of what we already know or think we know—a reflection that leaves no mark on our minds because it requires no risk and entails no cost. Rather, we are looking to be "blessed," and if we desire a blessing, we must "look into" the text, we must "persevere," we must wrestle like Israel in the night.

Accordingly, we have many choices to make as we journey from scene to scene, passage to passage, psalm to psalm, book to book. One of the adventures we must take is that of navigating our course between *philoxenia* and *xenophobia*. We have to interpret the Bible's conflicting tales of love and fear of the stranger. Readers who are Christian may desire to hold Jesus's teachings on love unforgotten and near the heart as they read, like a lantern to light their way on this winding path. Jesus himself was a skilled reader of the Bible, one who wrestled so passionately with God in the garden of Gethsemane that he sweat blood.

We who are Christian have him with us as a fellow Reader, a companion and fellow adventurer on the road. But he calls us to and accompanies us *on* the adventure; he does not remove it. The Word will still require difficult and brave choices from us.

PHILOXENIA IN THE NEW TESTAMENT: "DO NOT FORGET TO LOVE STRANGERS"

Philoxenia is a concept the first-century Jews in Diaspora—many of whom read the Old Testament in the Greek "Septuagint" translation—would have been deeply familiar with. It is a concept that reappears in the apostolic letters in the New Testament, whose writers define the Christian identity as that of refugees in a world whose "days are evil" but who have received refuge and safety in God's house, and who are now called to extend the same safety and salvation to others. We were lost in a dark world, but a *Soter* (a Deliverer, a Rescuer, a Savior) has granted us refuge (*soteria*), and we are now *sōs* (safe, rescued, delivered). To the early Christians, each member of their community is a *soterion*, a refugee granted refuge.

While on earth, Jesus's apostles taught, we are all strangers in a strange land, sojourners without citizenship, homeless travelers. In Hebrews 11, the analogy and example offered for the life of faith is the journey of Abraham across Mesopotamia. Abraham, as a *xenos* (an "other," a "stranger"), traveled across a wilderness in search of a new home, "hoping against hope" (Romans 4:18) for a better country, a country promised but as yet unknown. In the same way, the unknown writer of the letter to the Hebrews suggests, we are all *xenoi*—others, strangers, aliens in the world. We can endure any hardship on the journey because of the strength of our yearning and our faith that we will find "a better country":

> [Those before us] all died in faith, not having received the things promised, but having seen them and greeted them from afar, and having acknowledged that they were strangers [*xenoi*] and exiles [*parepidemoi*] on the earth. For people who speak thus make it clear that they are seeking a homeland ... they desire a better country, that is, a heavenly one. Therefore God is not ashamed to be called their God, for he has prepared for them a city.
>
> HEBREWS 11:13-16

In the New Testament, to be Christian is to be one of a group of exiles who have been offered a city—and who are then moved to bring other exiles in with them. The Christ himself was an outsider in the communities he visited, and being one, he was able to welcome all outsiders to break bread with him. The kingdom of heaven, he taught, is like a banquet to which all outsiders are brought in, dressed, fed, and made at home (Matthew 22). In *The Weakness of God*, radical theologian John Caputo describes an ethics of *philoxenia* in this way:

> To provide a place of respite and refuge, to offer bread and water, even to take the food out of one's own mouth in order to share it with the stranger—in short, to make the other welcome—that is the law of the land and the law of God. Hospitality could very well be taken as the very emblem of morality in the biblical sense, as Thomas

Ogletree argues. The traveler who appears at our door bears the mark of God upon his brow. God has signed the face of the stranger and placed him under divine protection. The one who receives the stranger, receives God, "the God who loves the stranger." … That same idea shows up again in the beautiful story in the New Testament in which the disciples ask the master, when did we find you hungry and feed you, or find you in prison and visit you, and the master says, whatever you did to the least of mine, you did to me (Matt. 25:35-40).

JOHN CAPUTO

The Roman poet Terence (who, according to the writers of antiquity, was himself a freed slave of foreign birth who became one of the great playwrights in the Roman world) famously wrote, *Homo sum; humani nil a me alienum puto*: "I am human; therefore I consider nothing human to be alien to me." There are no *xenoi* in Terence's thinking; all humans are in the *oikos*, in the house, together. There are no "others" who lack citizenship in humanity.

The early Christians, commenting on the Old Testament, arrive at a similar conviction, but from an opposite starting point. Rather than suggesting that *we are all inside the house*, the early Christians—speaking as and to the outcasts, often to those who have no secure place in a Roman world—suggest that *we are all outside the house*. We are all strangers in the land; knowing this, no human can be a stranger to us. We are all *xenoi*, and we are all refugees. Because we are *all* shivering in the cold outside the house, and because we are *all* passing through a strange land hoping for refuge, it is no longer either desirable or rational to wall anyone out. Loving the stranger—in recognition of our shared identity as strangers, our mutual alterity—is essential to New Testament ethics, and indeed it would be difficult to comprehend most stories about the early church without grasping this.

This was more than a metaphor for Paul, for Peter, and for the writer of the letter to the Hebrews. It was a way of describing the lived experience of a disinherited and diasporic people who believed they had been granted a new hope—a hope of citizenship in a city they had never seen, a city they had not built, a city to which they were being delivered by their *Soter,* their Savior. Having received such an unexpected, impossible gift, in gratitude they believed that their responsibility was to strive to live their lives in ways that would be worthy of that city, worthy of heaven. So when the apostle Peter urges the early Christians to avoid slavery to earthly desires, he abjures them by their identity as refugees:

> Beloved, I urge you as sojourners [*paroikoi*] and exiles [*parepidemoi*] to abstain from the passions of the flesh, which wage war against the soul.
>
> 1 PETER 2:11

A *paroikos* is literally a "dweller-near," one who lives outside the house (*oikos*) and is without citizenship, yet is dwelling near (*par*) it. A *parepidemos* is a "passer-through," one who is here for a time but was not born here and may not die here. Earth is not our country, Peter reminds us. We are passers-through, we are dwellers-near-but-not-of, and this identity must drive our commitments to ourselves and to others, and it must drive our choices, our actions.

Therefore, the writer of the letter to the Hebrews urges first-century believers:

Do not forget to love and provide for strangers, for some
have hosted angels, and this was hidden from them.

HEBREWS 13:1

"Some have hosted angels" is a reference to the story of
Sodom, that city that refused its travelers sanctuary. The
city that was utterly destroyed because of the violence it
offered to "the least of these," the city that was scorched
from the face of the earth because of the *tseaqah* or
"scream" of those who suffered in it. For readers of the
Bible, Sodom is not a city that is wildly different from
those we live in. Instead, Sodom is our "sister" city
(Ezekiel 16:49), a sister whose example we risk emulating.

It wounds me today to hear the vocal support and
encouragement from many quarters for bans on refugees
and for walling out the *xenoi*: the "others," the "aliens," the
"immigrants." If those of us who are men and women of
faith permit ourselves to "harden our hearts" against
refugees, if we who are *paroikoi* are deceived into thinking
of ourselves as proud owners of homes (*oikoi*), whose
homeland must be defended against all comers, then we
will have forgotten everything about who we are and what
we have been called to do.

Our path has often been the way of *xenophobia*—fear of
the stranger—but the New Testament calls us to lives of
philoxenia, of radical interdependency. Today, we can be the
church that gives sanctuary, or we can be the church that
kills—the church that leaves "the least of these" to starve,
that drives gay teens to suicide, that voices support from
the pulpit for bigger, better walls. We can say, self-

righteously, "ours is the house of God" while we sacrifice human lives, like the priests who earned Jeremiah's rage in ancient Jerusalem. Or...we can unforget who we are. If Christianity is to be not only "relevant" but critical and active in the years ahead, people of faith must remember *who we are*. We must remember—in fact, we must unforget, from hour to hour—that we are *sos* (saved). We must find ourselves again—as refugees on earth, as strangers in the land, as strangers to whom no other human being can be strange. As others (*xenoi*) who "other" no one.

Having forgotten this, we are hurting other children of God. In the United States, we live in a time when the question of whether to cage refugee children, whether to tear gas them at the border, is treated as a politically partisan position. Do not be deceived. We who love Jesus, we who are committed to live as citizens of heaven, we who have adopted the name the Romans gave us (the "little Christs," the Christians), we who serve a Refuge-Giver whose own family fled as refugees to a foreign land when he was only a baby or a toddler (Matthew 2:11-18)— we must not dispassionately excuse the mistreatment or slaughter of innocents, nor stand idly by while Herod soaks his hands in their blood and tears.

We must unforget *philoxenia*. We must do this for the survival of our neighbors. And we must do this also for the preservation of our humanity and our souls. Because, in the words of Jesus, what will it profit us if we gain "the world" and all its illusory security but forfeit our soul?

4. *EIRENE*: THE EGALITARIAN BODY OF CHRIST

WHAT THIS CHAPTER IS ABOUT

When the Body of Christ gets talked about today, we often express it in terms of head/body dichotomies and in hierarchical terms. But when we look closely at New Testament passages about the Body in ancient Greek, we find a radical dismantling of hierarchy, and the seeds for an egalitarian theology that is unlike anything we are living today.

"We are one body... If one member suffers, all suffer together with it."

THE FIRST LETTER TO CORINTH

IN THE YEAR 112, Pliny, in his official capacity as governor of the Roman province of Bithynia (in the north of what is now Turkey) wrote an exasperated and somewhat desperate letter to the Emperor Hadrian in Rome. In this letter, Pliny reports that the temples in his province are "almost forsaken" and that many locals are refusing to worship Hadrian as a god. Pliny undertakes the project of rooting out these Christians who refuse to acknowledge the deity of the Emperor. He writes of the difficulties involved in identifying who the Christians' leaders, or indeed in making sense of their religion or their way of living. He reports that he has found it necessary to "inquire by torments what the truth was." He gives the example of two slave women he imprisoned and put to torture, and expresses his shock that in their religious community "they were called deacons." To him, it is all but unthinkable that two domestic slaves would hold positions of honor and trust in the church. Surely a people who are capable of such disorder and such disregard for the structures of society might be capable of any anarchy, of any crime. But to his confusion, Pliny relates that after questioning these and other captives, the only "crimes" they would confess to were that they would sing a hymn at dawn, commit no theft or adultery, break no promises, and meet at evening with each other for a common meal. To the Emperor, Pliny pleads, "What am I to do?" It is his first time dealing with Christians; he asks how others have dealt with them, what punishments and verdicts they've assigned, and whether he is to treat teenagers, adults, and seniors differently, for it is not just young hooligans who have joined the new sect.

What to do with these people at whose common meal—the *agape*, or "love feast"—people of every ethnicity, gender, and social position gather? These people who refuse to acknowledge the hierarchies and values of the Empire?

I don't know if it is easy for a modern reader to grasp how radically egalitarian first-century Christianity tried to be, or to understand how flabbergasted Pliny was, writing to Hadrian that he had discovered two slave women who were *diakonoi* (ministers) of the underground church. Our communities today fall far short of the ideal that was expressed in the writings of the early church and that was apparently *lived* in second-century Bithynia. In several letters to early churches, Paul expresses the desired unity of the church in these terms:

> You have clothed yourselves with Christ. There is no longer Jew or Greek, there is no longer slave or free, there is no longer male and female; for all of you are one in Christ Jesus. And if you belong to Christ, then you are Abraham's offspring, heirs according to the promise.

GALATIANS 3:28-29

It might be easy to misread this letter thinking of our modern and callous idiom, where the more privileged among us say things like, "We don't see color," which we sometimes think is a noble-sounding sentiment but which, in the ears of people of color, may convey instead that you see everyone as *white*, that you don't see the unique needs, perspective, and suffering of your neighbors.

But in a first-century context, what Paul is saying to the Galatians in that passage is astounding. He is talking about equal access to the gift of "grace" and equal membership in a family that is as large as the world. And he is writing this letter to an ethnically diverse community. Galatia was founded by Celts who then intermarried with Greeks and other peoples inhabiting Asia Minor. They were conquered by Romans, and they were joined by Jews in Diaspora. And Paul is writing to people living under a Roman society that takes adoption and inheritance *very* seriously. To them he says: You are all heirs. If you are a woman, you are an heir. If you are a man, you are an heir. If you are a Greek, you are an heir. If you are a Jew, you are an heir. If you are a domestic slave, you are an heir. If you are a householder, you are an heir. Whatever your gender, your class, or your ethnicity, *you are a member of God's family, an heir in full legal standing*. It is in this spirit, too, that Peter advises Christian men to recognize women as "fellow heirs" of the gift of life (1 Peter 3:7).

But to *really* get how earth-shattering this idea was, you need to know about the Lex Falcidia. Let me tell you the story.

THE LEX FALCIDIA

This was a Roman law that was established forty years before the birth of Jesus and that still remained on the books six centuries later in the time of the Emperor Justinian. It was a strict regulation for how estates were to be inherited, and it was perhaps one of the ancient world's more just approaches to the problems of inheritance. For example, we might compare the Lex Falcidia favorably to the primogeniture of some feudal states a thousand years later. Under the system of primogeniture, only one son would inherit his father's estate. So a baron would leave his estate and title to his firstborn son, fund a second son's entrance to the priesthood, and leave any remaining male children (whether legitimate or illegitimate) to fend for themselves as "landless sons." Such men were prone to marauding the countryside; with no land to inherit, they might assemble a raiding party and set out to *take* some land. It was in response to such widespread marauding that the Roman Catholic Church proclaimed the Treuga Dei (the "Truce of God") in 1027 at the Council of Toulouges, demanding that armed conflict cease during holy days. Perhaps not by coincidence, under the Treuga Dei the church began adding a *lot* of holy days to Europe's religious calendar, commemorating the lives of various saints. A century after the Treuga Dei was signed, there were only eighty days left on the calendar that were *not* holy days.

Rome's Lex Falcidia, more civil than primogeniture, attempted to prevent fathers with large estates from passing them on entirely to one son and leaving the others without holdings. This law required that each living son receive a mandatory percentage of the estate. So a Roman family needed at least one son to pass the estate to; however, the more sons survived to adulthood, the more the estate would get carved up into smaller portions. And in Rome, your voting rights (and how much your vote counted), your social position, what businesses you were permitted to conduct, and what political offices you were eligible to run for, were all dependent on the amount of land you owned. Originally, during the years of the Republic, real estate also determined whether you could serve in the military. A little over a century before the Christian era, Rome's standing army was staffed only by men with property, reflecting a belief that such men would be less likely to desert and would fight bravely, because men with property have property to defend. But after a disastrous defeat in 107 B.C. in which much of the Roman military was slaughtered by invading Germans, the consul Gaius Marius changed the laws, recruiting military personnel from the *capite censi* or "head count," the impoverished and illiterate who lacked property, land, and voting rights. In return for military service, these new enlisted men would each receive a portion of the land conquered in Rome's campaigns. Rather than relying on men who had property to defend, Marius enlisted men without property who had property to win. Marius's restructuring of the military saved Rome from the invasion, precipitated an expansionist period in which Rome rapidly conquered the Mediterranean world, and contributed to the fall of the Roman Republic because it initiated a mechanism by which military leaders could amass enormous political and economic power by military conquest. For example, Julius Caesar carved up all of Gaul among his troops—creating a bloc of landowning (and voting) veterans loyal to their former commander. In the last days of the Republic, military service became the pathway to social mobility for many families—because if you could acquire land, that changed what you could buy and sell, what offices you could hold, and whether and to what extent you could vote.

Keeping real estate intact (and growing it) was a financial and social imperative for the Roman middle and upper classes. And because in Rome, unlike in medieval Europe, *all* sons would inherit, this made the question of having children a complex juggling act for well-to-do Roman families. On the one hand, high mortality rates meant you needed to make a lot of babies if you wanted a male heir who would survive to adulthood. On the other hand, if too many babies survived and grew up, your family would lose its wealth and its rights.

The solution that middle and upper-class Roman families found was adoption. This did not look anything like adoption looks today. In ancient Rome adoption, even more than marriage, was how affluent families established alliances. Suppose you had one family with one too many teenage sons, and another whose sons had all died in childhood or in the military. Family B might adopt Family A's extra son, who would then be the legal heir of Family B. The two families would now be allied, and both estates would be protected.

This also meant that you would always try to adopt from a family of equivalent or superior status, position, wealth, and bloodline. The whole purpose of adoption in the Roman world was social mobility. You wanted to make sure you had at least one male heir, but as few legal heirs as possible, so that the estate could continue to grow its wealth. You would be very unlikely to adopt a son from a class lower than yours; you would only do so in exchange for something quite remarkable from the other family. Maybe your family has the bloodline and the other family has the money, and that is the reason for the alliance. But in most cases, you're trying to adopt *up*. And you would be very unlikely to adopt a daughter.

Into this society comes the early church, whose apostles teach that all human beings are the adopted children of God the Father, and that all human beings—of all genders, classes, and ethnicities—are fellow heirs in the gift of the Father's estate. The good news preached by the first-century Christians is that they have a recklessly loving Father whose estate is infinite and who can therefore carve it up into endless portions. God gives all his heirs an inheritance, just as the *Lex Falcidia* requires—but rather than limit the number of heirs, God has adopted *everyone*. God is prodigal with his estate, like the prodigal father in the story Jesus tells. (See Tim Keller's book *The Prodigal God* to explore this idea further.) God gives everything, recklessly, to everyone. He isn't weighing whether the adoption improves his estate or not, because the only criterion for him is love, and when you adopt someone you *love*, you increase the only wealth that matters. (Remember the old childhood riddle: What do you have more of, the more you give it away?)

It is an idea that turns the logic of the *Lex Falcidia* and the economy and hierarchy of the Roman Empire upside down. God adopts women as easily as men, foreigners as easily as citizens of the Empire. To God, every single one of us is as worth adopting as an emperor's son. It is this reckless love of which Paul writes when he tells the church in Rome:

> In all these things we are more than conquerors through him who loved us. For I am convinced that neither death, nor life, nor angels, nor rulers, nor things present, nor things to come, nor powers, nor height, nor depth, nor anything else in all creation, will be able to separate us from the love of God in Christ Jesus our Lord.

ROMANS 8:37-39

119

And this love is what Paul writes about here, too:

> For all who are led by the Spirit of God are children of God. For you did not receive a spirit of slavery to fall back into fear, but you have received a spirit of adoption. When we cry, "Abba! Father!" it is that very Spirit bearing witness with our spirit that we are children of God, and if children, then heirs, heirs of God and joint heirs with Christ.

ROMANS 8:14-17

We are called to live as the dearly loved and loving children of a Father who would rather have *us* than all the wealth in the universe. And that means *all* of us. All of us who a Roman family would *never* adopt are cherished heirs in God's house. Slave women become apostles, and merchant women become ministers. Illiterate fishermen become prophets. Immigrants from a Middle Eastern desert country become teachers and healers. Husband and wife become no longer lord and subject but instead co-heirs in God's house.

THE RADICAL EXAMPLE OF THE EARLY DISCIPLES

The early Christians told a story about how this started. In that story, the Rabbi Jesus called together a group of students and apostles who were so diverse and so mismatched in the eyes of their culture that the religious leaders of the day found them alternately ridiculous, confusing, or threatening. There were Philip and

Nathaniel—fast friends, but one of them likely a Hellenized Jew (with a Hellenized name) and the other likely a more orthodox Jew (with a Hebrew name), who could often be found with his back to a tree meditating on the Torah. Just under two centuries ago, their ancestors had fought a devastating civil war, with one side sponsored by a foreign tyrant. Their very way of life, their identity as a people, had been at stake. The Hellenized faction had banned circumcision and defiled the Temple in Jerusalem. At one point, many Jews who faithfully observed the Sabbath were massacred on their holy day. It had been a brutal conflict. Eventually the orthodox faction won the war. When they retook the Temple, they rekindled the holy flame at the altar—the flame that must never go out. But there wasn't enough oil to keep the flame burning more than a single night. In haste, they called for more oil to be brought to the city, but there were still enemy encampments in the way. The arrival of the oil was delayed, yet the lamp did not burn out. It kept burning— for eight nights—until at last the oil could be brought to replenish it. It is this story that gets celebrated each year at the festival of Chanukah, and this is why the Jewish menorah has eight candles, a symbol to the Jewish people of hope and of faith that the light of Judaism will never burn out, no matter how many foreign oppressors might try to exterminate it.

The memory of those events was still fresh in the time of Jesus—as fresh as the American Civil War and its aftermath remains for us. And yet, these two men, Philip and Nathaniel, who initially may have been even more separate in their views and passions than an Alabama conservative and a New York liberal would be, somehow form a friendship and follow the Rabbi Jesus together.

Joining them are even more unlikely companions. There is Simon the Zealot, an activist who demands of his companions and his rabbi that they help him launch a revolt against the oppressor Rome. Judas the assassin is there too, for a while. He is one of the *sicarii* (in Greek, the "Iscariots") who carry the slender, curved blade known as the *sica*, a Roman knife used to kill Romans in the streets. When using it, you grab a Roman, cover his mouth, pull him into an alley, and slay him. Or you kill him at a public gathering while wearing a cloak and hood, so that you can disappear into the crowd after.

With them are Simon and Andrew and John and James, who are fishermen, small-town tradesmen. There is Mary Magdalene, an untouchable in her culture. There are Joseph of Arimathea and Nicodemus—two men of the priesthood, who unlike their colleagues do not feel threatened by this country preacher and who sponsor his work, one publicly and the other in secret. There is Matthew the tax collector, who makes his living collecting his countrymen's livelihood and sending it off to Rome; the only way he gets food on *his* table is by charging the taxpayers an extra collector's fee. You can just imagine how well he and Simon the Zealot probably got along...

And yet, these visibly incompatible people are the group Jesus chose to live with, travel with, dine with, and teach. *These* were the people he asked to "love one another, as I have loved you." These are the people whose feet he washed, and to whom at the Last Supper he promised a *pneuma aletheias*, a spirit of unforgetting, who would help them remember how loved they all were by Jesus and his

Father, and how much they were to love each other. On the night of his betrayal, as they break bread together, Jesus tells them that every one of them—from Matthew the tax collector to Simon the Zealot; Philip and Nathaniel both; the priests and the fishermen, all of them—are fellow heirs in God's house:

> Do not let your hearts be troubled. Believe in God, believe also in me. In my Father's house there are many dwelling places. If it were not so, would I have told you that I go to prepare a place for you? And if I go and prepare a place for you, I will come again and will take you to myself, so that where I am, there you may be also.
>
> JOHN 14:1-3

That was the promise, the very promise that led these people to work together for the rest of their lives, to build a community in which everyone shared equally (Acts 2:44-47), a community committed to living lives of faith and unforgetting. And what they told the world was that in the Father's house, there are rooms for us all. Everyone is a child of God and an heir in his eternal estate, everyone is cherished, everyone is loved and heard and advocated for. God's house is not a closed structure. In the book of Revelation, we learn that the city of heaven has not one gate but twelve, and that these gates are always open and *never shut*:

> Its gates will never be shut by day—and there will be no night there. People will bring into it the glory and the honor of the nations.
>
> REVELATION 21:25-26

WOVEN TOGETHER IN ONE BODY

Besides the house with open gates, another metaphor used throughout the New Testament is that the community of God's children are collectively the physical body of God on the earth, the lips through which he speaks love, the eyes through which he sees humanity's suffering and the ears through which he hears it, the heart which breaks at it, and the hands and feet by means of which he intervenes with compassion and justice.

> For just as the body is one and has many members, and all the members of the body, though many, are one body, so it is with Christ. For in the one Spirit we were all baptized into one body—Jews or Greeks, slaves or free—and we were all made to drink of one Spirit. Indeed, the body does not consist of one member but of many. If the foot would say, "Because I am not a hand, I do not belong to the body," that would not make it any less a part of the body. And if the ear would say, "Because I am not an eye, I do not belong to the body," that would not make it any less a part of the body. If the whole body were an eye, where would the hearing be? If the whole body were hearing, where would the sense of smell be? ... Let the members have the same care for one another. If one member suffers, all suffer together with it; if one member is honored, all rejoice together with it.
>
> 1 CORINTHIANS 12:12-17, 25-26

The writers of the New Testament teach that we are filled by the same *pneuma aletheias*, the spirit of unforgetting, the Holy Spirit. And our body that has this one spirit does not consist of a few privileged individuals but of many, all of us different. With all our different backgrounds and gifts, our calling is to share in one another's lives, to "rejoice with those who rejoice, weep with those who weep" (Romans 12:15), and to "have the same care for one another." In our family, in God's family, the Spanish-speaking immigrant who works as a maid in the last hotel you visited may be—and ought to be—as honored as a president. If those of us who call ourselves the body of Christ are *not* living this way, then we are falling short. We are literally sinning. (The Greek word for sin is *hamartia*, "falling short"—see Chapter 11).

To really "get" the ideal of the Body in the Greek New Testament, it's important to understand how the early Christians wrote about *peace*. I mentioned this briefly in Chapter 1, and I want to return to it here—because the word *eirene* in Koine Greek is profoundly different from "peace" in English, to such an extent that when we translate it as "peace" and read it in English, we may read from the text a meaning opposite to that a first-century Christian would have.

Consider what we often mean when we say "peace" in English. We tell our dead to rest in peace, we ask for peace and quiet, we "make peace" by ending a battle—because our "peace" is a descendant of the Roman *pax*, which means the absence of conflict. It means order, silence. Yet for many, the Pax Romana was a false peace and an oppression. The Greek word is *eirene*, which comes from the verb *eiro*, which means to "tie" or "weave." An appeal to *eirene* is not a call for order or the cessation of conflict; it is a call for interdependency—for a community "woven together." (Compare this to the Hebrew *shalom*, which has often been translated as "peace" and glossed as "full-flourishing.")

In a perfectly ordered *pax*, in a stable *status quo* with no conflict, people may find themselves stacked on top of each other in orderly castes and not woven together at all; lives may be prevented from full-flourishing because privileging the absence of conflict above all else keeps issues from being resolved, reconciled, or forgiven. But in *eirene*, we don't silence dissent or brush issues and conflicts under the rug—we *are* the rug. Woven together in community like a thousand colored threads in a brilliant tapestry.

Traditionally the first ancient verb that a student of Koine Greek learns is *luo*, which means both "I destroy" and "I loosen," a pairing that can confuse a modern student at first—until you realize the extent to which weaving was a potent metaphor for the ancient Greeks. Penelope, waiting for Odysseus's long-delayed return, weaves a funerary shroud by day and unweaves it by night. When we first encounter Helen of Troy in *The Iliad*, we find her at her loom. In Greek lore, the Fates weave our lives as a Greek woman might weave a carpet, and at the end of our life, Atropos snips our thread with her lethal shears. The spine is imagined as a cord to which are woven together all the threads inside our body. Once that spine is severed, all the threads fall slack, and a human body drops as limply as a snipped marionette. In epic poetry, when a warrior falls in battle, "his limbs are loosened."

When the threads of a beautiful coat of many colors are loosened from one another, the coat frays and then falls apart. To loosen is to destroy; to weave together is to make beauty. Weaving is a potent metaphor in the ancient world—in part because it takes so much time and effort and talent. A hand-woven rug with an intricate design might well take a young woman in the hills of Asia Minor a year to complete. Yet how easily a thing that took a year to make might be loosened and unwoven.

Thus the letter to the first-century church in Ephesus urges its members to bind themselves to each other in love, to allow nothing to loosen them:

> There is one body and one Spirit... Speaking the truth in love, we must grow up in every way into him who is the head, into Christ, from whom the whole body, joined and knit together by every ligament with which it is equipped, as each part is working properly, promotes the body's growth in building itself up in love.
>
> EPHESIANS 4:4, 4:15-16

To be one Body is to be woven together (*eirenê*) in selfless, giving love (*agapê*)—the kind of love that cares far more about reconciling conflict than avoiding it, the kind of love that would die on the Cross for one's friends:

> Love is patient; love is kind; love is not envious or boastful or arrogant or rude. It does not insist on its own way; it is not irritable or resentful; it does not rejoice in wrongdoing, but rejoices in the truth. It bears all things, believes all things, hopes all things, endures all things.
>
> 1 CORINTHIANS 13:4-7

The kind of love Jesus speaks of when he tells his disciples during the Last Supper:

> No one has greater love than this, to lay down one's life for
> one's friends.
>
> JOHN 15:13

And in the Sermon on the Mount:

> Blessed are the peacemakers (*hoi eirenopoioi*), for they will be
> called children of God.
>
> MATTHEW 5:9

That is the radical difference Jesus of Nazareth made in the cultures of the Near East 2,000 years ago. You could see his handprint, his teachings, his spirit, his *pneuma aletheias* (spirit of unforgetting), each time first and second-century Christians of varied ethnicities, genders, and castes dined together at an *agape*, a "love feast." You could see it when Governor Pliny arrested two house slaves and learned to his shock that they were ministers.

Rather than resting on top of each other in separate layers of society, the early Christian writers imagine an integration of all people into the warp and weft of a shared community. In David Mitchell's novel (and film) *Cloud Atlas*, the fugitive slave and revolutionary Sonmi 451 says, memorably:

> Our lives are not our own. From womb to tomb, we are
> bound to others, past and present. And by each crime and
> every kindness, we birth our future.
>
> *CLOUD ATLAS*

Though in *Cloud Atlas* this idea is voiced in a Buddhist context, it is an idea that first-century churches probably would have understood. Bound to others: woven together. By our every act, we are either weaving or unweaving our world—by strengthening or fraying the relationships in it.

We are "of one accord" (*homothumadon*, in Philippians 2:2) not when some have been silenced but when all have been heard. When we have listened and acted with compassion. Because the story of Christ's radical love defines our identity and models our action more than any other story of our lives. All the stories that divide and segregate us have been surrendered, because these are not the stories that tell us who we really are, and the values suggested by those stories belong to gods other than the one we serve. We are *homothumadon*, acting as one body, when it proves far more important to us to walk out onto the water together, helping each other over the waves, than it is to be right, or to be first, or to remain comfortable and secure in the rickety boat we have built using the planks of our cultural values and prejudices.

It is difficult to be the Body of Christ *and* live in a "bubble" of likeminded people who look like us and are all of the same class, ethnicity, sexual orientation, etc. I think it likely that the Body and the Bubble are incompatible concepts.

HEAD AND BODY: DISMANTLING HIERARCHY

When the Body of Christ gets talked about today within religious communities, we too often talk about it in terms of a head/body dichotomy. We say things like: The husband is the head of the household, Christ the head of

129

the church. But what we *mean* when we say this is very different from what first-century readers and listeners would have understood, hearing it. This is because the word "head" in Greek (*kephale*) does not mean what "head" means in English. In English, "head" conveys both the physical head and "a leader." It does in Latin, too (that's where we get this idiom from). So when we read "head of the body," we interpret it in a very Roman manner, understanding the metaphor to be one of hierarchy. The head makes decisions, the body gets them implemented. We see Christ as the Decider and the Body as the Implementer. We see the husband as the decision maker and the wife as the executive assistant, and so on.

But in Koine Greek, "head" doesn't suggest that secondary meaning of "leader"—not until centuries after the New Testament was written. *Kephale* does indeed have both a literal and a figurative meaning in Koine, but the figurative meaning is not "leader" but "source," like the source of a river. In Greek, the metaphor of Christ as "head of the church" is meant to suggest not *authority* in the modern, hierarchical sense but an *author* in the classical sense: an originator. The river has a source, and then a living, bubbling stream flows on to water the world from that point of origin. So also, Christ is a source of living water, and the church is called to be the vessel that carries that living water out to the world.

We might also take greater care with how we interpret and use the reference in 2 Timothy to the husband as the *kephale* ("head"), remembering that *kephale* implies origin, not power. For readings of that passage that take the nuances of Koine Greek into account, see Marg Mowczko's articles on the subject:

"Why Kephale Does Not Mean Leader"
https://margmowczko.com/head-kephale-does-not-mean-
leader-1-corinthians-11_3/

"Adam was Created First, and This Means…"
https://margmowczko.com/adam-created-first/

When we read a very Roman hierarchy into a text about
the Body of Christ, we shatter the entire point of the
passage. Paul writes to the church in Corinth that no part
of the body is less essential than any other. Such passages
call for the *dismantling* of hierarchies, for treating each other
as co-heirs of the kingdom of heaven, a community in
which God shows no "partiality" or "favoritism" (Romans
2:11; James 2:1-13), neither by gender nor ethnicity nor
social status nor wealth. For:

> Listen, my beloved brothers and sisters. Has not God
> chosen the poor in the world to be rich in faith and to be
> heirs of the kingdom that he has promised to those who
> love him?

JAMES 2:5

Have we not all one father? Has not one God created us?

MALACHI 2:10

It was this idea that all Christians are co-heirs that was so
liberating to the early Christians and so terrifying to some
officials of the Roman Empire. Because Pliny was
searching for church leaders among citizens of status and
high social position, he could not find them—until he
imprisoned and tortured two slave women and discovered

to his astonishment that *they* were ministers in the Bithynian church.

The egalitarianism that Jesus and his apostles longed for did not last long in history; yet ever since, it has haunted Christianity's teachings, its rituals, and its reform movements like a ghost, like the presence of the Holy Ghost—from the sister women of the New Testament to Francis of Assisi to Martin Luther King, Jr. And so this idea of One Body has poetic and profound implications for modern readers no less than for Roman ones. If we are one body—comprising all genders, all ethnicities, all social classes, and all degrees and types of physical and mental ability—and if *all our members* are essential (and *equally* so), then we cannot function as a body where some members reject others, or assault them, or impoverish them, or look away while such things occur. That is the opposite of peace.

> If one member suffers, all suffer together with it; if one member is honored, all rejoice together with it.
>
> 1 CORINTHIANS 12:26

That is something that we in our time need to unforget. It's something our community *needs* us to unforget. How differently might our churches today look and act, if we did unforget this?

5. *PISTEUO:* FAITH IS A VERB

WHAT THIS CHAPTER IS ABOUT

In Greek, faith is a verb. Yet the practice and doctrine of modern evangelical Christianity often treats *faith* as a transaction—forgetting that faith is a continuous activity. But what kind of activity? What does it look like to undertake the adventure of *faith*? To walk out into the wilderness like Abraham? To walk out onto the water like Simon Peter? Let's take a look.

I faith; help my unfaith!

THE FATHER OF A SICK CHILD IN MARK

I HAVE WALKED ON WATER with no solid ground beneath my feet. I have crossed the desert, not knowing where the next oasis could be found. And only love kept me going, and hope, and faith, which is in part the relentless commitment to those I love—"love, hope, and faith, these three" (1 Corinthians 13:13).

My daughter Inara was born suffering catastrophic seizures. I held her, an infant girl, in my arms as her body spasmed. We talked in hushed voices with doctors and

133

specialists who fought for her life like warriors. Many didn't think her likely to make it. But we hoped. We had faith. We fought.

She did too. Her middle name is Cahira, Irish for "warrior." Night after night at her bedside, I watched her fight. Not only to live but to *laugh*. I have never known a child who giggled the way Inara giggles, as if she sees in every hour a thousand joys and wonders and jokes that elude those of us who have reached adulthood without scarring in our brains.

Inara has been near death, drowning in neurological seizures, many times. Yet she lives exuberantly, climbing over couches, rolling her wheelchair, playing with toy dragons, painting with her feet on canvas, painting all the stories she cannot tell with speech.

When she began her long recovery, I wrote a book *Lives of Unstoppable Hope*, because words were pouring through my heart like fire. In it, I said:

> Now my daughter is improving, and we are on the other side of that time together. Yet those nights by her bed are recent in my heart, and they hurt. I don't know what this past year has meant, only that the love I now hold for those I call my own is fiercer than anything I have ever felt. I have learned that hope, which I had thought small and delicate like a moth in the night, can be hard as steel, a blade with which you cut your way through a press of moaning and hungry foes.
>
> *LIVES OF UNSTOPPABLE HOPE*

I wrote then about hope, which is the flaming blade we bear through the night. Now I want to write about faith, which is the will to go on walking, even in the dark, even in the desert, even across the surface of crashing waves.

THE ROAD TO EMMAUS

Long ago, two people were walking on the road from Jerusalem to Emmaus, an outlying town. We do not know who they were, except that they were acquainted with the Rabbi Jesus and were among his students. One church tradition holds that the two were Cleopas and Mary, a married couple who had been present at the Crucifixion. Having just witnessed the upheaval of everything they believed in and held dear, the brutal execution of their teacher and friend, the scattering of his followers, and the apparent death of his ministry, these two were going home, grieving and stricken to the heart. Along the way, they disputed the meaning of prophecies about the Messiah, the one who was to come and restore justice and peace to their people. The words that perhaps they could not speak, the words beneath their conversation, were: *How could we have been wrong? We thought it was Him. Now he is gone. What will we do now? Where will we look? Where will we hope?*

They were joined on the road by a stranger. "Why are you sad?" he asked them. When they answered, telling him of the defeat of all their hopes, he said, "Oh, you are slow of heart! But all of this had to happen. This is what the prophecies are about. Let me tell you the story again." And he did. They conversed until they reached an inn, where they broke bread together. Then suddenly, he was no longer there. Astonished, they looked at one another. "It was *him*!" they whispered to each other. "It was *Him*." And one of them says, "Didn't our hearts burn within us, while he talked with us on the road and opened the scriptures to us?" (Luke 24:32)

On the road to Emmaus, Jesus rekindled the fire of hope in their hearts by telling them their own story—the story of the men and women who had followed the Messiah and the hope of a Messiah into Jerusalem that Passover season. He told them their own story, but he told it differently than how *they* had been telling it—no longer a story of grief but one of unstoppable hope, if they would only have the faith to carry that story unforgotten and burning in their hearts, all the way back to their homes in Emmaus.

My friend and pastor Susie Grade once gave this sermon about the Road to Emmaus:

> We are the slow-hearted and the burning-hearted. We walk the road to Emmaus, catching glimpses on the way of the risen Christ. On the road to Emmaus, what defines us is not fulfillment but *hope*. We yearn for a "better country—that is, a heavenly one" (Hebrews 11). We hope that the justice and the beauty and the Christ that we see in glimpses "through a glass darkly" now, we will one day see face to face (1 Corinthians 13). That *hope* defines us. That hope burns in our hearts. That hunger, that thirst for justice, for peace, for *shalom*, for the "full flourishing" of all our lives, for a better country, for a world in which we are not exiles. A world that is as it ought to be. That hunger, that thirst, that hope is what defines us.
>
> SUSIE GRADE

The unknown author of the letter to the Hebrews in the New Testament speaks of that restless search for a "better country" in a passage about faith, which the author defines as the confidence in something hoped for but unseen (Hebrews 11:1)—something ahead, something across the water or across the desert. Something you must walk toward, through whatever perils may come, even if you are broken, even if you are terrified, even if you are carrying your daughter who may be dying in your arms—because the one ahead, the one asking you to follow, has your love. Because your love for him drives you, and your hope for the refuge to which he is taking you defines you.

Let's talk about faith.

DO NOT OUR HEARTS BURN WITHIN US?

Somehow, in our time, we have boiled all the flavor out of faith and turned it into mere "belief." But the faith Jesus required of his followers in the gospel stories was something distinct from and bigger than "belief." And in the stories of Jesus, faith—like any walk across the naked desert—is costly.

In one such story, a young man who had inherited considerable wealth came to Jesus and asked what he could do to inherit eternal life as well:

> As he was setting out on a journey, a man ran up and knelt before him, and asked him, "Good Teacher, what must I do to inherit eternal life?" Jesus said to him, "Why do you call me good? No one is good but God alone. You know the commandments: 'You shall not murder; You shall not

commit adultery; You shall not steal; You shall not bear false witness; You shall not defraud; Honor your father and mother.'" He said to him, "Teacher, I have kept all these since my youth." Jesus, looking at him, loved him and said, "You lack one thing; go, sell what you own, and give the money to the poor, and you will have treasure in heaven; then come, follow me." When he heard this, he was shocked and went away grieving, for he had many possessions.

MARK 10:17-22

This happened, too:

As they were going along the road, someone said to him, "I will follow you wherever you go." And Jesus said to him, "Foxes have holes, and birds of the air have nests; but the Son of Man has nowhere to lay his head." To another he said, "Follow me." But he said, "Lord, first let me go and bury my father." But Jesus said to him, "Let the dead bury their own dead; but as for you, go and proclaim the kingdom of God." Another said, "I will follow you, Lord; but let me first say farewell to those at my home." Jesus said to him, "No one who puts a hand to the plow and looks back is fit for the kingdom of God."

LUKE 9: 57-62

And to the first disciples he called, Jesus said this:

As he walked by the Sea of Galilee, he saw two brothers, Simon, who is called Peter, and Andrew his brother, casting a net into the sea—for they were fishermen. And he said to them, "Follow me, and I will make you fish for people." Immediately they left their nets and followed him.

MATTHEW 4:18-20

Leave all behind and follow me. Unless you are willing when called to leave your dead to bury themselves and to leave your property, your business, your tribe, can you really be said to be living the life of faith? Every comfort, every security, every thing in which you trust and rely that is not God, might need to be left behind. Here's another story about this:

> By this time the boat, battered by the waves, was far from the land, for the wind was against them. And early in the morning he came walking toward them on the sea. But when the disciples saw him walking on the sea, they were terrified, saying, "It is a ghost!" And they cried out in fear. But immediately Jesus spoke to them and said, "Take heart, it is I; do not be afraid." Peter answered him, "Lord, if it is you, command me to come to you on the water." He said, "Come." So Peter got out of the boat, started walking on the water, and came toward Jesus. But when he noticed the strong wind, he became frightened, and beginning to sink, he cried out, "Lord, save me!" Jesus immediately reached out his hand and caught him, saying to him, "You of little faith, why did you doubt?"
>
> MATTHEW 14:24-31

Lord, if it is you, command me to come to you on the water. Unlike those who approach Jesus asking to bury their dead first or to retain their property and real estate, Simon Peter understands something about how God works in the Bible. God always calls you out into the wilderness. He calls you away from the alleged security of the boat and out onto the waves. That is Peter's test for whether it is really Jesus, "the Son of God" (Matt 14:33) or a "ghost" whom he sees. He wants to know if Jesus will do the God thing and say, "Walk to me on the water."

Because that is what God does throughout the Old Testament, and such acts of reckless faith and loving obedience are the sacrifices God requires (1 Samuel 15:22). Thus Abraham departs from his home and his people, answering God's call and crossing a desert in search of a new land. He does not know where he is going. He does not know what he will find there. He knows only that he has been called. Unforgetting his hope of a new and better home, he braves great dangers and travels across many lands. He often falters, doubts, and makes terrible choices. Then he continues.

Similarly, Moses, after forty years living as a herdsman with the support and respect of an affluent family, is asked to travel back to Egypt to confront the Pharoah and demand that Pharoah release his labor force. "Why will anyone listen to me?" Moses asks God. And God says, *Here, I will give you a stick. Go to Egypt and take this staff. And also, I will be with you.*

That's really the only "assurance" God gives to any of these people: *ki ehyeh immakh,* "I will be with you" (Exodus 3:12). I will be in your midst. In the New Testament, Jesus is first introduced to the reader as *Immanuel:* "God with us" (Matthew 1:23). And Jesus promises his disciples, "Remember, I am with you always, to the end of the age" (Matthew 28:20).

I am with you. Come walk out to me, Peter, across the crashing waves. I'm here. If you fall, I'll catch you.

That "call" out onto the surface of the water is what we mean when we speak of a call to live a life of faith. In *The Weakness of God,* John Caputo writes eloquently of what he calls the "weak force" of God. Contrasted with "the strong force" of commandment or omnipotence (an idea that

Caputo finds both theologically and philosophically risky to stake either religious or intellectual commitments on), the "weak force" is the call, the invitation, the quiet insistence of the voice that we name God and that calls us to action. It is the "still small voice" that Elijah hears in that beautiful story in which God arrives not in power but in supplication, opening not with a command but with a question, with an invitation to *teshuvah* ("return"), to return to the work that needs doing in the world. "Elijah," God asks, "what are you doing here? There is work to do."

> Now there was a great wind, so strong that it was splitting mountains and breaking rocks in pieces before the Lord, but the Lord was not in the wind; and after the wind an earthquake, but the Lord was not in the earthquake; and after the earthquake a fire, but the Lord was not in the fire; and after the fire a sound of sheer silence. When Elijah heard it, he wrapped his face in his mantle and went out and stood at the entrance of the cave. Then there came a voice to him that said, "What are you doing here, Elijah?"
>
> 1 KINGS 19:11-13

That is frequently how God speaks in the stories in the Bible: with a voice in the quiet that requests our faith. Perhaps that very request testifies to God's loving, against-all-odds faith in *us*, God's faith that we will answer the call. Caputo describes the call as "a summons that calls and provokes, an appeal that incites or invites us, a promise that awakens our love."

Faith answers the call to adventure, whatever the cost, however great the risk. In faith, you walk out on the water—not because you have received a guarantee, not because you have total certainty of the outcome, but because you are so moved by the invitation or so provoked by the call that you can't *not* go. You accept the adventure. You don't really know what will happen, whether you will walk or sink; you simply trust, like Peter, that you do not stand on the water alone. Living in faith is being willing to face Pharaoh with nothing more than a stick in your hand and a message from an unnamed God. Faith is walking into the court of the King of Persia like Hadassah (Esther) when the lives of an entire people are threatened, to say, "My husband, I need to talk with you about something important," even though entering the court unsummoned might get you killed. Faith is being willing to speak truth to power, to leave your comfortable house and stand with slaves, to leave even your dead to bury themselves rather than delay. Faith is being willing to risk everything. And when everything is taken, and you are indeed thrown into a den of lions, faith is standing there facing their jaws and their hunger and praying, *I know you are with me and I am not alone. I'd really appreciate some help right now, but I trust you. I trust you. I love you. I am here, where you asked me to be. I am here.*

FAITH IS A VERB

Years past as a young student, I was delighted— overjoyed—to learn that in Koine Greek, you can "faith" someone, or more literally, "faith into" someone. The verb *pisteuó* takes the preposition *eis* ("to" or "into"), a preposition used for locations that you arrive at or journey into (or sometimes *epi*, "on"). *Pisteuete eis ton Theon, kai eis*

142

eme pisteuete, Jesus asks the disciples in John 14:1. "You have faithed into the Father, faith also into me."

Faith is a verb. It is not so in English. Our translators have to select from an array of possibilities—"I believe"; "I trust"; "I am committed"; "I am loyal"; "I am persuaded"; "I am confident"—but the Greek verb means all of these things, and more.

I crave being able to do that in English. I crave being able to look lovingly into my wife's eyes and tell her, "My love, I faith you." After all the battles we have fought beside each other; after all the long nights spent in vigil at our daughter Inara's bedside at the hospital; after the long struggle to get the ears of congressmen and protect Inara's care; after witnessing my wife, a valorous warrior, an *eshet chayil*, save our daughter and our family time and again; after the years of tears and laughter; after the many nights of reading stories to my wife to distract her just enough from chronic pain to make falling asleep possible; after all the mornings waking beside her and knowing I get to spend another day with her—I want to hold my wife close and whisper,

"My love, my love, I faith you."

In fact, I think I *will* do that today—even if the English doesn't quite work, doesn't quite do enough.

Faithing, in the Bible, is a process. It's a daily relationship, a daily living of the greatest commandment:

> You shall love the Lord your God with all your heart, and with all your soul, and with all your mind. This is the greatest and first commandment.
>
> MATTHEW 22:37-38

When I say I wish to faith into my wife or faith into my God, I am speaking of the fullness of love I have toward them: that I wish to do anything, commit my whole self to that love. My faith is not a belief *about* God, a conviction tucked away somewhere in my intellect. It is a willingness to step onto the water if he should call. Even if I sink. Even if, like Simon Peter, I sink. I want to trust, to commit, to believe, to follow, to faith *into* my God, deeper and deeper. Recklessly, illogically, passionately. I want to love God with all my heart, and with all my soul, and with all my mind. There may be specific times when I don't *feel* like doing that, but this is not about what I *feel*, moment to moment. It is about what I want—and *who* I want—in the deepest places of my heart.

METANOIA

But, being human, I am not very good at loving God with all my heart and all my soul and all my mind, and I am not very good at the second commandment either:

> And a second is like it: 'You shall love your neighbor as yourself.' On these two commandments hang all the law and the prophets."
>
> MATTHEW 22:39-40

I am bad at that kind of love. Easier to shiver in the boat with a chosen few than walk on the water or love all my neighbors so recklessly.

To love like that, to *faith* like that, to grow my tiny faith until it is even just the size of a mustard seed and might move a mountain if God wishes a mountain to be moved (Matthew 17:20), I need to be willing, even recklessly eager, to change and *be* changed in response to the insistence of God's call. I need to take the adventure he has for me.

Metanoia—"after thought" or "changing mind"—is what makes the walk of faith possible. It's what John the Baptist calls people to in the wilderness. Come out here and *metanoiete*, he tells them. We say "repent" in English, but repentance often carries for us the connotation of a quick transaction: Say we are sorry for a thing, and be forgiven. *Metanoiete* doesn't mean that. It means *Hey, all of you, change your minds.* The Greek word *nous* conveys more than just "intellect"; in Greek philosophy, *nous* referred to the faculty that allows a human being to perceive what's real and what's trustworthy. That is what we're being asked to change—what we put our trust in and what we see as real. So that, rather than trust in the "boat" of my culture, or my country, or my family tradition, or my current interpretation of religious texts, I will be willing to leave all of that behind and follow God's call across the water. And maybe God will not ask me to travel across a wilderness, like Abraham or Moses. Maybe God will ask me to leave behind everything I believe I know about my fellow human beings. Which journey is harder? Which is likelier to have me doubting and sinking into the sea?

But that change in what we trust and how we think and what we rely on—that is the transformative work that God pursues within us:

> For I am confident of this, that He who began a good work
> in you will continue to complete it [*epitelesei*] until the day of
> Christ Jesus.
>
> PHILIPPIANS 1:6

The Greek verb tense for *epitelesei* here is aorist—meaning that it conveys ongoing activity, rather than a one-time, transactional activity. This idea—that God is constantly at work within us, changing us—is such an important idea that Paul opens a letter to the church in Philippi speaking of it and giving thanks for it.

I have seen bumper stickers that proclaim things like, "I am a Christian; you can persecute me, but you cannot change my mind." I think the makers (and users) of such stickers think they are advertising *steadfastness*, but I will admit I find the message on these stickers unsettling at best. In the New Testament, to follow Christ is to surrender to ongoing *metanoia*. Against this is contrasted *sklērotēta sou kai ametanoēton kardian*, "your hardness and unchanging heart" (Romans 2:5). Unchanging hearts and minds are what the apostles did *not* want.

That is the conundrum for those of us who are Christians in today's world: the process of "faithing into" Christ is one of ongoing *metanoia*, yet our culture has taught us that faith is about holding one's mind unchanged and unchangeable. The New Testament ideal is to change one's mind, heart, and behaviors constantly according to compassion and the need to live lovingly in community with others. Paul describes behaving as the Romans behave when in Rome, and speaks harshly of people who, in their "hard and unchanging heart," judge others.

Christians, like Christ, are not sent out into the world to judge but to love and to give refuge. And to do so, we must allow God to continue his ongoing work in us.

Perhaps that is frightening. Is not a *little* work, not a little change. One of our most cherished Christian sacraments, baptism, expresses that, in a ritual act of recognition that following Christ requires the death and annihilation of our old life and our rebirth into a new life:

> Do you not know that all of us who have been baptized into Christ Jesus were baptized into his death? Therefore we have been buried with him by baptism into death, so that, just as Christ was raised from the dead by the glory of the Father, so we too might walk in newness of life.

ROMANS 6:3-4

LEAVE ALL BEHIND

Jesus's demand that we be ready to change our minds and hearts when called to follow him and imitate him is repeated in passage after passage. He speaks eloquently—and dismayingly—about the costs of discipleship:

> Whoever comes to me and does not turn from his father and mother, his wife and children, brothers and sisters, yes, and even life itself, cannot be my disciple. Whoever does not carry the cross and follow me cannot be my disciple. …and none of you can become my disciple if you do not give up all your possessions.

LUKE 14:26, 33

To *faith into* God is to be willing to relinquish all else—one's people, one's culture, one's material security, and one's tradition. In fact, one's culture and tradition may place a cross on your shoulders for you to carry with you—in other words, may outcast and punish you—if you decide to follow God. That is a consequence that disciples of Christ are urged not to be naïve about. "When Christ calls a man he bids him come and die," Dietrich Bonhoeffer preaches in *The Cost of Discipleship*. His commentary has all the more weight for me because Bonhoeffer *did* die in his discipleship, not only in the sense of leaving behind the expectations of his people and his culture and the dictates of his government when he decided to resist Hitler in Third Reich Germany, but also in the sense that he literally died in a concentration camp because of his discipleship.

Bonhoeffer understood that Christianity is not a culture; it is a choice to follow and imitate the living Christ *instead of* your culture and your tradition. Our sin of pride and idolatry in the United States is that we have often conformed our Christianity to American values and prejudices, rather than allowing our Christianity to upend our allegiance to our culture and challenge our tradition. To follow Christ is to step outside the boat of our culture, leaving the illusory security of its planks behind and step out onto the water instead. That is the adventure. We may prefer staying put. We may prefer the idolatry of trusting in the timbers and planks of our culture, but we are called to walk on the water with nothing solid under us, without security, without prejudice, just faithing, just unforgetting who we follow and what he asks of us. Even if this means leaving our father and our mother, even if this means leaving the culture that bore us. We are to cross the wilderness, even if it means carrying a cross on our shoulders while we do. This is how the New Testament defines the children of Abraham. To *faith* is to abandon comfort and embrace vulnerability because you love someone and trust that they love you, and that love is of more worth to you than all the world. Being worthy of that love is more important to you than upholding religious or cultural tradition. That love becomes worth risking it all. Even dying for. That is the adventure, one that will require unexpected choices and wild risks of us—as readers, as followers of Christ, as human beings. That is what *faithing* is.

6. *PARAKLETOI*: THE ADVOCATES

WHAT THIS CHAPTER IS ABOUT

In the New Testament, the same word is used for the Holy Spirit and for Christians. That word is *parakletos* (plural: *parakletoi*). It means "one called beside." It is also the word for a lawyer, the word translated into Latin as *avocat*, "advocate." The teaching of the early church is that Christians are to act as advocates and defenders of their fellow human beings—that, in doing so, they carry out the activity of God the Paracelete. We are called to be *parakletoi*—to stand for each other, in each other's moments of need, just as God stands for us. To do this, to love one another actively and as advocates, is to carry the name and the action of God into the world. It is what Jesus asks of those who follow him.

———————

Blessed be...the God of all consolation, who advocates for us in all our suffering, so that we may be able to advocate for those who are in any suffering with the same advocacy with which we ourselves are consoled by God.

THE SECOND LETTER TO CORINTH

———————

ONCE UPON A TIME, A TRAVELING RABBI visited the temple and began to teach. A group of religious scholars interrupted him, dragging a woman with them and shoving her into the middle of the temple courtyard. They make her stand there with everyone staring at her; as she cries, they tell the Rabbi Jesus that the woman was caught in the act of adultery. They haven't bothered to bring the man along. Maybe he coerced her. Maybe he seduced her. Maybe they fell for each other, but when "caught," he abandoned her and fled. Regardless, he is not here. She stands alone, perhaps wrapped hastily in a blanket or a cloak, shamed in front of all her people, surrounded by the shouting faces of angry and judging men. The religious scholars, adept at picking and choosing verses that, in isolation, appear to support their own prejudices and desires, quote Scripture and suggest that legally, they are entitled to stone the woman. That is, to brutally strike her with heavy rocks until she dies. "Now what do *you* say?" they demand of the rabbi.

They want him to say either *Yes, stone her* or *No, don't, what on earth is wrong with you?* If he says Yes, he will be exposed as cruel, and some people will stop following him. If he says No, they will drive a wedge between the rabbi and his students by suggesting that the rabbi does not care to follow the law. It is a political game they are playing, and the unnamed woman who they've shoved into this public space—they have done a terrible thing to her, making her pain and fear serve their political purpose and making her life an object for political opponents to gamble for. That is one brutality; the actual stoning would be a second.

The rabbi does not say *Yes* or *No*. In fact, he doesn't say anything. He does not play the game. Instead, he crouches and writes in the dust with his finger. Maybe he is buying time to think. Maybe he is doodling possible ways out of this trap. Maybe he is too angry or too upset at the cruelty of the religious scholars, and needs a moment to breathe and calm down before he answers them. Maybe he is simply listening. Maybe he is being kind and lowering his eyes so that at least one man present is not staring, gawking, shouting at this half-naked woman whose entire life has not only been torn apart but has also been dragged into this religious facility to be put on display for the mockery or hate of strangers.

Whatever the case, the scholars won't desist. They continue to decry the shamefulness of this woman they have dragged out of bed. They continue to demand answers of the rabbi. Finally, he straightens up. He doesn't stare at the woman. He doesn't question her. He doesn't accuse her. He doesn't demand that she tell her story. Instead, he looks at each of the religious teachers. And he says, "Let he among you who is without sin be the first to throw a stone at her." Remember that in Greek, sin is *hamartia*—"falling short" or "missing the target." He is literally telling these men of religion that if there's someone among them who has never made a mistake, that person should be the first to throw the stone.

None of them can meet the rabbi's eyes.

They came here, each of them, to shame and torment this woman as a means of finding an opportunity to shame *him*.

But now they are shamed.

Each of them, in that moment, has been shoved back to reflect on his own mistakes, his own sins. Maybe they see those memories reflected in his eyes before they drop their gaze. They have been given this one kindness: their sins, at least, are not dragged out into the public eye. *Their* lives can be weighed in the privacy of their own hearts. The rabbi has not done to them what they did to that woman.

One by one, they slip away. They leave. None of them can stand in front of his community and say, "I have never erred. Not once." None of them has a moral high ground to stand on, from which to justify judging, stoning, and brutalizing this woman.

At last, only the Rabbi Jesus and the woman are left. Alone. Only now does he face her. He asks, "Woman, where are they? Has no one condemned you?"

"No one," she whispers.

"Neither do I condemn you," he says. "Continue your journey [*poreuou*] and sin no more."

STANDING WITH AND FOR EACH OTHER

That story does not appear in any of the first, second, third, or fourth-century Greek manuscripts of the Gospel of John; it first appears in the Codex Bezae, a fifth-century text. This means it was probably added sometime late in the fourth century; during the fifth century, church leaders refer to it in sermons. Do you realize what that probably means? It suggests that this story and its message was *so important* to late-antiquity Christians that they inserted it ("retconning" it) into the gospel, and then kept it and gave sermons on it. That's how much it mattered to them.

And I can see why. This story, beautifully and quickly told, enacts and illustrates what it means to live "in imitation of Christ"—the idea of living and acting as a paraclete.

Parakletos is my favorite Greek word. It means one who is "called beside" another. Sometimes you see it translated "advocate," "comforter," or "intercessor"; it conveys both *attorney/legal advocate* and *confidant/comforter*. It is the word used in the New Testament for the Holy Spirit. In 2 Corinthians, it is also the word used to describe *our* role and responsibilities to each other, the specific way in which we are called to imitate Christ and to live lives that are filled with and fulfilled by the Spirit of the living God:

> Blessed be ... the God who advocates (*parakalōn*) for us in all our suffering, so that we may be able to advocate (*parakalein*) for those who are in any suffering with the same advocacy (*paraklēseōs*) with which we ourselves are consoled (*parakaloumetha*) by God.
>
> 2 CORINTHIANS 1:4

The verb *paraklein* means to call to one's aid, and the *parakletos* is the one called to aid others. I have seen the word translated many ways, because no one English word does a good job of capturing its full meaning. Sometimes it is rendered "helper" in English texts, and I like this best. It reminds me of the Hebrew *ezer* ("helper," one who gives refuge), a word often used to describe God in the Old Testament. God is the ever-present *ezer* in time of trouble (Psalm 46:1); God is an *ezer* and a shield (Deut 33:29;

Psalm 33:20; Psalm 70:5; Psalm 115:9), and an *ezer*, a refuge and deliverer from enemies (Exodus 18:4; Deuteronomy 33:7, 33:26).—And by the way, in the story of the creation of Adam and Eve, Eve is also described as an *ezer* (Genesis 2:18). Human relationships and community are created at the moment when a second human being arrives to be an *ezer* to another. Far from being subservient as some readers assume, Eve's role (and by extension, her descendants' roles, the role of any human being who becomes a companion to another) is compared to God's.

Because *ezer* gets translated into English as "help" or "helper" in many passages in the King James Bible, "helper" as a translation for the New Testament *parakletos* reminds me of *ezer*. *Ezer* (in Hebrew) and *parakletos* (in Greek) are both words used to describe both God's relationship to us *and* our relationship to each other. "Helper" also reminds me of the famous words of minister, educator, and children's television host Mr. Rogers, describing what would happen when he was a child and would see scary things on the news:

> My mother would say to me, "Look for the helpers. You will always find people who are helping." To this day, especially in times of disaster, I remember my mother's words, and I am always comforted by realizing that there are still so many helpers—so many caring people in this world.
>
> FRED ROGERS

All my life, I have found that to be true, as well, and a thing worth unforgetting. There are still helpers in the world. So I like that translation of *ezer* as "helper" quite a bit. I have also read English translations of John 15 where at the Last Supper Jesus promises his disciples a "helper." He promises to send the *parakletos*, the *pneuma aletheias*, the spirit of unforgetting, who will help them bear witness (John 15:26). That is how the Holy Spirit is introduced in the New Testament. When the apostles wrote of the "Holy Spirit," they didn't mean some amorphous presence but an active advocate, intercessor, and consoler who is "called beside" us in our moment of darkness.

Relevant to this understanding of God, there is a beautiful passage in the twelfth-century *Historia Calamitatum* by Peter Abelard (the same monk who wrote such famous letters of love and spirituality to the nun Heloise), where Abelard defends his choice of naming a medieval oratory after the Paraclete. He opens the passage by telling the story of a time of great poverty in his life:

> This time it was poverty more than anything that drove me back into teaching. Since "to dig unable and to beg I was ashamed," I returned to the art I knew, working with my tongue instead of my hands. My students happily provided for all my basic needs—food and clothing, work on the land or help with the cost of building... Since my oratory could not hold even a fraction of their number, they had to enlarge it and build a solid new construction of stone and wood. The building had been founded and first dedicated in honor of the Holy Trinity, but since I had taken refuge there in my despair and found some consolation by the grace of God, I renamed it for the Paraclete in memory of the gift I was given.
>
> HISTORIA CALAMITATUM IX
> (LEVITAN'S TRANSLATION)

Abelard's naming of his refuge draws ire from some religious authorities. Defending his decision, he argues passionately that the name of the Consoler and Helper is a name by which we honor all the persons of God, a name by which we know all of God in his fullness:

> This new name struck many as odd, and some even attacked me for it with considerable violence, charging that by ancient custom a church must not be named for the Holy Spirit alone ... but only for the Son or the Trinity as a whole. ... But just as the Trinity or any of its members may be called *God* and *Sustainer*, so it is correct to address each or all of them as *Paraclete,* or *Consoler.* ... [Paul writes,] "Know you not that your body is the temple of the Holy Spirit who is in you, whom you have of God, and you are not your own?" ... Is it at all strange then to name a material temple for the member of the Trinity to whom Saint Paul has specifically ascribed a spiritual one? ... At any rate, it was not my intention to honor only one member of the Trinity when I named my oratory for the Paraclete. It was, as I mentioned before, simply in memory of the consolation I found there.

HISTORIA CALAMITATUM IX

For Abelard, to know God was to know one who gives shelter when you starve and consolation when you sorrow. To him, God *is* the Paraclete, and each of us is a living temple to the spirit of the living Paraclete.

Like Abelard's students giving him shelter, we in turn are to be *parakletoi* to each other, called to each other's aid, to stand with each other, to console and help each other, and to intercede and bear witness on each other's behalf. In this role we are called beside anyone who is vulnerable, starving, oppressed, or grieving. In 2 Corinthians 1:4, Paul writes that we who have been advocated for and consoled by the Paraclete must now "be able to advocate for those who are in any suffering." The Greek word *thlipsis* in this verse gets translated "suffering," "distress," or "affliction," but it literally means "pressure"—the pressure on the heart and soul that comes from feeling that you are hemmed in with no escape, or that the pain, injustice, poverty, or suffering you endure will never cease.

In the letter to the Ephesians we find this call to live as Christ lived:

> Therefore be imitators of God, as beloved children, and live in love, as Christ loved us and gave himself up for us…

EPHESIANS 5:1-2

To live in love—even to the point of giving up your lives to love and defend others. The verb used for "give" here is a form of the Greek verb *paradidómi*, which means to give oneself into an oppressor's hands so that another might go free. For the writers of the New Testament, followers of Christ are *those who are there* when others are suffering. In Chapter 4, we learned that we are the *sos*, the saved, the refugees who have been given refuge and are now called to give refuge to others. To be the helpers and the advocates—for the apostles, this is fundamental to our identity and purpose as Christians, and I believe that those of us who follow the Way of Jesus must recover that. We must unforget it. To be *parakletoi* is to be the agents through which the active presence of God, the Paraclete, operates in the world.

Our English word "compassion" literally means "suffering together" (from the Latin: *com-* "together" + *patio* "to suffer"). In our compassion and our *paraklesis*— our advocacy for each other—we get closest to imitating God. In his lament for his son (2012), Yale theologian Nicholas Wolterstorff writes:

> Through the prism of my tears I have seen a suffering God. It is said of God that on one can behold his face and live. I always thought this meant that no one can see his splendor and live. A friend said perhaps this meant that no one can see his sorrow and live. Or perhaps his sorrow is his splendor.
>
> NICHOLAS WOLTERSTORFF

It is of the Father's compassion for us, his suffering for and with us, that we speak when we tell the story of Jesus, the "man of sorrows" who bears the sin and pain of the world. "Love one another," Jesus urges us, asking that we join one another in each other's pain, so that none of us need bear it alone. In Paul's words:

> Bear one another's burdens, and in this way you will fulfill the law of Christ.
>
> GALATIANS 6:2

By this bearing of each other's burdens, this sharing in each other's suffering, the paracletes are contrasted with the Pharisees, those teachers and preachers of religious tradition of whom Jesus tells his students:

> Do not do as they do, for they do not practice what they teach. They tie up heavy burdens, hard to bear, and lay them

159

on the shoulders of others; but they themselves are unwilling to lift a finger to move them.

MATTHEW 22:3-4

When the religious leaders, in their hardness of heart, bring the full weight of law or custom crashing down on the shoulders of the vulnerable, the paraclete intercedes. The paraclete says, "I stand with her. I bear witness to her pain. You will not throw rocks today."

However, bearing one another's burdens is not always about standing in the street or in a court battle in defense of another. It is not about playing the hero. Nor is it the opposite: passively feeling pain on behalf of another. Sometimes when others are suffering, we rush to action *too* immediately, and we do so for the wrong reason: to get their suffering to end because of the discomfort it causes *us.* Other times, we rush to outrage and *don't* act when action is needed, because we are too busy feeling and not listening.

Remember Jesus writing in the dust with his finger, just listening. Advocacy always begins with active listening, with hearing another, learning what they need and being there in the way that they need, not in the way that we ourselves "judge best." As paracletes, we are called to be each other's witnesses (Greek *martyroi)*, and we can only do that if we are listening.

In Judaism there is a custom called sitting *shiva*, where mourners simply sit in silence with one who is grieving. Yet in our culture, people often try to meet someone's suffering with words, with arguments, with dismissal, or with quick fixes. Within the church, this tendency can take many forms. We may tell someone "it is all part of God's plan," which is a callous and cruel thing to say to someone who is in pain. Or we may suggest that they did something wrong, that their pain was something they brought on themselves. But this kind of victim blaming is a way of setting on someone's shoulders "heavy burdens, hard to bear." Too frequently, the suffering of others is something we would rather not see or deal with. Even death itself is something we prefer to hide away and hide from, locking away the aged in assisted living campuses and locking away our dead in cemeteries, out of sight. By contrast, some medieval towns buried their dead beneath the floorstones of the church, so that when you took Mass, you stood in the community of all your people, living and dead.

What if we *didn't* dismiss or flee the suffering of others? What if we met each other only with compassion and advocacy? What if we were paracletes? A paraclete hears a woman who reports her assault and listens to her with compassion for her pain, and is there for her, and does not rush to dismiss her. A paraclete kneels with a protesting athlete in compassion for the lives lost in his community. A paraclete's heart breaks at a recording of children's cries at the border or at a border station's case of crucifixes that no longer have bodies to wear them, and a paraclete calls their representatives to plead on behalf of those children and those immigrants. A paraclete removes her shoes and hands them to a child whose feet are bleeding. A paraclete joins a caravan to take supplies to people suffering after a hurricane. A paraclete is not driven by politics or pundits; a paraclete is found, as Mr. Rogers suggested, wherever people are suffering.

"For just as the body without the spirit is dead, faith without works is dead," James warns us in his letter to the early church (James 2:26). If our activity as paracletes is subtracted from our faith—if we do not act as those "called beside" others—then we have drunk from the waters of *lethe* (forgetting) and have not listened to the *pneuma aletheias* (the spirit of unforgetting), the Paraclete who bears witness within us. Having drunk from the river of Lethe, we hold to a faith that has died inside us and in our community. Yet, like zombies, we keep shambling on, going through the motions of following Christ without actually *being* the body of Christ that carries the Paraclete into our world.

Our neighbors today report being persecuted by Christians. Have we forgotten that we are called to be the opposite of persecutors? That we are called to stand beside one who is suffering, *no matter who they are* (as Jesus stands beside us—even to the Cross—regardless of who *we* are), and in fact to be their advocate, standing between them and their persecutors? How have we forgotten this? How have we so often become the stone-throwers, rather than the ones who lift our beaten neighbor from the dust?

Let's unforget these words Jesus spoke 2,000 years ago, as he called a community of paracletes to their work:

"...for I was hungry and you gave me no food, I was thirsty and you gave me nothing to drink, I was a stranger and you did not welcome me, naked and you did not give me clothing, sick and in prison and you did not visit me." Then they also will answer, "Lord, when was it that we saw you hungry or thirsty or a stranger or naked or sick or in prison, and did not take care of you?" Then he will answer them,

'Truly I tell you, just as you did not do it to one of the least of these, you did not do it to me."

MATTHEW 25:42-45

Please hear this. This is the radical heart of the gospel, the story we must unforget. We who say we follow Christ are not called to be "good people." We are not called to live comfortable American lives. We are called specifically to be paracletes. To be those who intervene. Those who sit *shiva*. Those who step between the woman and the men lifting stones. This is who we are. This is what the very earliest Christians lived, and for it they were beaten, starved, jailed, crucified, tortured, killed. They were not living safe lives. They were living the lives of paracletes.

PART 3: THE TASK AT HAND: TO BECOME BETTER READERS—OF THE BIBLE, AND EACH OTHER

7. To Read Each Other with More Compassion

What This Chapter is About

Christianity began not with the sharing of doctrines or creeds but with a gospel—literally a *god-spell*, a "good story." In Greek, *euangelion*, "very good news." Yet we often speak of ethics and compassion as though these are motivated or determined by creed or moral code. In fact, compassion and ethical action are a response to hearing the stories and perceiving the experiences of others. This is something crucial for Christians, as witnesses to the good story (the story of Christ, of grace, of God's gift), to unforget.

———

As God's chosen ones, holy and beloved, clothe yourselves with compassion ... Above all, clothe yourselves with love, which binds everything together in perfect harmony. ... Let the word of Christ dwell in you richly.

The Letter to Colossae

———

ONCE UPON A TIME, THERE WAS A RABBI who stopped to hear everyone's story and respond to each person's need. Walking through a crowd on his way to heal a young girl who was dying, Jesus felt someone touch his robes, and he stopped:

> Now there was a woman who had been suffering from hemorrhages for twelve years; and though she had spent all she had on physicians, no one could cure her. She came up behind him and touched the fringe of his clothes, and immediately her hemorrhage stopped. Then Jesus asked, "Who touched me?" When all denied it, Peter said, "Master, the crowds surround you and press in on you." But Jesus said, "Someone touched me; for I noticed that power had gone out from me." When the woman saw that she could not remain hidden, she came trembling; and falling down before him, she declared in the presence of all the people why she had touched him, and how she had been immediately healed. He said to her, "Daughter, your faith has made you well; go in peace."
>
> LUKE 8:43-48

In that culture at that time, a woman bleeding or menstruating was regarded as unclean and could not be touched physically by others; she had to conceal herself indoors and remain separate from community until the bleeding stopped. This woman whose bleeding does not stop has lived isolated and alone for a *long* time. It is the wound in her heart—living separate from her people, untouchable—that drives her to seek a miracle-worker in secret. And it is that wound in her heart, not just the wound in her body, that Jesus stops to heal. At first, her worst nightmare occurs—she is called out of the crowd, put on display for her neighbors, she who cannot be spoken with or touched. In that moment, she anticipates cruelty but receives an inexplicable kindness: a public declaration by a rabbi that she is well. That she can be touched. That she can have meals with others in her community. The words are not for her alone but for all those within earshot, an implicit demand that everyone who hears welcome her back into the community.

The word translated "well" here is one we have encountered in this book before, in Chapter 3. It is *sesōken*, a form of the verb *sózó*, "to save," "to grant refuge." This woman's story is the gospel story: the story of being delivered and reintegrated into community with God and with one's neighbors. And hers is the story of the person of faith; in her outrageous courage and trust that Jesus can heal her, she dares the unthinkable and receives the impossible. This is a story of *soteria* (refuge-giving, the word we translate "salvation"). And the pattern of this story is the basic pattern of the stories of Jesus. Like the Doctor in *Doctor Who*, Jesus travels somewhere (on foot, though, not in a TARDIS), sees someone suffering and alone, and stops to help. And someone who is suffering and alone, someone who has suffered ostracism and cruelty all her life, dares to seek his help, either secretly (as in this case) or publicly (in others). This is the story that gets told again and again throughout the gospels, in many variations.

Another time, while Jesus is "passing through" a town, he stops to talk with a man in a tree. The man's own town ignores him, because he is very short and can be overlooked by the tall, and shuns him because he is a civil servant collecting taxes for the Roman Empire, and his neighbors want as little to do with him as possible:

> He entered Jericho and was passing through it. A man was there named Zacchaeus; he was a chief tax collector and was rich. He was trying to see who Jesus was, but on account of the crowd he could not, because he was short in stature. So he ran ahead and climbed a sycamore tree to see him, because he was going to pass that way. When Jesus came to the place, he looked up and said to him, "Zacchaeus, hurry and come down; for I must stay at your house today." So he hurried down and was happy to welcome him. All who saw it began to grumble and said, "He has gone to be the guest of one who is a sinner."

> LUKE 19:1-7

People in the gospels are always overlooking "sinners," but Jesus didn't overlook people. And by his example, he insisted that others stop overlooking their neighbors, too. Jesus was rarely content just to "pass through" a town. He'd stop by a well and talk, find the nearest outcast and say, "Let's do dinner," or turn aside from his road to take notice of someone in pain. Jesus notices people.

Another time, he calls his disciples' attention to an impoverished widow. "Do you see her?" he asks them, and invites them to emulate her generosity:

> He looked up and saw rich people putting their gifts into the treasury; he also saw a poor widow put in two small copper coins. He said, "Truly I tell you, this poor widow has put in more than all of them; for all of them have

contributed out of their abundance, but she out of her poverty has put in all she had to live on."

LUKE 21:1-4

Another time, Jesus is at dinner with his friends, and this happens:

> One of the Pharisees asked Jesus to eat with him, and he went into the Pharisee's house and took his place at the table. And a woman in the city, who was a sinner, having learned that he was eating in the Pharisee's house, brought an alabaster jar of ointment. She stood behind him at his feet, weeping, and began to bathe his feet with her tears and to dry them with her hair. Then she continued kissing his feet and anointing them with the ointment. Now when the Pharisee who had invited him saw it, he said to himself, "If this man were a prophet, he would have known who and what kind of woman this is who is touching him—that she is a sinner."

LUKE 7:36-39

Like the woman who bled, this unnamed woman is also untouchable in her community. But Jesus tells a brief parable about how those who have suffered most often love the most and how those who have borne the greatest burdens appreciate the lifting of burdens more than others do (Luke 7:41-43). Then he turns to his disciples and says simply, "Do you see this woman?"

Do you see her?

The Greek verb *blepó* is more than just passive sight; it is to *look* at, to perceive. Had the other people in the room—any of them at all—really *seen* her?

171

Jesus goes on:

> Do you see this woman? I entered your house; you gave me no water for my feet, but she has bathed my feet with her tears and dried them with her hair. You gave me no kiss, but from the time I came in she has not stopped kissing my feet. You did not anoint my head with oil, but she has anointed my feet with ointment. Therefore, I tell you, her sins, which were many, have been forgiven, for she has loved so much.
>
> LUKE 7:44-47

The other men in the house think that Jesus should have known *tis kai potapē hē gynē*—"who and what this woman is." But Jesus, seeing her, sees a woman who *ēgapēsen poly*—"she has loved so much."

In story after story, encounter after encounter, Jesus asks his contemporaries that question: *Do you see her?*

DO YOU SEE THEM?

That question—*Do you see them? Do you see their pain?*—has been key to all of my work as a storyteller. It's the question I have most wanted to ask, again and again, ever since I heard Jesus ask it when I read stories of him as a youth. Jesus's question haunts me. It is the whisper in my ear in the dark. It is the blade in my heart.

In my series *The Zombie Bible*, which retells biblical and ecclesiastical tales as episodes in humanity's enduring struggle against hunger and the hungry dead, the zombies are those who can no longer see anyone as anything other than food. When you look at the dead, they don't look back. They don't see *you*. In one of the novels, *What Our Eyes Have Witnessed*, Polycarp practices the Apostle's Gift by granting the dead absolution; he does this by *seeing* them:

> To give the dead rest, he'd needed to look first into each one's blind eyes and find beneath the gray scratches the remnant of the soul locked within the shambling corpse. He'd needed to witness each one's secrets, each one's sins, each one's suffering—all that each one had loved and feared and regretted in their brief lives. Only then might he absolve them and set them free and let the corpses slide lifeless to the alley floor.
>
> *WHAT OUR EYES HAVE WITNESSED*

In *No Lasting Burial*, a young man with a disability has been denied his rite of passage into adulthood; in one scene, he gets into a conversation with this alternate history's Jesus, who says:

> "You must not hate them, Koach."
> "They hate *me*," Koach said.
> "No." Yeshua gave a vehement shake of his head. "No, they don't. They do not hate *you*. Because they…they have *never* seen you. They look at you and see only what they fear, only that. They do not hate *you*."
>
> *NO LASTING BURIAL*

And in *Death Has Come Up into Our Windows*, one cannot love one's God without also loving and unforgetting one's neighbor:

173

If a people could forget the pain in the eyes of children, they could forget God. And if a people could forget God, they could forget the words she gave. If they could forget the words she gave, they could forget the pain in the eyes of children.

DEATH HAS COME UP INTO OUR WINDOWS

In the novel, the Old Testament prophet Jeremiah, speaking truth to power, pleads with the monarch, the priesthood, and the merchants who rule a dying city, asking them to unforget God and each other:

No nation, though it have decorated tombs taller than mountains and all the world's perfumes—no nation can be called great if some of its people starve, or are sold to beds in other cities, or are forgotten, or sacrificed to the dead to make a few men feel safe.

DEATH HAS COME UP INTO OUR WINDOWS

At the time that I'm writing this, the federal government in the United States, under an administration whose campaign slogan has been "Make America Great Again," is determining whether to define gender as a binary (determined by assigned biological sex) and, with the stroke of a pen or the tap of a keyboard, remove civil rights protections from transgender and intersex Americans by simply denying that they exist.

If you can't see people's existence, how will you see their hurt?

If you can't see their hurt, how will you respond with love, compassion, and justice?

WHERE DOES COMPASSION COME FROM?

I would propose to my brothers, sisters, and others in the Christian faith that it is not *belief* that moves us to be ethical or kind people, but *our capacity for seeing or hearing others with compassion.*

The accusation Jesus makes against the Pharisees is not that they have beliefs that are incorrect, but that they have *sklērokardía*, "hardness of heart" (Matthew 19:18; Mark 10:5), an unwillingness to hear others' needs with compassion. *Sklērokardía* literally means "dry heart," a heart unwatered by love, shrunken and shriveled, dried up until it becomes hard and unyielding, likelier to respond to others' pain with callousness and unthinking cruelty than with compassion. A reader of mine once suggested we translate *sklērokardía* "prune-heartededness." The prune-hearted see the world in terms of sin and judgment, forgetting what the first disciples taught, that:

> Indeed, God did not send the Son into the world to condemn the world, but in order that the world might be saved through him.
>
> JOHN 3:17

And the prune-hearted forget that when Jesus's disciples leapt to deliver judgment to those who believed or lived differently, he rebuked them:

> On their way they entered a village of the Samaritans to make ready for him; but they did not receive him, because his face was set toward Jerusalem. When his disciples James and John saw it, they said, "Lord, do you want us to

command fire to come down from heaven and consume them?" But he turned and rebuked them. Then they went on to another village.

LUKE 9:52-55

In the New Testament, it is the Pharisees who are concerned not with the stories of individual children of God, but with placing people into prim, neatly organized, manageable categories, some of which earn heaven and some of which do not. How easily we in the twenty-first century fall into that same trap of dividing the world in our heads into churchgoers and sinners. It is nonsense.

I have lost count of the times when people have insisted to me that you cannot be a moral person if you do not believe in God, if you do not follow a set of moral absolutes because he told you to. And all this insistence does is build a wall between the church and everyone else. It also reduces our faith, insultingly, to following a set of instructions, as if the only reason we treat people well is because Daddy told us to and we're just following the house rules.

Though I am myself a religious man, the notion that religious belief is a prerequisite for ethical behavior has always struck me as really odd. It's neither logical (because a moment's reflection will reveal that a majority of human beings appear to possess a conscience whether or not they possess religious beliefs) nor biblical (in both his speech at the Areopagus and in Romans 1, Paul insists that ethical behavior and a longing for goodness is written into the world, and later in Romans he argues that the law is written on our hearts, whether we have it in our conscious mind or not). "Love each other" and "Do unto others as you would have them do unto you" are not difficult concepts to grasp, even if they are apparently difficult to *do*.

So why *do* we want to treat each other ethically? And is it necessary to believe in a Divine Being in order to answer that question?

There has been a vigorous conversation and study of this going on for the past sixty years, but because it has been going on in French and on the other side of the world, very few people in the U.S. outside of academia have been a part of it. In the 1950s, in his book *Totalité et Infini,* the philosopher Emmanuel Levinas proposed what in retrospect seems a very simple but powerful idea. Here is the short-short version:

Levinas suggests something happens when we meet each other's gaze. When two people have a face-to-face encounter and neither avoids the other's gaze, there is an intimacy that occurs. When I look into the eyes of another person, someone who is not-me, who is in fact different from me, who may have a different gender, religion, race, or class from my own — when I look into her eyes and see her looking back, there is an implicit "demand" in her gaze.

The demand is that I recognize her as akin to me. In this meeting of our gazes, we are both human. In this moment, I can recognize that she loves, hopes, fears, and desires, even as I do. That gaze bridges, briefly, our separateness and our aloneness. In other words, when I meet her gaze and she meets mine, her eyes communicate, implicitly, the demand that I respond to her as a fellow and equal human being. It is a demand for ethical behavior: for just and compassionate treatment of the other.

This is why we ask others to look us in the eye so that we can see if they are communicating the truth to us. It is harder to lie (not impossible, alas, just harder) when you are gazing into the eyes of the person you're lying to. It's also why a hierarchical caste system in which society's lowest layers consist of "untouchables" is often paired with a cultural restriction on eye contact across castes. When you don't meet the eyes of untouchables, you are less likely to perceive any demand that you treat them justly, equally, and compassionately. Thus, you are less likely to respond, and the system is less likely to change. Similarly, Gandhi's project of *ahimsa* (nonviolence) was about facing the oppressor assertively but non-aggressively, eye-to-eye, making it difficult for the oppressor to avoid your gaze—in short, making it difficult for them to deny your essential human kinship.

As we saw in Chapter 6, *compassion* is derived from a Latin word meaning "to suffer with." At the meeting of the eyes, we are invited to perceive, empathize, and respond to another's joy or another's pain. It is with that heart that Dietrich Bonhoeffer, before his death in a concentration camp in WWII, wrote to other Christians, "We must learn to regard people less in the light of what they do or omit to do, and more in the light of what they suffer."

THE HUMAN OTHER & THE DIVINE OTHER

This is why ethics is possible whether the universe has a God or not: ethics is a response to that demand in the other's gaze. It's why both religious people and atheists *feel* when they see photos of a child dead on the beaches of Syria. It's why both religious people and atheists may, or may not, stop to help an old grandmother across the street.

In Judaism, Christianity, and Islam (the Abrahamic religions), God is the ultimate Other: the Other who is *most* "other," most different from us, and yet who calls to our heart with the deepest yearning for union with us. God is the divine Other who responds to *our* demand for love, compassion, and justice, and who calls out to us with his own demand that we love him and love our neighbor. A core tenet of Jewish ethics is *tzelem elohim* ("the image of God," from Genesis 1:27): that all human beings are made in the image of God, and that when you look into the eyes of another person, you see the face of God. Emmanuel Levinas was an atheist Jew, and his philosophy is deeply influenced by Judaism's approach to ethics.

Whether or not you hear *God*'s call (that is, God's insistent request for your love and for your justice), whether or not you believe God exists, whether or not you care, you will likely hear the demand of *human* others for your love and your justice. You will encounter that demand at the meeting of the eyes. And at other occasions, too—we'll get to that in a moment.

So no, it is not necessary to believe in God in order to find reason to behave in an ethical, just, or "moral" way.

That is not to say that faith in God might not *add* something to ethics; it simply isn't a prerequisite for ethics. If empathy and our response to empathy is hard-wired into most human beings on a level much deeper than belief, then belief and religion can either augment or detract from our capacity for empathizing and responding to the demand of the other. What Christianity might add to our ethical life is a demonstrative story about a relationship between two who are other (those two being *homo sapiens* and *God*) and a story of one (Jesus) who responded to the other's demand for love even to the point of sacrificing himself for the other. And, of course, a call to *live* that story ourselves.

HOW STORIES TEACH US COMPASSION

Emmanuel Levinas' explanation of ethics is useful but does have its limitations, too. Other thinkers have questioned the implication that only the face-to-face encounter can communicate the other's demand for justice and provoke our response to that demand. After all, blind people have consciences just as sighted people do. And we often respond to requests for love or for just action from people we have never actually seen. So perhaps there are other communications that can serve as proxies for a meeting of the eyes.

Jacques Derrida, for example, suggests that a written text might convey that demand, too. A letter, a speech, a narrative, words spoken to your ears: any of these might also invoke a moment of intimacy and relay the other's demand for love and justice. Similarly, C.S. Lewis, in *An Experiment in Criticism*, argues passionately that reading a great story can be one of those acts—like love or just action—that permits us to "be more than ourselves," to be united with others:

We want to be more than ourselves. Each of us by nature sees the whole world from one point of view with a perspective and a selectiveness peculiar to himself... In love we escape from our self into one other. In the moral sphere, every act of justice or charity involves putting ourselves in the other person's place and thus transcending our own competitive particularity... The primary impulse of each is to maintain and aggrandize himself. The secondary impulse is to go out of the self, to correct its provincialism and heal its loneliness. In love, in virtue, in the pursuit of knowledge, and in the reception of the arts, we are doing this... The man who is contented to be only himself, and therefore less a self, is in prison. My own eyes are not enough for me, I will see through the eyes of others. Reality, even seen through the eyes of many, is not enough. I will see what others have invented. Even the eyes of all humanity are not enough. I regret that the brutes cannot write books. Very gladly I would learn what face things present to a mouse or a bee; more gladly still would I perceive the olfactory world charged with all the information and emotion it carries for a dog. Literary experience heals the wound, without undermining the privilege, of individuality. There are mass emotions which heal the wound; but they destroy the privilege. In them our separate selves are pooled and we sink back into sub-individuality. But in reading great literature I become a thousand men and yet remain myself. Like the night sky in the Greek poem, I see with a myriad eyes, but it is still I who see. Here, as in worship, in love, in moral action, and in knowing, I transcend myself, and am never more myself than when I do.

C.S. LEWIS

"In reading great literature I become a thousand men," Lewis writes. When you have a good story, you get to walk around the world for a while in another's skin, taste life through another's senses—and that's powerful. In his famous essay *A Defense of Poetry*, Percy Shelley suggests that imaginative stories train us to experience "sympathy" for others—that, in fact, all empathy begins with imagination: with the imaginative act of identifying with the other and picturing to ourselves what it would be like to experience and feel what they are experiencing and feeling.

In real life, when you run into something or someone who is different from you, someone who speaks differently or believes differently or looks different, or a place or culture or organism you don't fully understand, you have a mix of instinctive responses. You have a mix of wonder and fear. One of those two reactions is going to take priority.

If the *fear* response takes priority, you are driven to increase the distance between you and what's different from you. There are different ways to seek or enforce that distance. You can pick up an axe and smash the other who frightens you in the head. You can run away. You can freeze in stark terror, like a character in a weird fiction story confronted by a mass of tentacles and eyeballs slithering near. Or you can take what's different and put it in a cage, confine it and control it so that it stays where you want it while you move about. That's the *fear* response.

That's a powerful instinctive response that we have, and it is a biologically useful response if you're facing a charging tiger or a tentacle beast or some alien elder god with a thousand eyes. But if you're facing another human being who looks different, fear may not be the best response. If what you perceive as different from you is a black college student taking her nap in a dorm, you don't call 911, as one white student at a dorm in Yale recently did. That woman sleeping on the sofa is not a tiger or a tentacle beast. She's a human being. She's one of your kin. You just happen to feel that she looks different from you, and this frightens you.

The fear response isn't the only instinct we have. We have a *wonder* instinct as well: curiosity, the desire to decrease the distance between us and what's different, to draw near and find out more and get to know that other person or culture or place. Stories give us opportunities to explore these two instincts that we have and to practice negotiating these instincts during the encounter with the other.

So even when we cannot meet each other's eyes, we can still communicate in stories. Stories can cut deep. They can help us feel what others have felt, even others long past. Even imaginary others who have never been born.

Why do I want to respect and be kind to other people? Because I can imagine *being* them. Because when I see their eyes, I realize we are both human. Because when I hear their story, I am moved.

In my novel *Strangers in the Land*, the ex-slave Hurriya tells an aging judge and prophetess this:

> When you see another's face—the face of a child, or another woman, or the face of the goddess, or the face of someone hungry or hurt—their eyes, they look back. They look at you. They ask your love, they ask you to hear their crying and know that you and they are both alive, and some day you may be hurt, you may be hungry. It may be your child carried dying in your arms." Hurriya choked a

moment, then went on. "When I look at you, you look back. Only the dead don't look back. You think the Law is a pact with your God, a pact with others of your People. But it's not just a pact. It's an answer. You have rules for everything. But it's not the rules that matter. It's that you want to make them. You want to answer the suffering you see in another woman's face. You want to give her safety, or justice, or comfort. That's what matters. That's why you have your Law, why you love it.

STRANGERS IN THE LAND

The story of Christianity—if we have the courage to unforget it—is that God is on the Cross gazing at us, inviting us to gaze back. That he who responds to our pain with his love asks us to do likewise, responding to *his* pain with *our* love. Similarly, our fellow human beings (whether through a silent gaze or a spoken story) demand our response to their pain. It may be that this call is fundamental to human communication, and that most of us are wired—as relational, communal, social animals—to *want* to respond. The question demands its response. We are uncomfortable with silence for an answer.

But we are *also* wired for other, contradictory responses that may motivate us to avoid meeting the other's gaze or hearing their story. Self-defense. Satisfaction of our basic appetites. Tribal identity (to the exclusion of others). Such impulses that drive against answering that call for compassion and justice. So the call frequently does go without response, and we have crime and conflict. We start to create laws, rules, or moralities to try to limit the destructive consequences of such conflict. But it is not the morality or the law that makes us *want* to be good. Moral codes and laws and religious creeds and institutions are the *response* to our desire to be good or to our failure to be good; they are not the *cause* of that desire. We desire to be good to each other because we see in each other's eyes and hear in each other's stories that call to kinship. Religious people might say that demand for kinship is because in each other's eyes we see the likeness of God (*tzelem elohim*); atheists might say it is a primal instinct for empathy inherited from our primate origins. But whatever you want to *call* it, that demand is there.

STORIES SHAKE THINGS UP

I yearn to hear more stories, and to tell the stories I hear—to tell and retell and pass them on—because in stories I encounter others who are so different from me and yet are human, just as I am. I want to hear everyone's story. I wish I had the time and immortality and patience to hear everyone's story. And like C.S. Lewis, I yearn also to know what the world sounds like to a whale or what it smells like to a wolf. To hear the stories of all the souls in the world who are not me. To see the universe with a thousand faces, and to treat the wearers of those thousand faces in the way we treat people when we have taken their stories into our hearts. The encounter with the other—in life, or in story—is a *kairos*, an opportunity, a moment of choice, where the enlargement of our hearts and the healing of our separation from each other is made suddenly, unexpectedly possible.

The Jews say *Tikkun olam—tell the story, heal the world.* And Christians say (when they unforget to), *Here is the good story. See the man in this story, this man who loves you, who died for you and everyone. Be like that man.* It is that story that I love; my desire to live that story is what my Christianity consists of. Our word "gospel" comes from the Anglo-Saxon word *god-spell*, which literally means the "good story." As I recounted in Chapters 2-6, in the early centuries of the Christian era the gospel was a story that transformed lives, that got slave women and businesswomen and fishermen and tax collectors and zealots all sharing meals together, all talking together about a better way to live. It was a story that broke walls, that taught people to walk on water, a story that threatened an Empire—not with the promise of a rival but with the absence of one. Our Great Commission in Christianity is not to teach people rules or to propagate moral codes or to build church buildings or to form political coalitions. Our Commission is, and has always been, to tell the good story. To tell a joyous story, a story that gives people hope. A story that can wake the lethargic, forgetful dead to new life. And to help each other be good readers of that story, "hearers and doers" of it: disciples and students who live the good story.

Yet have we not become, increasingly, a culture of people who spend more of our time talking and soapboxing and less and less of our time reading, listening to, and sharing stories? This will not do. In our generation, we have to become better at reading each other with compassion, the way Jesus did in so many stories that we have of him. How do you fix the world? I have no idea how to answer that question in full, but I do know that one of the things we will need along the way are millions and millions of compassionate, skilled *readers*, by which I mean skilled and open-hearted hearers of each other's stories. We need people who will hear stories from diverse others (both real and fictional others)—people who approach everyone's story as eager, curious hearers and readers.

They say that when your one tool is a hammer, sooner or later, every problem looks like a nail. I may be guilty of that; *my* tools are storytelling and reading. Yet I do believe that what the world needs are really, really good readers and really, really good stories that can move into our hearts and do in there the *god-spell* work of reconciling and reuniting us readers with each other and with God.

Stories present us with new possibilities by hitting us right where we *feel*, not just where we *think*. This is not always a comfortable experience. Jesus's own stories don't comfort or affirm what his listeners already know. They *unsettle*. They demand that we reconsider things. They don't even always have an ending or resolution; in many of his parables—such as the tale of the Good Samaritan or the tale of the Prodigal Son—Jesus simply ends the story when a choice is just about to be made or a riddle is just about to be solved, and he tosses the choice back to his listeners. The *kairos*, the opportunity, is not only for the characters in the story but for those hearing it; Jesus insists on his listeners' active involvement in the adventure. "Now *you* tell *me* how it ends," he says.

For example, in the parable traditionally named "The Prodigal Son," we are left to decide for ourselves whether the elder son who stands resentful on the porch outside the house will enter and join his younger brother at the feast, setting aside his self-righteousness and resentment and coming again to the father's table. Jesus's audience of lawyers and religious scholars, many of them uncomfortably in the position of the elder son, are left to address that question. (If you want to take a closer look at that story, Tim Keller's book *Prodigal God* gives a fresh and invigorating exploration of it.) In the case of "The Good Samaritan," we are left to answer the question: For the man who was beaten in the road, ignored by the priest and the levite, and then rescued by the sworn enemy of his people—who acted as his neighbor? The priest, the levite, or the sworn enemy? In yet another parable: What if the kingdom of heaven, where grace is given freely, is like a vineyard where the workers who came in the morning and the workers who arrived an hour before dusk receive the same full-day wage at the end of the day? These are not *comfortable* questions. Jesus's stories shake things up—just as the story *of* Jesus shakes things up.

We have tried so hard in our culture to tame Jesus. We make him white and well-groomed. We tack quick morals onto the end of his stories for convenient use in our sermons, like Aesop's fables. We skip over stories of miracles as if embarrassed by them—or as if we know in our heart of hearts that hearing tales of wonder is risky and dangerous. That such tales invite us to adventure, that they can change us. We don't want to be changed. We want things to stay as they are. Comfortable. Safe. Surrounded by pictures of Jesus but making as sure as we can that he won't stagger, sweaty and bloodied, into our peaceful church sanctuary.

That is also why some of us react with such consternation when we encounter other untamed stories—stories with Gandalfs or Aslans or Harry Potters or Mrs. Whatsits in them. It's ironic to me that most fantasy novels that have been "banned" or restricted from church or school libraries at one time or another were penned by devout Christians, by Christians who knew the wild, unleashed power of a good story. J.R.R. Tolkien, C.S. Lewis, J.K. Rowling, Madeleine L'Engle—at various times, their novels have been unwelcome in some religious communities, in communities that have swallowed the idea that to live in imitation of Christ is to be a rule follower rather than an adventurer and a hearer of impossible stories.

My calling in life is fiction, and I want to tell outrageous, imaginative stories. Stories of others' lives, stories of other worlds, stories almost as outrageous as the gospel. I want to crew starships along with people of every gender, ethnicity, and social class. I want to time travel and walk the road to Emmaus, or see the first pyramid raised. I want to drink water changed into wine and see people raised from the dead. I want to ride tyrannosaurs.

My dear fellow Christians, let's be once again the people who tell and hear stories *daringly*. Let's recover and unforget that facet of our identity, as Tolkien and Lewis and L'Engle and many others did. Let's be daring again. That's so important. I think in our culture, the stories we are being asked to swallow so much of the time are not daring stories. They're stories that make us smaller. I want to tell stories that make us bigger—together.

And let's not only *tell* stories. Let's *hear* stories. Let's relearn how to sit in silence and listen to the stories of others—in fact, to those people who we think are most different from us. Let's hear *their* stories. Let's listen for the invitation to adventure that their stories offer. Let's get so good at hearing others' stories that in response, we become people who go out of our way, people who stop the hard of heart, the dry and prune-hearted, in their tracks and demand of them, *Do you see her? Do you hear her story?*

8. TO READ THE BIBLE AS CHILDREN—AND AS ADVENTURERS

WHAT THIS CHAPTER IS ABOUT

In our modern tradition, we often read the Bible as if it is an assembly manual (*we* are what is being assembled, and we either affirm or reject what we read based on what we think the Bible is trying to assemble us *into*). Partly for this reason, we place enormous emphasis on finding the one correct interpretation, holding to it, and resisting challenges to it. But what if our goal was not to arrive at a definitive and final interpretation, but instead, to seek, each time we read, new insights into the heart of God?

———————

Our sufficiency is from God, who also made us sufficient as ministers of the new covenant, not of the letter but of the spirit; for the letter kills, but the spirit gives life.

THE SECOND LETTER TO CORINTH

———————

Truly I tell you, unless you change and become like children, you will never enter the kingdom of heaven. Whoever becomes humble like this child is the greatest in the kingdom of heaven.

JESUS

ONE DAY, JESUS'S DISCIPLES were hungry. That's something that happens on a long walk, and they were often walking. Jesus rarely *hurried* anywhere, but he was always in motion, traveling out of one story and into another. "Let us go on to the neighboring towns," he tells his disciples when the crowds urge him to stay, "so that I may proclaim the message there also; for that is what I came out to do" (Mark 1:38). And so he and his companions traveled—often weary, often hungry. One such afternoon of walking fell on the sabbath, their people's holy day of rest from work:

> One sabbath he was going through the grainfields; and as they made their way his disciples began to pluck heads of grain. The Pharisees said to him, "Look, why are they doing what is not lawful on the sabbath?" And he said to them, "Have you never read what David did when he and his companions were hungry and in need of food? He entered the house of God, when Abiathar was high priest, and ate the bread of the Presence, which it is not lawful for any but the priests to eat, and he gave some to his companions." Then he said to them, "The sabbath was made for humankind, and not humankind for the sabbath..."

MARK 2:23-28

This is a fascinating story to me, though I want us to be careful with it; too often the church has used these lines—and the verse that follows ("for the son of man is lord of the sabbath") to prop up anti-Semitic prejudices. But Jesus's reading of the Torah here is very Jewish, and it anticipates the Talmud and two millennia of Jewish ethics and discourse. It anticipates a long cultural and rhetorical tradition that privileges disputation and dialogue and resists the reduction of the Torah to a mere set of declarative statements.

What Jesus is urging the Pharisees to do is read the law of Moses as a living document, something that guides action but that needs to be interpreted in light of each specific occasion rather than reduced to general absolutes that are expected to fit every occasion. Reducing God's Word to a set of absolutes does not work. Paul warns the early church of this when he writes that the new covenant:

> ...is not of letter but of spirit; for the letter kills, but the Spirit gives life.
>
> 2 CORINTHIANS 3:6

The letter kills. Focusing on what we take to be the literal meaning of a single passage—without considering context, without asking what we may be missing—may land us in a place where what we take away from the text is opposite in spirit to what may originally have been proposed. For example, the Sabbath is for a day of rest and laying down of burdens, a day to spend time with God and your family rather than with your business and your daily toil. Therefore, the day is not intended for harvesting food.

That is what the Pharisees in the story focus on. But though the Sabbath is not a day of toil, it is *also* not a day for going hungry unwillingly. It is a day created for us, rather than we for it; that is the interpretation Jesus proposes.

Jesus also implies that when we read one passage strictly and legalistically, we are often leaving some other scriptural passage out of our reckoning—like that story of David entering the house of God and eating the priests' bread on the sabbath. Once that overlooked passage is pointed out, it is likely to upset our rigid interpretation, because no rigid interpretation can account for every case. When we read the Word rigidly and reductively, our conclusions always leave out something (or some*one*).

And that, in the New Testament, is what the Pharisees do. They leave people out. In their hardness of heart and their strictness of interpretation, they divide people into categories. Then, in their pride, they define themselves as the righteous category, excluding all others:

> "Two men went up to the temple to pray, one a Pharisee and the other a tax collector. The Pharisee, standing by himself, was praying thus, 'God, I thank you that I am not like other people: thieves, rogues, adulterers, or even like this tax collector. I fast twice a week; I give a tenth of all my income.' But the tax collector, standing far off, would not even look up to heaven, but was beating his breast and saying, 'God, be merciful to me, a sinner!' I tell you, this man went down to his home justified rather than the other; for all who exalt themselves will be humbled, but all who humble themselves will be exalted."
>
> LUKE 18:10-14

By knowing your religious responsibilities exactly and keeping careful record of whether you and others are fulfilling them—by knowing exactly who you are holier than—you risk losing all sight of where you actually are and what God does expect of you. In fact, the man who enters the temple at a complete loss and just cries, "have mercy on me, a sinner!" is nearer to encountering God, because he is more interested in pleasing God than in justifying himself.

What Jesus often suggests is that the Pharisees' pride effects how they read their scriptures. The Pharisees think they have everything figured out, that God is on their leash and can be relied on to shower them with appropriate and hard-earned blessings. The modern prosperity gospel is the descendant in spirit of this kind of thinking: Do X, Y, and Z and do them perfectly, and you will earn both the kingdom of heaven and earthly blessings; those who do not do X, Y, and Z will fail to earn the kingdom of heaven and will be consigned to the poverty they deserve. In this way of thinking, the love of the Father becomes a thing to be purchased rather than a gift freely given to all.

How do we learn again to read our Bibles humbly? Jesus gives us the answer, in this sermon and in others: Come to the text, to prayer, and to God with as few assumptions as possible. Leave what you think you know at the door. Leave behind your tradition, your credentials for righteousness, all the reasons why you think you are approaching and comprehending God in just the right way—leave all that behind you. Like the tax collector, like the outcast in the story, come empty-handed. Come humbly. Come ready to learn and be changed. "Truly I tell you," Jesus teaches his students:

> ...unless you change and become like children, you will never enter the kingdom of heaven. Whoever becomes humble like this child is the greatest in the kingdom of heaven.
>
> MATTHEW 18:3-4

Children ask questions that adults think are obvious and already answered—and children find answers that startle us. Children approach things adults have seen a thousand times with fresh wonder, as though everything is new. Some things that we see every day, a child sees more clearly than we do, the first time. And some details of heaven and earth they see more clearly because they are *closer*: a bee, a crack in the sidewalk, a blossoming flower that is at the child's eye level.

And children play and take risks. I allow my children to play outside, to climb things, to explore. I may be watchful, but I am not going to smother them in rules and expectations until there is no child left inside them. Why do we who are followers of the Way think the Father is any different? Why shouldn't we think that he desires us, his children, to adventure and climb and play and take risks as we explore his Word? Why do we so rarely approach the Word as children?

There are adventures to be had, if we can remember how to have them! As Umberto Eco suggests in his book *Six Walks in the Fictional Woods*, to read a story is to make choices. That is why reading can be an act of adventure. Some of these choices are acts of inference—"What will happen next? What will this character do?" Others are acts of prioritization—"What will we notice? What will we ignore? What will we treat as *most* important in the passage?" For example, in modern times, when we look to the book of Judges, we have been taught to treat the story of Samson and Delilah as being the story in that book that is most important, relevant, and worth remembering—indeed, to treat *specific moments* in that story as important and worth remembering. But on the other hand, readers in other centuries regarded the story of Deborah and Jael as vitally important, worth reciting and discussing, worth painting and illustrating. In Hebrews 11, Samson is just one of four figures from the book of Judges to appear in a list of Old Testament heroes. Or what if we turned our attention to the tale of the murder of the Levite's concubine and its consequences, a gruesome episode from Judges that has been neglected both by us *and* previous generations? That story is arguably as dramatic as Samson's and might be as important.

It is for us, as readers and as children, to choose where we will walk through the "woods" of these stories—to choose our paths through the text—as wisely as we can, making the most informed choices we can. But also as playfully as we can, because if we forget to play and roam and climb into the unexplored places, if we forget to be children, so much will go unnoticed. And also as humbly as we can, unforgetting the fact that we *are* making choices. That what we select as central and what we neglect as peripheral are choices we have made, and that there is a risk that we've chosen foolishly, or that choices that appear wise to us at the time may prove foolish for another reader at another time.

THE BLADE, THE ASSEMBLY MANUAL, AND THE LAMP

One of the things that most restricts us is the way we talk *about* the Word and how we understand the activity of reading it. Possibly the first choice a reader makes—often unconsciously—is how to use the text, what relationship we want to have with the text. For example, will the reader encounter the text eisegetically—coming to the text with their own prejudices and questions—or exegetically—looking to the text to provoke unanticipated questions? To what use will the text be put?

We are told in the Bible that the Word is to be "living and active and sharper than any two-edged sword"; that it pierces "until it divides soul from spirit, joints from marrow"; that it is *kritikos*, able to put to the test "the thoughts and intentions of the heart," like a court examining a case (Hebrews 4:12). Such a blade can cut through our assumptions, our cultural prejudices, and our sinful habits of thought like Alexander's blade through the Gordian Knot. That is one purpose that the Bible itself proposes it be put to. Unfortunately, in our culture we're not taught to use the Bible as such a keen-edged tool. Instead, we're taught to mine the Bible for snippets of information or models for behavior; the Bible is treated as a static document, like instructions on how to assemble a bookcase. Maybe it is recognized to be more difficult to read and interpret than the typical bookcase assembly instructions, but in the end, we treat it as that kind of document—except that *we* are what is being assembled—and we either accept or reject the Bible depending on whether we like the shape we think these instructions will assemble us into.

In fact, we're taught to read almost everything that way. Unless we have escaped this trap either by means of voracious reading on our part or some college instructor's insistence, we tend to read even works of great literature in search of the "moral" of the story—or their one right, or best, interpretation. We go into stories looking for their end result, whether that end result is "True love conquers all" or "A good man is hard to find" or "Jesus saves."

We aren't often taught that reading can be an act of adventure, or play, or wrestling. As I mentioned in Chapter 3, *Israel* is Hebrew for "he wrestles with God," and for Jewish readers, the Torah has often been a set of texts out of which readers must wrestle meaning together. What meaning they find is always provisional, not permanent, because this world God has set spinning in space is always changing, plunging us from one context to the next. So we must continually return to the text with fresh and childlike eyes.

If you look at a standard, American Christian study bible (let's say the ESV Study Bible), you find text at the top of the page and annotations at the bottom, where one preacher or editor has footnoted difficult passages and explained exactly what they mean. Not various possibilities of what the passages might mean, but what one minister or group of ministers insists they mean. In this way, study of a singular human interpretation is substituted for an encounter with the living and active Word. It's a way of carefully keeping the sword of the Word in its sheath and preventing it from cutting its way through our carefully arranged and restricted communities and our orderly lives.

I remember a particular afternoon when I was shopping for a Bible at a religious bookstore, and the woman shopping next to me asked for my advice. "I want a study bible with clear notes," she said, "so I'll know what it means and I won't have to think about it." I think we are often taught to read this way—as though every question in the book has an answer and only *one* answer, and as if one of our fellow, fallible human beings can tell us exactly what that answer is.

Consider, by contrast, a popular rabbinical study bible—the *Etz Hayim*, a Hebrew/English parallel text of the Torah. It, too, has annotations at the bottom; it is laid out much like a Christian study bible. But there's a big difference. The footnotes here on a difficult passage here are likely to consider not one but five examples of how different people in different centuries have read it. Some of it is brilliant. Some of it is beautiful. Some of it is thought-provoking. It's all meant to prompt you to wrestle with the text yourself, to ask smart questions and to look for more than merely the most readily apparent answer— in fact, to hold multiple possible answers in mind at once and consider their possibilities. To actively wrestle with the text, not just be told "what it means."

The introduction to the *Etz Hayim* describes this tradition of *midrash* commentary:

> D'rash (or *midrash*) is a traditional nonliteral way of reading sacred texts. The term comes from a Hebrew verb meaning "to inquire, to investigate," and it refers to a process of close reading of the text to find insights that go beyond the plain meaning of the words. In Jacob J. Petuchowski's felicitous simile, Jews read the Torah as one reads a love

letter, eager to squeeze the last drop of meaning from every word: Why was that word used rather than another? What is the significance of the repetition of certain words? What does the choice of a word reveal about the speaker's innermost thoughts? ... The *d'rash* commentary has approached the text with reverence, asking not "Do we approve of this passage?" but "Because this was sacred to our ancestors, what can it teach us?"

ETZ HAYIM

That's a beautiful, intelligent, exciting way to read. Imagine if we, too, read the Bible not as an assembly manual but as a love letter! If we held its parchment close to our heart, *unforgetting* it, as a young lover *unforgets* the love letter she has tucked into her blouse near her heart, taking it out often to read, to consider each word, to reflect and ponder and try to get, moment by moment, nearer the heart of the one we believe sent us the letter. Then the Bible would be the "living Word" indeed.

Here is another passage to illustrate the *midrash* tradition, this time from a novel, James Michener's *The Source*. In one chapter, a rabbi is teaching his students during Roman times:

It was therefore each student's responsibility to ascertain God's intentions, and to help them in this task Rabbi Asher proposed certain drills: "If our desire is to uncover God's wishes, we must develop minds that can penetrate the shadows, for the mists produced by living obscure the truth and you cannot discern it unless you sharpen your wits." At this point he would unroll a scroll of Torah and read from Leviticus: "These also shall be unclean unto you among the creeping things that creep upon the earth: the weasel, and the mouse, and the tortoise after his kind, and the ferret, and the chameleon, and the lizard, and the snail, and the mole. These are unclean to you." Having read this, he would say, "God Himself forbids His people to eat the lizard. I want you to find one hundred reasons why the lizard should be eaten." When his students protested that this might be blasphemous, Rabbi Asher explained, "Again and again the great rabbis have warned us that when God handed Moses the sacred law, He placed it in the hands of men so that it might exist on earth and not in heaven, to be interpreted by men. The Torah is what we say it is, you and I in all our frailty, and if God made a mistake in forbidding the lizard, we had better find out about it."

JAMES MICHENER

Rabbi Asher wants his students to sharpen their minds on the whetstone of the living Word. How different that is from a tradition in which we seek a single authority to tell us "what it means." In Chapter 5 we talked about *metanoia*, "after thought" or "changing mind," the Greek word for repentance. *Metanoia* is an active response to an encounter with the unexpected—like Saul's encounter with the risen Christ or like our own encounters as we read. *Metanoia* can happen if we read in such a way that we are open to the unexpected, to the *kairos*, to the unanticipated opportunity, to the call to adventure.

What if the Bible is not our assembly manual? What if it is a love letter, as Jacob J. Petuchowski suggests? Or what if it is a blade, as the author of the letter to the Hebrews suggests, a sword that can cut through the tangle of assembly notes we've been trying to live by? The metaphors we choose matter; they describe and define our reading methods and traditions. Here is another metaphor:

Your word is a lamp to my feet
and a light to my path.

Psalm 119:105

In Psalm 119, the Word sheds light on whatever path you walk. It is a tool that helps you notice things about your environment or your situation that you would otherwise miss. In this metaphor, the Word is not the path itself; it is a device for increasing what you can perceive as you travel.

How do we let the Word shine again as a light to our path, rather than making it a path that we tread on in the dark? How do we make room for the Word to cut its way, bladelike, through the hard, dry shells we've grown around our hearts?

We need to practice more ways of reading our Bible, so that we *can* unsheathe the Word as a blade or unshutter the Word as a lamp, rather than just keeping it in our house (or in the clutter of our minds) as a mere decoration. In this chapter, I want to suggest one way of reading that I believe helps us approach the Word again like playful adventurers and like humble children, as Jesus asked us to. A way of reading that, for a religious reader, allows God room to do the ongoing work of *metanoia* in us—changing our minds and hearts in a continual process of making us more like Christ.

The Tower of Babel, the Confusion of Language, and the Remainder

For our generation, encumbered under much tradition, I want to recommend deconstructive reading, which is a methodology described by the French Jewish philosopher Jacques Derrida. It's not the only reading method available to us; I think we would also gain much if we did more group reading in the form of *lectio divina* to learn simply to sit in the presence of God and contemplate his Word together. And we might gain a lot if we looked more deeply into the tradition of *midrash*. But I'll talk about deconstruction because it is a useful method of cutting through the veils that our tradition places before our eyes. And it's a methodology of reading that I have been trying to use throughout this book.

For brevity, I am going to focus on just two ideas—the fallibility of human language and Derrida's idea of a *remainder*. (For those who are well-acquainted with Derrida, this really is only going to touch on a tiny piece of the play of methods he proposed. Otherwise this chapter would itself be as long as a book, or likely longer still. For those less well-acquainted who would like to dig in more deeply, I recommend John Caputo's book *The Prayers and Tears of Jacques Derrida: Religion without Religion.*) Then I'm going to offer a deconstructive reading of Genesis 1:1-5 to show how this way of reading can present us with new and significant possibilities.

Derrida suggests that all language is fluid and indeterminate. This is an idea that has since permeated the humanities and the social sciences, but has been met with skepticism or even derision in other quarters. In America, we have a tendency to assume *(a)* that after a bit of mental work you can identify, beyond doubt, the complete and final meaning of a written sentence, and *(b)* that everything that matters can be expressed accurately in "common" language, or language that everyone can understand.

Jacques Derrida ruffles our American feathers by suggesting that language is a less reliable tool than we believe, and that the task of deriving fixed meaning from language is a project that can never actually be completed.

But while our feathers may be ruffled, I'd suggest that the fallibility of written communication isn't (or needn't) be an idea that is unfamiliar to Christian readers. After all, Christian scholars for centuries—from Augustine to Aquinas—have remarked on the fallibility and fluidity of language. (Derrida responds to and revises their work.) Indeed, right there in the Bible, we have our own story of the Tower of Babel. In this ancient story, the confusion of languages serves the explicit purpose of preventing human beings from building a tower to heaven and becoming like God, comprehending everything and achieving anything. In Genesis, languages are invented to confuse and scatter us:

> Now the whole earth had one language and the same words. And as they migrated from the east, they came upon a plain in the land of Shinar and settled there. And they said to one another, "Come, let us make bricks, and burn them thoroughly." And they had brick for stone, and bitumen for mortar. Then they said, "Come, let us build ourselves a city, and a tower with its top in the heavens, and let us make a name for ourselves; otherwise we shall be scattered abroad upon the face of the whole earth." The Lord came down to see the city and the tower, which mortals had built. And the Lord said, "Look, they are one people, and they have all one language; and this is only the beginning of what they will do; nothing that they propose to do will now be impossible for them. Come, let us go down, and confuse their language there, so that they will not understand one another's

speech." So the Lord scattered them abroad from there over the face of all the earth, and they left off building the city. Therefore it was called Babel, because there the Lord confused the language of all the earth; and from there the Lord scattered them abroad over the face of all the earth.

GENESIS 11:1-9

This tale is near the beginning of the Bible, like a tower-shaped reminder on the horizon of the past, set there lest we grow arrogant and proud, lest we treat that language as a reliable tool, like a hammer we might set down and pick up again and put to predictable uses. Language is not a hammer. Language is a tool that shifts its shape, a tool that shapes us. According to Genesis 11, it is confusing, as befits the communication technology used by ungodlike, humbled, scattered people who live on the earth and build no towers to heaven. Language is like the flaming sword of the cherubim outside the garden of Eden; it is an obstacle in our path back to Paradise. Yet, by the beauty and the blaze of its flames, it is simultaneously a beacon, lighting the borders of Paradise, teasing us with the possibility of finding Paradise. The texts we write down, from the humblest love poem to the holy Bible, might prove either a lamp to light our path through the dark forest of life—or a forest fire, sending the cedars up in flames all around us, trapping us to burn.

Our languages are both a source of confusion and the means by which we strive to navigate our confusion. In Chapter 1, I suggested that translation is a beautiful and tragic act of compromise. Beautiful because by translation from one language to another or simply from one context to another, we try to reduce confusion and convey things worth knowing, worth unforgetting. Tragic because we create confusion even as we work to dispel it.

We lose meaning when translating between languages. We have seen that in this book, from *aletheia* (the activity of truth that is "unforgetting") to *eirene* (the "peace" that is a love weaving) to *eshet chayil* ("woman of valor"). We also lose things translating across time, even within a single language. Commonly understood meanings for a word shift, sometimes rapidly; "condescend," for example, used to be a beautiful word, borrowed into our language from Latin; it meant "to step down with" someone—to join them in their moment of vulnerability, lift them up on their feet, and climb out of that moment together. It meant being a paraclete. But because of the way Victorian charities "condescended" to the poor, that word began to suggest very different (and far more negative) meanings to us. The meaning of words doesn't stay fixed.

We lose things in translation even within the same hour. The English word "liberal" suggests certain things to an academic studying in the liberal arts. It may suggest entirely different things to three neighbors—one politically progressive, one moderate, and one conservative—each of whom will define the word differently. We even lose things in translation in conversations between people with the most similar backgrounds, beliefs, and values. How many times have you written an email or a post on social media that was construed differently than how you had intended? How many times have you tried to convey something to your spouse and been startled at how they took it? For that matter, if you have ever tried to express your love or express extreme grief in words, you know how extremely limited a technology language actually is—though I am thankful that we have it.

The meaning of words isn't absolute, located out there in some ideal space, something that we can refer back to with complete assurance and accuracy. The meaning of words, Derrida cautions us, is something that is *constructed* in the moment, by the hearer. When we construct the meaning of what we read or hear, we are both informed by and limited by our context, and by the influence of past occasions in which we've encountered similar words and ideas, by our knowledge of the language, by our own values and views, by our opinion and understanding of the writer or speaker, by what we notice or fail to notice in what was said, and by many other things. For this reason, when we construct the meaning of what we have just heard or read, we *always* leave something out of our interpretation. There is something we neglect to consider—some remainder that is left over. That is how we get an interpretation; we emphasize some things and exclude other things.

WHAT DOES IT MEAN TO READ IN THE RUINS OF BABEL?

What happens if we read the Bible while keeping it in mind that language is rarely trustworthy and that our interpretations (whether religious or secular) are created by selecting what we will attend to and forgetting what we have ignored? Deconstruction is one method to seek meaning in what we read without ever forgetting that we stand in the ruins of the tower of Babel and that the meaning conveyed by human language is forever contingent.

Deconstructive reading entails a stance of humility toward the written text, an acceptance that no matter how thorough our interpretation, we will leave things out of it—probably important things. The interpretation immediately prior to ours did that, too; it left things out. So will the next interpretation to follow.

The deconstructive method is to start any reading of the text by seeking what was left out previously. This can be playful or it can be serious. Maybe it is both. I would approach a text with these four probabilities in mind:

1. The interpretations others have offered for this text *have left something out*. There is a remainder.
2. If I find what was left out, that finding will deconstruct the established interpretation. It will take that interpretation apart, to one degree or another.
3. If I find what was left out, I might discover so much through this text that I never noticed before. There will be opportunity for a deeper understanding and another interpretation.
4. However, my new interpretation will *also* be fallible, because I am *also* leaving something out. While I may understand more or differently, my new reading of the text can also be deconstructed.

This might sound alarming to some readers, because you could take this to mean, "We will never finally know what this passage *means*."

But that very objection reveals a secret arrogance in our culture, an arrogance by which we assume that to approach God, we need to fully understand and comprehend his word, completely, without mistakes or uncertainties—an arrogance that assumes it is actually possible for us to do that. Yet in our sacred texts, God sets no requirement that we fully comprehend him. It is prideful to think that we can. It's a very modern pride, I think. In the past, our religious traditions have often acknowledged the incompleteness of our understanding of God and our inability to convey holy matters effectively in language. Medieval mystics spoke of approaching God through "the cloud of unknowing," and the book of Exodus relates that at Mount Sinai, while most of the Hebrews stayed back "at a distance," Moses walked alone into "the thick darkness where God was" (Exodus 20:21).

In our modern tradition, however, we find it uncomfortable approaching God in the "thick darkness" or through the "cloud of unknowing." We don't like to draw near to God (or anything) in the dark. We like to *know*. And we really like to have definitive answers. When we don't have them, we get frustrated. And when we do have an interpretation that seems good to us and someone approaches us and deconstructs that interpretation, it may annoy us enormously, or even appear threatening to us. We simply don't like having our interpretations deconstructed. We are often either proud of our interpretations or very reliant on them.

But there is no reason this needs to be so. Why not read our text the way scientists strive to read the more extensive text that consists of the data and phenomena of our natural world? I have heard some of my neighbors voice the perception that scientists are constantly "changing their answers." But of course they are, because they're constantly testing what they've learned, uncovering new evidence, deconstructing a previous theory or interpretation, and arriving at new insights into the natural world and how and why it works. That new understanding may also be fallible if there is evidence that it left out—if, in Derrida's terms, there's a "remainder" that didn't get noticed or considered. Newton's interpretation of how the universe worked was a pretty deep and effective interpretation...until Einstein suggested that something was left out. A dedicated scientist adopts a strikingly humble perspective toward knowledge; like the poet Goethe, the scientist's heart starts at *Many things I know; yet many things I do not understand*—and then goes on to add, *But it's going to be so fun and rewarding to step into the space I don't understand, ask questions, test what answers I get, and learn more.*

We could undertake the work of reading and interpreting religious texts in a similar spirit. There is a humility and even a joy in looking deeper. I spoke of this a little in Chapter 3; it is what Roland Barthes would call "the pleasure of the text," the pleasure of wrestling meaning from a nuanced text that could suggest many meanings. There can be pleasure and excitement and adventure in looking for what was *left out*, in finding the remainder, and in approaching the word with the base assumption that our revised interpretation is also going to be fallible. That doesn't have to be a scary thing. It can be a position that glorifies God and humbles man.

In Christianity, there is a belief and a trust that all the scripture is God-inspired (2 Timothy 3:16-17). But Scripture is written down and translated by fallible people

211

using flawed and imperfect language, and the *interpretation* of Scripture is likewise developed by mortal, fallible, flawed human beings. It *always* leaves something out. In deconstructing a traditional interpretation, we find a *kairos*, an opportunity for encountering a wildly impossible and recklessly loving God who, like Gandalf in *The Hobbit*, is always ready to invite us to an unexpected banquet and an unexpected adventure.

DID JESUS READ DECONSTRUCTIVELY?

I opened this chapter with the example of the confrontation on the Sabbath. *You claim to be a religious teacher,* the Pharisees demand of Jesus, *so why are your disciples gathering up wheat as they walk through this field, on a day when all work is prohibited?* Jesus responds not with a direct answer but by deconstructing their choices of how to interpret and apply the laws about the Sabbath. *You've left something out,* he says. *Don't you remember the moment in the Old Testament when David took holy bread from the tabernacle on the Sabbath? What can we learn from that moment? That the Sabbath is not a day for going hungry. Man is not made for the Sabbath; the Sabbath is made for man.* That is the *remainder*, a non-trivial item that the Pharisees in the story left out while they were focused on other details.

In the gospels, only on rare occasions does Jesus make definitive interpretive statements about the Old Testament (which, for a Christian reader, is a striking circumstance, because traditional Christian theology and metaphysics hold that Jesus, as God's Word incarnate, would have been the one person in history who might claim an absolute right to do so). Instead, what we see Jesus doing is continually deconstructing established interpretations by pointing out the remainder. The Pharisees, as portrayed in the gospels, desire to work out, in exactitude and in fine detail, what is meant in the levitical law. They like to have definite answers—answers that don't shift when you have your back turned. Jesus angers them in part because he upsets that stability; he has a tendency to charge in and overturn their interpretations and conclusions as abruptly as a man flipping over tables and chasing money-changers out of the temple.

This is why radical theologian John Caputo playfully calls Jesus a deconstructionist, in his book *What Would Jesus Deconstruct?* In his teachings and parables, Jesus invites his listeners to deconstruct their previous understanding of how the world works, how God works, and how *they* might work. He challenges them with the possibility that in focusing so intently on certain things (like the prohibition of work on the Sabbath), they may be leaving out other things, even *big* things. Jesus also points out that when you arrogantly assume that your interpretation is final and that there *is* no remainder, that arrogance has real-world ramifications. You make big mistakes. You start to leave *people* out. You judge when it is God's role alone to judge—and often you judge unjustly.

"The letter kills, and the spirit gives life." Encountering the "spirit" in the text means approaching scripture not with the intent of arriving at a definitive and final and *literal* answer, but with the intent of encountering the heart of God and having your assumptions shaken up—as they certainly will be, if we believe that what we are encountering in the text is the living Word of God, the Word that once walked incarnate on the earth.

A DECONSTRUCTIVE READING OF GENESIS 1:1-5

Let's *do* some deconstructive reading. Let's go to the start of the Bible, read Genesis 1:1-5 (the first day of creation), and start with the humble stance that when we read it previously, *we left something out.* Let's take that as a given—and approach the text searching attentively for what we left out before. In doing this, our goal isn't to arrive at a definitive and final interpretation, but we may hope to gain new insights into the text. For those of us who are religious readers, we may hope to gain new insights into the heart of God. In other words, we are not out to control the Bible and what it means, but to be moved and stirred by it. Reading in this way might challenge our assumptions. It might waken our hearts and minds. It is worth doing.

Many readers are likely familiar with Genesis 1:1—"In the beginning, God created the heavens and the earth"— but how often do we read the rest, and how attentively do we read it? Here is the opening in the NRSV translation:

> In the beginning when God created the heavens and the earth, the earth was a formless void and darkness covered the face of the deep, while a wind from God swept over the face of the waters. Then God said, "Let there be light"; and there was light. And God saw that the light was good; and God separated the light from the darkness. God called the

light Day, and the darkness he called Night. And there was evening and there was morning, the first day.

GENESIS 1:1-5

What have we left out of our traditional interpretation of this passage? What have we neglected to notice? I'll draw attention to two things that have profound implications. But as I do—as I call our attention to these two things—I will likely be ignoring other things. That means that my interpretation, like all others, is deconstructible; it can be taken apart and shown to be incomplete. I hope and yearn that the next reader after me will notice more, will offer us a still deeper journey into the Word and into the heart of God. I hope that a few months from now, I myself will find my reading of this passage incomplete—that I will have noticed something further, or someone else will have noticed and shared it with me. Like a lover holding close to his breast the letter from his betrothed, I will keep reading and unforgetting the Word, yearning after every nuance, every possibility that might be teased out of its concealment in the text.

But for today, let's read Genesis 1:1-5 with fresh eyes. We will look at the two of the actions in the story—*creating* and *calling*. There may be an invitation to adventure hidden here in plain sight.

1. *Bara: How God Creates*

"The earth was a formless void and darkness covered the face of the deep." This passage has always excited me as a reader. In my tradition, I have been taught—as many

Christians have been taught since the fifth century—that God created the universe *ex nihilo*, "out of nothing." There was nothing at all; then *bam,* there was something. The idea of *ex nihilo* was attractive to Roman thinkers, who liked to focus on absolute power and authority—omnipotence—as divine attributes. But this idea is an anachronism introduced by late-antiquity theologians writing in Latin. This idea of a universe created out of nothing isn't present in the Hebrew text, nor even in the English translation. In the Genesis text, something is already there—a formless empty place, and the deep, the waters stirred by God's breath. What does it mean that these are there in the dark, predating light, predating speech from God's lips?

There are things we can do to investigate this. We can hunt through commentaries. We can take a look at an interlinear Bible, look up specific vocabulary in Strong's concordance, or look up a Hebrew lexicon and dig up the etymologies of some of the words appearing here in this passage. We can investigate where else those words appear in the text, looking for contextual clues about how these concepts might have been read and interpreted by readers long ago who were closer to the text. We can look to other Mesopotamian creation stories for analogues. Because Genesis 1 is a Hebrew text, we can also look to the rabbinical tradition. We can pluck *Etz Hayim* off the shelf and see if it has commentary on these passages. We can visit the nearest academic or research library, either in person or online. We could send an email to a professor in Jewish Studies, Religious Studies, or Hebrew at a local college or university; their names, areas of specialty, and email addresses are posted publicly on their departmental websites. Reflecting back on my own time on a university faculty, I can vouch for the fact that most faculty are delighted to receive earnest requests about the area they have devoted their lives to studying. All one has to do…is ask.

In this case, one of the most enlightening resources I have found on this passage is Catherine Keller's *Face of the Deep*. I found quite a few insights in that book. One of them provides a key to unlocking a new story (new to me, that is—maybe new to you) that is hiding in this passage, hiding just under the surface of the water, hiding out in the formless waste.

Keller points out that *bara* (the Hebrew verb for creating) doesn't mean *creatio ex nihilo* (making something out of nothing). Instead, *bara* suggests taking raw materials and shaping them into a new object that has purpose, use, and beauty. For example, when you take a hollow reed and poke holes in it and turn it into a flute, you are doing the kind of creation that is *bara*. When you take a rock and carve it into a statue, that is *bara*. When you take twelve people of diverse classes, traditions, and motivations, and weld them into a team of apostles, that is *bara*. When you take dust and form it into a human being and breathe life into it, that is *bara*. The poet John Milton, having read his Old Testament in Hebrew, described God creating worlds out of "his dark materials" in *Paradise Lost*.

Our Latin tradition of reading *ex nihilo* into the Genesis story influences the rest of our translation in other, subtle ways. For example, we translate *tohu vavohu* as a "formless void," where the Hebrew suggests not a void but a desert. The universe before God touches it is not empty like a blank space but empty like a lifeless desert. A desert isn't *nothing*. It is just, in this verse, a dry waste without life

217

and without form. The original writers of this passage were the agrarian descendants of a people who had traveled across deserts. Reading Genesis, an ancient Hebrew might have pictured the wilderness beyond their farmlands and imagined God taking all that emptiness and making it fruitful, filling it with light and life and green, growing things. For that Hebrew reader, this story of creation implies incredible hope—because a desert is not a dead space. A desert is raw materials.

By reading Genesis 1:1-2 as a narrative about *creatio ex nihilo* (creation out of nothing), we have missed out on the story of *bara* (creating by taking raw materials and shaping them into something purposeful and beautiful). These are two different stories. One of these is about emphasizing God's *power*. The other emphasizes God's *purpose*. One emphasizes *what God can do*, while the other is suggestive of *how and why God does things*. After all, much of the rest of Scripture is concerned with how God goes on creating and re-creating the world. God calls water out of the rock, makes springs bubble up in desert places. God visits the desolate with new life—from Naomi in the book of Ruth to Elizabeth in the book of Luke. God visits the bitter, the grieving, or the hard-hearted and turns them into apostles, prophets, healers, teachers, and even kings who dance naked before the Ark in an extremity of joy. *Bara* is what God does with us, taking the "dark materials" of each of our hearts and making all things new. If the way God creates is *bara*, then we who take this creation story to heart can live in the unstoppable hope that no matter how formless and desertlike a life might seem, it might yet flower again.

Seeing five thousand people following Jesus into the wilderness to hear him teach, the disciple Philip asks how food will be found for so great a multitude, "for we are in a desert place" (Matthew 14:15). Jesus's reply—and the miracle of the feeding of the five thousand with a few loaves and fishes—implies that for God, there are no desert places. Not truly.

In the opening lines of the Hebrew Bible, we are introduced to God as the one who stirs the desert and makes a whole universe out of it. I am so moved by that story. It is what my pen name means, the name I have taken as my life motto, the words I have inscribed on the door of my life since I was a teen. You can find my legal name on the copyright page of this book. It's no secret. *Stant Litore* is not a concealment for me but a daily unforgetting of a story I hold in my heart.

The phrase *stant litore* is Latin, and it is from the Roman epic *Aeneid.* In that story, while the city of Troy burns, Aeneas leads the survivors fleeing toward the shore. Someone ahead of him shouts: "Hurry! Hurry! The ships stand at the shore!" In Latin, *stant litore puppes*! "The anchor is already drawn up! Hurry! The ships are here to take you away!"

As far as the refugees from Troy know, this is the end of their world. Where there were homes and gardens and markets, there is nothing now but smoke and ash. Where there was a city, there will now be ruins and desert. What they *don't* know is that once they embark on those ships and cross the sea, they are going to found Rome, a civilization that will last for thousands of years. They have a breathtaking future ahead of them that they can't even imagine. That doesn't change what they have lost, but their loss does not define the totality of their future. An entire civilization might be born out of the ashes of their city, an entire universe might be summoned forth out of a desert. That story of impossible hope, of endless creating—of *bara*—speaks deeply to me.

Seven years ago, I sat vigil for long months beside a hospital bed while my infant daughter Inara fought for her life. We were cautioned, her mother and I, that she might not make it through her first year. That if she did, she would be unlikely ever to see, stand, or walk. All of these, she has done. She is a fighter, and she has done the impossible. That is the meaning of *her* name; she is named for a crew member on the fictional spaceship *Serenity*, whose captain said of his crew, "We have done the impossible, and that makes us mighty."

The story of the past seven years might so easily have been written differently and more darkly, but Inara's survival and her conquest of life has been a reminder to me that the possibilities of tomorrow are always uncharted, that tomorrow is always being created anew. I try to live my life continually unforgetting that no matter how desolate the night, the ships still stand at the shore—in Latin, *stant litore*.

In the holy Bible that I read and love, the story of the universe begins with a desert place bursting into sudden life and potential, and the story of humanity begins with life breathed into something that a moment before was only dust.

2. "Called": How God Invites

We have seen that when we focus all our attention on one thing, we miss other things that may be just as—or more—important. This also happens when we have been taught in our tradition to read something *into* a text (like *creatio ex nihilo*), so that we don't think to try reading the text *without* it. The Romans chose to read a Hebrew creation story as a tale of the omnipotence of God, though the ancient Hebrews had likely written it as a tale about *how* God creates. It was a tale of hope, but the Romans reinterpreted it as a tale of power. If I might pun, we miss such a "powerful" story this way!

There's more to that story. Because I am a languages nerd, I have always been struck by the fact that in Genesis, God creates in the subjunctive mood instead of the imperative mood. In other words, God creates by invitation, not by command. The subjunctive mood is "Let there be light"; the imperative mood is "Light, be! Happen! Right now!" The invitation is "Let's!" and the imperative is "Do!" Because we have learned to read Genesis 1 as a story about divine power and omnipotence (expressed by the act of creating everything from nothing), we typically read God's words in this passage as though they are commands. But grammatically, they are not. So the deconstructive question is: What do we miss out on, when we read them as commands?

What does it mean that God *calls* or *invites* the universe to be, rather than *commands* it? What if, in *bara* creation, God took the raw materials of the universe and *called* them to be something of purpose and beauty? What if God is like Isaiah's "voice crying out in the wilderness," calling us to change the world? What if God's voice is a "still, small voice" that approaches us not with a command but with a call? In Chapter 5 (the chapter on faith), we looked at the story of Elijah on the mountainside in 1 Kings 19; when Elijah hears the voice of God, he hears it not as a shouted imperative, "Elijah, get your butt back into action!" but as a quiet voice calling to him: "Elijah, what are you doing here?" In Genesis 3, God walks through the garden in the evening, calling for Adam. In the gospels, Jesus calls the disciples—"Come and see!" (John 1). In 1 Samuel 3, God calls Samuel into his presence in the middle of the night. And so on. The Bible is full of calling. Today, in both religious and secular contexts, we talk about having "a calling."

The New Testament idea of the redemption of the heart is that God takes a heart that has become a wasteland and calls it to purpose, justice, love, and faith. Grace—the freely given gift—isn't just that God forgives; it's that he remakes. He calls us to "newness of life" (Romans 6:4) and begins to make us into something beautiful that we did not expect. Just as a reader of Genesis 1 might imagine God taking stardust and forming it over time into planets and trees and people, we might think of God taking the raw materials of a life and shaping it into something new. That activity continues the work of creation and calling that we see in Genesis 1. "Let there be light." "Let there be waters above the waters." "Let there be living things." And so on. That's God standing at the edge of a formless waste and calling forth life. That's Jesus standing on the waters calling Peter out of the boat. That's Christ calling to a desolate heart.

It's not a command; we can always ignore it. It's a call. In *The Weakness of God*, John Caputo refers to the call as a "persistent" and "insistent" invitation, one that can be refused but one that sometimes gets inside us and gets more and more difficult to ignore.

This idea of "calling"—this big idea at the start of the Bible, which suggests so much about the nature of God's work of creation described throughout the Scriptures—frequently gets left out of our readings of Genesis 1. This idea is one remainder, a part of the story left over and largely forgotten.

TAKING THE ADVENTURE

To read deconstructively:

1. Start with the hypothesis that something has been left out.
2. Look for that remainder.
3. Once you identify it, ask questions. See what you can find out.

Such reading provides us with opportunities to encounter the unexpected—and also to relinquish our pride and set aside our modern tendency to "lean on our own understanding" (Proverbs 3:5). It empowers us to avoid the trap of *ametanoeton kardian* ("unchanging heart"), which in the Bible is not something to be prized (Romans 2:5).

If we *don't* go in looking for what has been missed, if we go into the Bible reading only what we expect to, only

223

what we've been taught to read—if our only "takeaway" from Genesis 1:1-5 is to reinforce the established interpretation that the Genesis narrative is all about and only about the omnipotence of God, then we are missing *so much* of the story. We are missing big things like *bara* creation and how God creates and recreates us by invitation.

The function of deconstruction isn't to destroy. It's to take apart an incomplete and flawed interpretation (which, because it's flawed, might miss opportunities or even prove dangerous). Having done so, you might then *re*construct. You might develop a new interpretation that takes into account and is partly shaped by the remainder you've noticed. But, because you are developing that interpretation using a flawed technology (human language), it would be wise to realize that your new interpretation is *also* tentative and *also* deconstructible—just as the interpretations I've shared above as examples remain tentative and deconstructible. That is, I am convinced that I have left things out. I know I have—because I am not God but a human being using human tools. There are things I haven't even looked at. Reading a second time, deconstructively, I might identify some of the remainder I've left. Or others will. There will be more questions to ask, and the interpretation I've offered in this chapter— like every interpretation—necessarily stands on shaky ground. But as I've suggested, that can be a joyous thing, not a scary thing. We must fall in love with *learning* again, coming to the Word like wide-eyed, inquisitive children. And like adventurers, we must unforget that it is *the journey there*—the risky walk across the wilderness or over the surface of the water—that changes us, enlarges us, and redeems us.

If we approach the Bible (or indeed, any written text) with a willingness to deconstruct the interpretation we have received, that is a humble act. For those of us who are followers of Christ, it may even be a devotional act. It is a way of letting go of our desire to master God and his Word, and instead open ourselves to encounter God's heart and his word anew, each day. It is a way of letting go of our desperate, clinging need for certainty, a way of saying, "God, I will not lean today on my own understanding. Before you, what I think I know is insignificant. I am going to approach your Word and your kingdom like a small child, with questions and new eyes and a willingness to notice things for the first time. Whatever adventure you have for me, Lord, I will take it. God, what do you want me to notice today?"

That is how I yearn to read.

PART 4: WHAT GETS IN OUR WAY

9. "FOR THE SAKE OF YOUR TRADITION"

WHAT THIS CHAPTER IS ABOUT

In Christianity, each of our denominations and sects is one tradition among many. We do not always share doctrine or ritual. We *do* share a story—the story of Jesus. When we lose sight of that story and we privilege our one tradition and our sect's doctrine above all else, we start to forget what's most important, and in place of a life-changing story we easily substitute our own cultural traditions and prejudices.

———————

"And why do you break the commandment of God for the sake of your tradition?"

JESUS

———————

A FEW YEARS AGO, before my son was born, my wife and I took our two daughters River and Inara, piled into a car, and did a road trip from Colorado to the Pacific Coast and back. My oldest and I walked through caverns of glistening stone far beneath the earth; my wife and my youngest stood inside a house carved into the side of a cliff, a house deserted for a thousand years. We climbed sand dunes. We drove through "dry" towns in Utah during the middle of the day, and past an Area 51-themed brothel in Nevada in the middle of the night, to our amusement and bemusement. We stayed a few nights at the Grand Canyon, where I laughed and told stories with my children at the edge of the world, and talked with my God under the midnight stars. At dawn, I pointed to the bottom of the canyon as it emerged from the dark; a little ribbon of blue could just barely be seen. "Look how little that river is," I told my daughter River. "That little river *made* this giant canyon. Never forget that. A little river can do anything." My daughter Inara sat beside us in her wheelchair, feeling the sunrise on her face—because difficulty walking should be no impediment to exploring the world.

We were traveling to California to attend a friend's wedding on San Francisco Bay. Literally *on* the bay—the wedding was on a boat. None of us had ever been there, and the trip was a time for wonder and storytelling and good company. A few days after the wedding, we went to the Muir Woods. Jessica and I took turns wheeling Inara down the broad path until we reached the cathedral trees—redwoods a thousand years old, trees that were young when Marco Polo crossed Asia to report that he saw the skeletons of dragons in the Gobi desert. Trees that were saplings when the great libraries of Morocco and Bokhara were established, and when Pope Urban called the first crusade. They had grown old and tall. Redwoods are wet trees, absorbing moisture into their spongy bark, genetically prepared to withstand forest fires. The fires that had swept through over the centuries had hollowed out the insides of these trees, leaving dark, scorched caverns inside them. But those same fires killed the trees' competitors and burned rot and insects out of their wood. After the fires, the trees kept growing, ever taller, ever wider at the base, reaching toward the sun with their branches and reaching toward the heart of the earth with their gnarled roots. And always, the trees clone themselves—little clusters of cells growing on their bark, prepared to burst into new life if the old tree should ever fall crashing to the ground. River, Inara, and I spent a little while inside one of the most massive trees, just listening. It was so quiet. Even the footsteps of other people walking by were hushed. Medieval mystics or Puritan poets would have said that we stood inside one of God's own cathedrals. I marveled to see Inara, only a few years old, leaning from her wheelchair and kicking her feet inside such an ancient living creature.

The church traditions within Christianity are like those trees. It's customary to describe Christianity as a family tree with many flowering branches. But after my return from the Muir Woods, my friend Todd Bergman, a United Methodist pastor, told me that Christianity is much more like a cathedral grove of redwoods than it is like a single tree. Each of the mighty trees of the Christian family has its own story. Yet our roots are intermingled, because all of our roots dig down and drink deeply of the living water that is the story of Jesus. Our trees have grown tall over the centuries like adjacent redwoods, and each has survived many forest fires.

Consider the history and variety of Christianity's many cathedral trees. Besides the varied Protestant sects and the many orders of the Roman Catholic church, there is the Eastern Orthodox church, with its greater emphasis on monastic community and mystical spirituality. There are the churches of East Africa, which trace their tradition back to the earliest days of the faith. There are the Syrian churches and the Coptic churches in Egypt, and there are the Nestorians, who continued practicing the Christian faith in communities throughout central Asia during late antiquity and the Middle Ages. It is a mistake to live inside one of these ancient trees and think it is the only one whose roots drink deeply from the soil of the Christ story.

It is also a mistake to look at our Bibles translated into English and sold by U.S. publishers and suppose that what we hold in our hand is the only Christian Bible. We have 66 books in most American Bibles. But there are 73 in the Bibles used by the Roman Catholic church, the Anglican church, and the Episcopalian church. There are 81 in modern Greek Bibles used by the Orthodox church. And there is a little further variation in the Slavonic Bible (which includes additional deuterocanonical books) and in the Coptic Bible, which includes the second-century letters of Clement. There's a risk in forgetting that the Bible is not really *a book*, but is instead a library of books. Different Christian sects have chosen to define the boundaries of that library differently. There are also the Mishna and the Talmud—extensive commentaries and interpretations of the Hebrew scriptures that were developed by rabbinical scholars during the same centuries that saw the canonization of a 73-book Christian Bible in Europe and

Asia Minor. These Jewish texts were not consulted by the Christian teachers of late antiquity and have been rarely consulted by Christian teachers since—with the result that in our own traditions, we often operate partly in the dark, reading our Old Testament without the benefit of centuries of recorded learning and discussion by scholars who read and spoke the language in which it was written and who were much closer to the original texts.

Besides developing different canons of Scripture, we have also developed different traditions for how to read and interpret our Scriptures—and what to emphasize. This is because each of our traditions arose out of a particular cultural moment with particular issues at stake. For example, eighteenth and nineteenth-century Methodist circuit riders in the U.S. preached moderation as a core biblical virtue, partly in response to an epidemic of alcoholism precipitated by the increased availability and affordability of unwatered booze. But other sects, most notably the Pentecostals, emphasize not moderation but frequently its opposite—ecstatic spirituality. While Methodist services lean toward stately, dignified music and a measure of decorum, services in more ecstatic church traditions might include glossolalia (speaking in tongues), prophecy, and the sharing of personal visions. One sect might take David's naked dancing before the Ark as a model example of the religious experience, whereas another sect within our same religion may regard dancing as inherently sinful and "of the devil." The Bible never forbids dancing, but some churches have—that's an example of a tradition created in response to a specific cultural concern and then handed over from one generation to the next, continuing to hold authority long after the situation that originally provoked it has passed. I'll talk more about that in a few pages.

Each sect by itself is a minority within the faith, each redwood but one in a vast grove. According to the most recent Pew Research Center data, Christians in the U.S. account for only 11% of all Christians in the world. Only 33% (about one third) of Christians in the world are white. There are more Christians in Brazil than there are in the American "Bible Belt," and there are the same number of Christians in the Philippines as there are in the Bible Belt. Roughly 25% of the world's Christians are black, and the oldest continuously operating churches on the planet are in Ethiopia (which was a great surprise to the first European missionaries to visit them). 26% of Christians live in Latin or South America. So our Christianity in the United States, in all its diversity, remains a very tiny portion of the whole picture, the whole community of our faith.

If we insist that our generation or our tradition's biblical interpretation is the only true one or the *most* true one, that is both haughty and anachronistic. It is haughty because by our insistence, we remove ourselves from communion and conversation with others in the faith, both here in our own cities and around the world. Then we start to behave like the elder brother in the tale of the Prodigal Son, certain that we have everything right; we begin to look down on our siblings in the faith, to resent them. And it is anachronistic, because no sect of Christianity that exists today existed at the time of Christ. We are all descendants, all trees growing together out of the fertile soil that is the good story, the gospel.

As Christians, we don't have one true doctrine or one true biblical interpretation; we have one true story. It is a story of *aletheia*, a story of God's unforgetting of us. It is to that story and the person in it that we commit ourselves as Christians; the commitment to One Tradition is often an idolatry. Our deep investment in orthodoxy can make it too easy to miss the *kairos*, the opportunity for an encounter with the impossible, the encounter with an impossible and loving God. Too easy to ignore the call to adventure. Too easy to substitute our own prejudices and momentary cultural concerns for the teachings of the Word. In the end, our tradition becomes more sacred to us than the two greatest commandments—to love God and to love one another. When this occurs, we give our time, effort, and worship to our traditions and our theology instead of to Christ. And, staring at the interior of our one tree, the one cathedral tree inside whose hollowed trunk we have chosen to stand and live, we stop seeing either the forest or the water-rich, Christ-filled soil beneath our feet. We miss the forest for the tree.

PARADOSIS AND *ENTOLE*—THE TRAP OF TRADITION

In the gospel according to Matthew, the religious scholars of first-century Palestine confront the Rabbi Jesus, demanding to know why his disciples were breaking the tradition (in Greek, the *paradosis*) of their religious elders. Tradition required the disciples to wash up to their elbows before eating; not all of them were doing so. Jesus, ever the teacher, does his typical thing of answering a hostile question with a keen question of his own:

> And why do you break the commandment of God for the sake of your tradition? For God said, "Honor your father and your mother," and, "Whoever speaks evil of father or mother will surely die." But you say that whoever tells father or mother, "Whatever support you might have had from me is given to God," then that person need not honor the father. So, for the sake of your tradition, you make void the word of God. You hypocrites! Isaiah prophesied rightly about you when he said:
>
> > *This people honors me with their lips,*
> > *but their hearts are far from me;*
> > *in vain do they worship me,*
> > *teaching human precepts as doctrines.*

MATTHEW 15:3-9

It is one of those passages in which Jesus speaks very harshly to the religious teachers and biblical interpreters of his day. He accuses them of prioritizing their religious tradition over seeking after the heart of God. For them, upholding religious tradition has become more important and more essential to living a righteous life than treating others as God would have us treat them.

In the example Jesus gives, the Pharisees have maintained that tithing to God is paramount. Tithe first, *then* tend to your worldly needs. At first glance, this tradition makes sense; by devoting tithes to God first above all other financial needs, the Pharisees propose a more total devotion to God. The Pharisees may be thinking of the words of the prophet Haggai:

> Is it a time for you yourselves to live in your paneled houses, while this house lies in ruins? ... Go up to the hills and bring wood and build the house, so that I may take pleasure in it and be honored, says the Lord. You have looked for much, and, lo, it came to little; and when you brought it home, I blew it away. Why? says the Lord of hosts. Because my house lies in ruins, while all of you hurry off to your own houses. Therefore the heavens above you have withheld the dew, and the earth has withheld its produce.

> HAGGAI 1: 4, 8-10

Or perhaps this passage from the book of Malachi:

> Will anyone rob God? Yet you are robbing me! ... Bring the full tithe into the storehouse, so that there may be food in my house, and thus put me to the test, says the Lord of hosts; see if I will not open the windows of heaven for you and pour down for you an overflowing blessing.

> MALACHI 3: 8, 10

Take care of God's house first, *then* your own. It's right there in the Bible. But the traditional interpretation and the priority the Pharisees have given to these passages now needs to be called into question, because their tradition has led to a circumstance where those who follow their teaching neglect the financial needs of the elders in their family. Their *paradosis* or tradition has led them to leave their father and mother destitute. It has become an obstacle to carrying out the second of the two greatest commandments—to love one another.

An interesting thought: In this situation, honoring father and mother and honoring the traditions handed down by your forebears are set in opposition to each other. Honoring one's parents does not necessarily entail honoring your parents' *traditions*. The two are not equivalent, and that may be an important thing to remember. We saw in Chapter 5 that Jesus tells those who would follow him that they may need to leave their parents or even their dead behind; to follow God, to love God and one's neighbor recklessly, one often has to challenge or abandon tradition.

In this passage, Jesus contrasts *paradosis* and *entole*—which we often translate "tradition" and "commandment." *Paradosis* is a Greek word that compounds *para* ("close beside") and the verb *didomi* ("to hand something over"). *Paradosis* conveys that which is handed over from one generation of religious elders to the next. *Entole*—the word translated "commandment" above—literally means "in the end." It is *en* ("in") + *telos* (an "end," an objective, a final result). Jesus is accusing the Pharisees of breaking the "in-the-ends" of God for the sake of upholding what has been passed down to them from the previous generation. That is, they are butchering the desired final result, outcome, or objective—the *entole*—of God's Word. In doing so, they "make void" the *logos* (word, idea, intention) of God.

The verb we are translating "make void" is *akuroó*, which is *a* ("not") + *kurios* ("master"). *Kurios* is Greek for the master of a house; we often render it "Lord" in English. In the Greek text, Jesus is saying that the

Pharisees' choices "un-master" or "un-Lord" the word of God.

Jesus also accuses the Pharisees of being "whitewashed tombs," bleached and pure on the outside but filled with decay within (Matthew 23:27); he says that they are hard-hearted or "prune-hearted" (Matthew 19:8), and that they set burdens on other's shoulders that are heavy to bear and then lift no finger to help (Matthew 23:4). He says that they—the very teachers of religion—are like vipers that bite and poison their people (Matthew 23:33). The passage we are looking at right now is fascinating because in it, Jesus suggests *how* and *why* the Pharisees have come to this pass. How did people who care deeply about religious law and about living devout lives become "vipers" who poison the people? How did that happen?

It happened because their allegiance shifted. The first of the ten commandments is to place no other gods before God, but one step at a time, the Pharisees shifted their worship to another god—Paradosis, or Tradition. Moses cautioned against this in Deuteronomy, urging that one engage with God's word actively each day, at each hour—because:

> ...not with our ancestors did the Lord make this covenant, but with us, who are all of us here alive this day.

> DEUTERONOMY 5:3

> You shall love the Lord with all your heart, and with all your soul, and with all your might. Keep these words I am commanding you today in your heart. Recite them to your children and talk about them when you are at home and

when you are away, when you lie down and when you rise. Bind them as a sign on your hand, fix them as an emblem on your forehead, and write them on the doorposts of your house and on your gates.

DEUTERONOMY 6:5-9

The Pharisees we meet in the book of Matthew have taken these instructions literally; they have bound phylacteries on their foreheads, tiny containers with scraps of parchment inside, on which are written portions of the law. But Jesus charges them with having missed the *spirit* of the law, with having neglected its in-the-ends. They have fulfilled the *letter* of what Moses said, reciting the law and keeping it on their persons. But they missed the intent, the spirit— because the goal was not to know the law simply by rote but to *live* the law, each day, and to love the Lord closely, not at a distance. (Although the Pharisees get a "bad rep" in the gospels, it's important to note that Jesus's teachings here anticipate the writings of the rabbis who, in the following centuries, would assemble the Mishna and the Talmud commentaries on the law of Moses.)

Consider Jesus's teachings on prayer in the Sermon on the Mount:

And whenever you pray, do not be like the hypocrites; for they love to stand and pray in the synagogues and at the street corners, so that they may be seen by others. Truly I tell you, they have received their reward. But whenever you pray, go into your room and shut the door and pray to your Father who is in secret; and your Father who sees in secret will reward you.

MATTHEW 6:5-6

Jesus warns that prayer—which should be your time with your father in heaven who loves you—is frequently reduced by the religious teachers to a rote activity, a performance in public. Instead, he urges his students, meet with God privately, spend time with him, and he will reward you. Because time with you, his beloved children, is what God desires.

For the "prune-hearted" Pharisees, everything is by rote. God's word has become an artifact, rather than a living and sharp two-edged sword. A relic to preserve and look at, not a lantern to take with you on a journey. It becomes prized not because God's in-the-ends matter to you—not because the deepest desires of the Father's heart move you and inform *your* desires—but because it is your tradition. And bit by bit, Tradition itself becomes the god you serve.

THE ONE TEST: DO WE LOVE?

I think those of us who follow Christ sometimes become like the Pharisees in the gospels, serving Tradition rather than God. Our commitment to pursuing the right doctrine, ritual, or practice (while not intrinsically a bad impulse) can easily get in the way of unforgetting the right story—the story and person of Jesus.

I said in previous chapters that we have been taught to go into the Bible looking for what we expect to see, and that what we read gets filtered through both translation and our own cultural fears, prejudices, and context. We make our reading of the Bible an encounter with our *paradosis* (with what has been handed down) rather than an encounter with God. Therein lies danger—because eventually it becomes more important to us to affirm and uphold our tradition than to love God and love our neighbor. We defend traditions—or even legislate adherence to them—in ways that cost both lives and souls. Just as the Pharisees did. When we un-Lord God's word, we risk making the church an instrument of hate rather than a community of radical and reckless love.

How do we know that we have done this? How do we know when we have read our own prejudices aggressively into the text, substituting our own attitudes and traditions for God's in-the-ends? Not everyone gets to read Greek and Hebrew, nor does everyone have access and time to peruse hundreds of commentaries. But I think we can avoid our worst traps by choosing to hold our traditions lightly, by being ready to relinquish them when needed, and by keeping the "in-the-ends" near our heart:

> "'You shall love the Lord your God with all your heart, and with all your soul, and with all your mind.' This is the greatest and first commandment. And a second is like it: 'You shall love your neighbor as yourself.' On these two commandments hang all the law and the prophets."

> MATTHEW 22:27-40

> By this everyone will know that you are my disciples, if you have love for one another.
> JOHN 13:35

If loving God and loving one another are Jesus's "in-the-ends," that means that when our interpretation gets in the way of loving each other, it is time to question our tradition and take a second look. That stance, far from being heterodox, is biblical.

I want to point out that this desire to hold religious dogma and traditional doctrine lightly—even to be quite skeptical toward it—is also loyal to the historical spirit of the Protestant Reformation. We have the opportunity to read our Bible in translation today because people before us questioned their religious tradition and called for reform. They also believed that interpretations needed to be wrestled out of the text by each generation, and that this could only happen if everyone had access to read it, so many reformers worked tirelessly to translate the Bible into languages besides Latin. There was tremendous resistance to this. In the sixteenth century, translators were burned at the stake with copies of their translated Bibles tied around their necks. There is a story that translator William Tyndale (who suffered just such a fate) once argued with a clergyman over dinner. The clergyman insisted that the Bible could only be understood properly in Latin. Since none of the Bible was written originally in Latin, I wonder at that clergyman's logic—but then, so did Tyndale. As the conversation grew more heated, Tyndale pointed to a boy working outside in the field and declared, "I will make it so that plowboy knows more of Scripture than you do!" And indeed, today—though he died for it—we could suppose that William Tyndale's dream has come to pass: anyone who is literate in English can read the Bible in translation, regardless of their class or their level of education.

Tyndale's desire in translating the Bible was that in reading it, we would question the tradition of our elders and our priests, and that we would seek each time we read to encounter the heart of God. To seek God's "in-the-ends" and not trust our tradition naïvely. In our time, we have gained the resource Tyndale desired us to have—but we do not always practice the skepticism toward tradition that drove his efforts.

William Tyndale and other scholars of the Protestant Reformation were reacting against abuses they saw in church institutions in their century. They noted how in many cases religious authorities would either take verses out of context in ways that harmed their neighbors, or would claim that certain traditional interpretations—especially ones that brought money into the church—were directly validated and authorized by God. *Sola scriptura* ("by the text alone") was one of the theological tenets and rallying cries of the Protestant Reformation. Look to the text, never to tradition. Read rather than simply accept doctrine. It's why the Reformation sparked the creation of hundreds of new Christian sects and denominations; in a short space of time, *many* people were reading and reinterpreting and questioning tradition.

That was centuries ago. Ironically, what some of those rebellious readers of the first Bibles in English concluded has since been handed down from one generation to the next, as a new *paradosis*, traditions that many now follow as unquestioningly as others once followed the traditions that these supplanted and replaced. In our own time, we have nearly lost the desire and the will to go into our Bibles with Tyndale's fiery need to question our interpretations and to seek new insight. Yet I have faith that this is the adventure to which each generation of readers is called anew: not to carry on the march-step of tradition from one day to the next (*chronos*), but to seek a *kairos*, an occasion or opportunity for an encounter with the impossible through the text. (For a Christian, an encounter with the impossible and living God.) To seek the occasion that makes this moment, this day "the right time." To make *today*'s choices—both interpretive and ethical choices—and not merely repeat previous generations' choices that have already *been* made. To adventure with God once again across the wilderness of this world.

When defending our tradition loudly against all comers gets in the way of imitating Jesus and loving one another, we become merely noisy gongs and clanging cymbals, and we cease growing together into a community of radical love. In the end, the criterion for any interpretation or tradition is not whether our ancestors thought it correct or whether today's most numerous or simply most vocal religious teachers do, but whether it empowers us to carry out the commandment to love one another:

> And I will show you a still more excellent way. If I speak in the tongues of mortals and of angels, but do not have love, I am a noisy gong or a clanging cymbal. And if I have prophetic powers, and understand all mysteries and all knowledge, and if I have all faith, so as to remove mountains, but do not have love, I am nothing. If I give away all my possessions, and if I hand over my body so that I may boast, but do not have love, I gain nothing. Love is patient; love is kind; love is not envious or boastful or arrogant or rude. It does not insist on its own way; it is not irritable or resentful; it does not rejoice in wrongdoing, but rejoices in the truth. It bears all things, believes all things, hopes all things, endures all things.

1 Corinthians 13:1-7

STANT LITORE

The Prophets of the Old Testament, confronting the calcified and hardened religious traditions of their own era, asked their people this:

> And what does the Lord require of you
> but to do justice, and to love kindness,
> and to walk humbly with your God?

MICAH 6:8

We in turn can ask such questions about the doctrines and actions of our churches today: Is it just? Is it kind? Are we walking humbly with God? Most of all, are we *loving?*

This book is about unforgetting (*aletheia*), which is the activity and the adventure of truth. Each generation faces its own prejudices and its own sins, its own forgetting of the greatest commandments. This fourth section of the book—the chapters that follow—are intended for peeling away a few traditional interpretations to which some church communities today cling too closely. These are artifacts of *our* culture that get in our way, that bar us from doing justice, loving kindness, and walking humbly with our God. These artifacts include vestigial late twentieth century homophobia; the belief in humanity's primacy and "dominion" over the earth, which is in part a legacy of the British Empire; a mythology about "hell" that we inherited from the Middle Ages; and a belief in the efficacy of conversion through fear that was left to us by the Puritans of the seventeenth century. And others. We *need* to peel these traditions loose from our practice of Christianity because they keep us from loving, and we *are able* to peel these traditions loose because Christianity predates them. We need to take an honest look at what (and who) our

246

traditional interpretation makes it easy for us to forget—and we need to be willing to depart from our tradition, to venture across the wilderness again. We need to grasp our traditions very lightly and loosely; we have to be willing to let our dead bury their dead and let our traditions go when needed.

In the gospels, the Pharisees forgot to provide for elders in the community; are there human beings *we* are leaving unloved, unprovided for, or even persecuted? Some of our traditions have permitted atrocities. As a people and as the body of Christ, we bear responsibility for the atrocities we permit. We need to let go of interpretations and prejudices that prevent us from unforgetting and loving the Father and each other.

10. GOD DOESN'T CONDEMN LGBTQ+ PEOPLE (HUMANS DO)

WHAT THIS CHAPTER IS ABOUT

In the U.S. since the 1950s, many have accepted that contemporary cultural attitudes sexual orientation and gender are mandated by the Christian faith. This is odd to me, as these are not things of which Jesus taught, and the ways in which we express our cultural beliefs about gender are neither consistently biblical, nor informed by empirical evidence; nor are they loving and Christlike. And though the biblical texts we revere are *ancient*, many of us don't realize how *modern* our beliefs about our neighbors are.

———————

"Those who say, 'I love God,' and hate their brothers or sisters, are liars; for those who do not love a brother or sister whom they have seen, cannot love God whom they have not seen. The commandment we have from him is this: those who love God must love their brothers and sisters also."

THE FIRST LETTER OF JOHN

———————

ONCE THERE WAS A PRINCE who fell in love with a shepherd, and a shepherd who fell in love with a prince. As a reward for slaying a giant, the young shepherd received the hand of the king's daughter in marriage, but the scenes of disrobing and intimacy that follow the saving of the kingdom do not occur between David and the princess, but between David and the king's son:

> Then Jonathan made a covenant with David, because he loved him as his own soul. Jonathan stripped himself of the robe that he was wearing, and gave it to David, and his armor, and even his sword and his bow and his belt.

1 SAMUEL 18:3-4

You are my life. He loved him as he loved his own soul. It is Jonathan who fights by David's side in battle and who helps engineer David's escape later from his father the king's murderous wrath. And the king is incensed at his son's choice of where to pledge his heart:

> Then Saul's anger was kindled against Jonathan. He said to him, "You son of a perverse, rebellious woman! Do I not know that you have chosen the son of Jesse to your own shame, and to the shame of your mother's nakedness? For as long as the son of Jesse lives upon the earth, neither you nor your kingdom shall be established. Now send and bring him to me, for he shall surely die." Then Jonathan answered his father Saul, "Why should he be put to death? What has he done?" But Saul threw his spear at him to strike him; so Jonathan knew that it was the decision of his father to put David to death. Jonathan rose from the table in fierce anger and ate no food on the second day of the month, for he was

249

grieved for David, and because his father had disgraced him.

1 SAMUEL 20:30-34

Grieving, Jonathan goes out to the field where David is hiding and sends his servant on a wild goose chase so that he can be alone with his beloved friend. Their parting is as tender as any I have ever read:

> David rose from beside the stone heap and prostrated himself with his face to the ground. He bowed three times, and they kissed each other, and wept with each other; David wept the more. Then Jonathan said to David, "Go in peace, since both of us have sworn in the name of the Lord, saying, 'The Lord shall be between me and you, and between my descendants and your descendants, forever.'" He got up and left; and Jonathan went into the city.

1 SAMUEL 20:41-42

They never see each other again in waking life.

After long years apart, the prince and his father the king both fall in battle on the same day, and David, still banished, is not there to hold Jonathan's head as he dies. David is heartstricken when he gets the news; in his grief and rage, he slays the messenger. And he sings a funeral song for his friend:

> I am distressed for you, my brother Jonathan!
> delightful you were to me;
> your love to me was wonderful,
> more than the love of women.

2 SAMUEL 1:25-27

Was this a tale of deepest friendship or of a bond between soulmates? Bromance or romance? We can't know for sure; too many centuries separate us from the storyteller who gave us this account, and our culture treats affection between men as suspect, where other cultures on our earth have celebrated it.

But the original language does gives us clues here, as the vocabulary used in the story to describe this relationship is unapologetically romantic; the words chosen for this funeral song appear elsewhere in primarily romantic or even erotic contexts. "For as he loved his own soul, so he loved him," we are told of Jonathan, and to him David sings, "Your love to me was wonderful, more than the love of women." The words used here are *ahabah* and *aheb*. *Ahabah* is the same word for "love" that we find used repeatedly throughout the Song of Songs by the Shulammite woman yearning for her lover:

> He brought me to the banqueting house, and his banner over me was love.

> O daughters of Jerusalem, please, if you find my dear one, tell him I am faint with love.

> Set me as a seal upon your heart, as a seal upon your arm, for love is strong as death.

> SONGS 2:4, 5:8, 8:6

Imagine David singing those lines to his Jonathan! Such passion. And the verb *aheb* is the same verb used in Genesis repeatedly to describe Jacob's overwhelming passion for Rachel, and in Deuteronomy to describe the passion with which the Hebrews are to love their God (with all their mind, and with all their strength, and with all their soul). And when David sings, "Delightful you were to me!" he uses *na'amta*, which means "very dear" or "lovely." It is the same word used by the young woman in the Song of Songs to describe either the bed where she gives herself erotically to her lover, or to describe her lover himself (the grammar in Hebrew leaves it ambiguous which):

> How beautiful you are my love how lovely and green our bed.
>
> SONGS 1:16

WE NEED LARGER HEARTS

Continually we bind our small hearts inside the tight, restrictive wrapping of our cultural prejudices. And we try to read our own modern prejudices and fears back *into* holy texts that are thousands of years old and that predate our prejudices. Doing this, we become guilty of the *sklerokardia* of which Jesus accuses the Pharisees—that hardness of heart that makes callousness and casual violence toward our neighbor not only possible but inevitable. Jesus warned his disciples at the Last Supper:

> They will put you out of the houses of worship. Indeed, an hour is coming when those who kill you will think that by doing so they are offering worship to God.
>
> JOHN 16:2

This violence and exclusion from religious communities (in the belief that such actions serve God) has been happening in our country, in our time, to teens who suffer dysphoria and to gay teens. Our youth have every reason to expect love and compassion from the adults in their community, yet they receive fear, contempt, and condemnation instead. "There is therefore now no condemnation to them which are in Christ Jesus," the apostle Paul advises us (Romans 8:1), and yet we condemn our youth, at the very time in their lives when they are most vulnerable. Suicide rates among gay teens are epidemic, and in some communities, gay teens are even sent to conversion therapy camps, a form of legalized torture that has been proven repeatedly to be both cruel and ineffective. My people, this is not acceptable.

And this condemnation of our youth is grounded not in the Greek New Testament but in our contemporary cultural prejudices and our modern cherry-picking of verses out of context. Notably, the Bible doesn't refer to committed and loving same-gender relationships (except—possibly—David and Jonathan, whose relationship is described in romantic language). Our culture's conflation of sex acts or even of sexual violence with love and relationships is repulsive and an illness in our modern world. And to deny people any romantic relationship at all—to enforce celibacy on them—is in direct contradiction to Paul's teachings on celibacy (which, he stresses, must be a choice, not a mandate imposed by others—see 1 Corinthians 7:7, 7:17, 7:25). It is a modern way of acting as the Pharisees do, laying on others' shoulders "heavy burdens, hard to bear" and then afterward lifting no finger to help.

A FEW BONES TO PICK WITH THE CHERRY-PICKERS

Those who condemn same-gender relationships often appropriate a few biblical verses to validate their view, but the use of these verses for that purpose is highly suspect. Let's take a look.

Sodom

> This was the guilt of your sister Sodom: she and her daughters had pride, excess of food, and prosperous ease, but did not aid the poor and needy.
>
> EZEKIEL 16:49

We make a great deal of Sodom and Gomorrah, but we read that story today in ways that are profoundly anachronistic. We have even written our prejudice into our vocabulary by coining the word "sodomy" in English. We read into that story a homophobia that no one in the Bible shares with us, and we completely neglect the teaching that *does* get proposed each time the story of Sodom is mentioned by a biblical writer. As we saw in Chapter 3, the prophet Ezekiel defined "the sin of your sister Sodom" as neglect and cruelty offered to a community's most vulnerable members (the orphan, the widow, and the immigrant), and Jesus referenced the story of Sodom in the gospels in the context of criticizing communities that do not welcome and provide for strangers (Ezekiel 16:49, Matthew 10:15). The writers of the Bible did not read the story of Sodom as we do.

One possible exception to this is Jude, which may have been the last book in the Bible to be written. In Jude, there is a brief reference to the men of Sodom *ekporneusasai kai apelthousai opisō sarkos heteras*, "having sold themselves to fornicating and having pursued other flesh." Since the twelfth century, some readers have chosen to read *sarkos heteras* ("other flesh") as referring to men pursuing men, but the passage in Greek doesn't provide any hints that we should interpret "other flesh" in that way. Sometimes we support our modern interpretation by exaggerating *sarkos heteras* in English, with translations like "strange flesh" or "unnatural flesh"—conforming our translation to our prejudices—but the Greek is simply "other flesh." *Hetera* means "other"; I might compare it with *phylēs heteras* ("another tribe") in Hebrews 7:13. (There is even a pun embedded here for the modern reader: because that same *hetero, hetera* is the root for our modern word "heterosexual," where to desire "other flesh" literally means to desire someone with a gender other than your own.) In context—and knowing how other biblical writers describe the "sin of Sodom"—it is more likely that Jude is criticizing Sodom for losing themselves to their sinful appetites and attempting to rape visitors from another tribe (*sarkos heteras*) as it is that Jude is proposing what we would recognize in our culture as homophobia. In Ezekiel and in the gospels, the Bible's teaching on Sodom is not about sexual acts at all—certainly not about sexual orientation—but about the peril of violence toward those who lack the security of a home, and the necessity of *philoxenia* (love and provision for the stranger). If our linguistic ancestors had been better readers of the Old Testament, the word "sodomy" in English would not have been coined as a reference to anal intercourse but as a reference to acts of violence against immigrants and refugees.

Toebah

Besides referring to Sodom, people today will pluck two verses out of the Levitical code to describe specific sex acts as an "abomination." However, these same apologists for homophobia are unlikely to deal with the fact that Christians don't tend to regard themselves as subject to anything else in the Levitical code, or that the Hebrew word *toebah* that we translate "abomination" doesn't refer to a thing that is morally abhorrent, but rather to a practice forbidden to the priesthood. In Leviticus, various sex acts, the eating of shellfish, and the wearing of clothing made from mixed fabrics are all *toebah* (forbidden). Although there is no direct linguistic relationship between *toebah* and the Polynesian *tapu* or "taboo," the two words share both a coincidental similarity in sound and a similarity in meaning, conveying that which is forbidden.

Finally, to pluck a prohibition of sexual activities from Leviticus out of context and apply it to a judgment of relationships in our own community requires that we treat a sex act and a romantic relationship as the same thing. I hope I do not need how wrong *that* is.

Arsenokoites

There is a word that appears only twice in the New Testament—*arsenokoites*—that sometimes gets translated as "homosexuals" in recent English versions of the Bible (beginning with the RSV in 1946), but no one knows with certainty what the word actually means. It is a compound of "man" and "beds," and it may have been coined by Paul in the moment; it doesn't appear anywhere else in ancient Greek. It could be a reference to gigolos, or to pederasts, or could conceivably be translated as something not sexual at all.

Some commentators have chosen to read *arsenokoites* ("manbeds") as "manbedders," concluding that *malakoi* (the word that appears immediately prior to *arsenokoites*) refers to the recipients of anal penetration and *arsenokoites* to the givers of it, but this doesn't quite work, because first-century Koine Greek doesn't have a verb "to bed someone," the way modern English does. In English, we can take the noun "bed" and use it as a verb, and it is understood that when we're "bedding" someone, we're having sex with them. That isn't necessarily the case in Koine Greek.

To illustrate the difference, suppose that in English, we were to take the noun "food" and make it a verb (the way we can with "bed"), so that we are "fooding people." In this case, it is no longer clear in English what we're doing. What is a manfood or a manfooder? Is that a reference to a cannibal, a glutton, a chef, a gourmand, or a grocer? I have no idea, but I would be reluctant to start persecuting gourmands on the basis of an oblique reference to manfoods. In Greek, "manbeds" reads like "manfoods" in this way, and so *arsenokoites* presents us with a similar puzzle. It may or may not be meant sexually, and if it is a sexual term, it's not clear whose sexual activities are being described. We have simply assumed.

(I once had a conversation with an earnest young man who insisted that the English word *coitus* "proved" that *arsenokoites* must be read as a sexual term. But this confuses two languages. *Koite* is Greek for bed; *coitus* comes from the Latin verb *co* + *ire*—to "go together." It's a lovely word, but it isn't Greek and it isn't related to the noun *koite*.)

In the list of people engaged in problematic activities that we find in 1 Corinthians 6:9, *arsenokoites* ("manbeds") is preceded by the word *malakoi* ("soft ones"). A *malakos* ("soft one") is someone who loves luxury. By extension, in some classical Greek texts, a *malakos* is a coward; in other texts, a *malakos* is someone effeminate. In a few texts, a *malakos* is the recipient of anal intercourse—though it is not the most common term for this. The traditional interpretation that *malakoi* and *arsenokoites* are paired labels for 'submissive' and 'dominant' partners in acts of sex acts remains guesswork, and other interpretations are also plausible. For example, *malakoi arsenokoites* ("soft ones, man-beds") could easily be a colorful reference to pleasure-loving rich men who loll about on bed eating grapes all day and ignore the suffering of their impoverished neighbors. That's a type of vice that the New Testament lectures on frequently and at length, and to which the letters in which these words appear devote considerable attention. Jesus warns that it is not easy for the rich and avaricious to reach the kingdom of heaven, and in Paul's second letter to Corinth, those who have wealth but are slow to contribute are taken repeatedly to task for abstaining from giving or for giving only sparingly when they see others in need (2 Corinthians 8-9). Rich, luxurious, gaudy living was also a vice that Greeks and

Romans alike tended to scorn and treat with mockery. (They would have found Trump Tower hilarious.) Reading *malakoi arsenokoites* in this fashion is conjecture—but so is every other proposed reading of *malakoi arsenokoites*. That's the point. This term that no one is able to define with certainty prior to its medieval usage is arguably the flimsiest of all pretexts for justifying fear and abuse of our neighbors.

This word *arsenokoitia's* travels from antiquity to the present have been especially convoluted, to say the least. The first time *arsenokoites* appears outside the Greek Bible is in the writings of John the Faster over five centuries later; he does read it as a sexual term, but he understands it as a reference to any anal intercourse in which a man is involved, not specifically to sex between men: "If any man perform *arsenokoitia* upon his wife, he shall be penanced for eight years." It wasn't until the twelfth century that ecclesiastical laws were written specifically to condemn sex between men. England's first such law, the 1533 "Buggery Act"—was, irony upon ironies, established as a pretext by which Henry VIII, in his strife with the Roman Catholic Church, could arrest gay monks and lesbian nuns and seize the affected monasteries and convents as possessions of the crown. I just want to underscore the historical irony: England's first written law against homosexuality was *an attack on the church.*

Romans 1-2

Finally, there is a passage in Romans 1:20-32 that is often read as referring to same-gender sex as one item on a list of "unnatural" and "degrading" consequences of idolatry, but we nearly always read this in English without reading the continuation of the passage—that is, the opening verses of Romans 2, which offer a rebuttal to the preceding statement. Remember that the chapter breaks and verse numbers you see in the Bible are arbitrary; these did not exist in the original text. The chapter breaks we use today did not exist prior to the year 1205, and those earlier churches that also divided their biblical books into sections for more convenient reference (such as the Byzantine church's use of *kephalaia*) divided them in different places than modern churches do. So if we stop reading at the end of Romans 1, we're actually stopping mid-argument.

That's important in this case. Some biblical scholars (among them Calvin Porter and Don Burrows) think it likely that the closing verses of Romans 1 are among Paul's many paraphrases of positions held by other preachers whom he wants to rebuke. (For other examples of Paul's state-an-argument-then-knock-it-down method, see all of Romans 3 and 4, where Paul continues this to do this but at a brisker pace.) It's likely that Romans 1:20-32 is *not* Paul's own position, because in the lines that immediately follow this passage, Paul addresses whoever was just speaking—*O anthrope*, "O man"—and rebuts that person's argument:

> Therefore you have no excuse, whoever you are, when you judge others; for in passing judgment on another you condemn yourself, because you, the judge, are doing the very same things. You say, "We know that God's judgment on those who do such things is in accordance with truth." Do you imagine, whoever you are, that when you judge

those who do such things and yet do them yourself, you will escape the judgment of God? Or do you despise the riches of his kindness and forbearance and patience?

ROMANS 2:1-4

In the next verse, Paul speaks of the self-appointed judge's *sklērotēta sou kai ametanoēton kardian*—"your hardness and unchanging heart." If that sounds familiar, it's because it's the same language with which Jesus rebukes the Pharisees. Once again, we are encountering the dry-hearted, the prune-hearted. Romans 1:20-32 may well be a paraphrase of someone else's sharply worded condemnation of Gentile converts to the church. Someone in the early Roman church was criticizing them for both their polytheistic past (Romans 1:20-23) and their allegedly aberrant sexuality (Romans 1:24-32). Note that immediately after Paul's rebuttal of this, he segues to a defense of Christians who grew up Greek rather than Jewish (Romans 2:13-16).

In other words, Paul recited a very prejudiced rant against Greek converts and their culture, a rant that he didn't like, then pivoted, *addressing the very self-appointed judges he was just paraphrasing*, to demand, "How dare you pass judgment? Do *you* keep every commandment in Leviticus perfectly? Are you God? Do you doubt the riches of his kindness? Why do you have such hardness and such unchanging hearts?" (Romans 2:1-11). He goes on in the same vein:

...if you know his will and determine what is best because you are instructed in the law, and if you are sure that you are

261

> a guide to the blind, a light to those who are in darkness, a corrector of the foolish, a teacher of children, having in the law the embodiment of knowledge and truth, you, then, that teach others, will you not teach yourself? While you preach against stealing, do you steal? You that forbid adultery, do you commit adultery? You that abhor idols, do you rob temples? You that boast in the law, do you dishonor God by breaking the law? For, as it is written, "The name of God is blasphemed among the Gentiles because of you."

ROMANS 2:18-24

Humbly, I submit to you the likelihood that the opening chapters of the letter to the Romans were not written as an incitement to homophobia but as a furious rebuke of it—a rebuke of *sklerokardia*, hardness of heart.

The gist of Paul's case for many paragraphs to follow is that the heart's commitment to following God and to loving one another is of far greater importance than adherence to the letter of the law. He writes, "a person is a Jew who is one inwardly, and real circumcision is a matter of the heart—it is spiritual and not literal" (Romans 2:28-29). Remember that Paul describes himself and his fellows as "ministers of a new covenant, not of letter but of spirit; for the letter kills, but the spirit gives life" (2 Corinthians 3:6). He explicitly does *not* want the early churches cherry-picking Leviticus to create strife and marginalize Gentile converts. Paul here is not concerned with what is *toebah* (forbidden) for Levites; he is concerned with getting a group of people from diverse ethnicities and traditions to love one another.

Another indication that Romans 1:20-32 is not a statement of Paul's own position but instead a paraphrase of another's position that he is about to spend the entirety of Chapter 2 dismantling—is that this passage is the only place in his writings that we are certain alludes to sex between people of the same gender. And it appears in a letter to people living in Rome, a place where there is a strong cultural prejudice against sex acts in which one man occupies a "submissive" position. By contrast, the issue never comes up in any letter to the Greek churches, despite the fact that in many Greek cities, bisexual romantic and erotic relationships were normative. In fact, one of the two most popular lyrical poets and songwriters of the ancient world, whose songs had been hits for centuries and still were at the time that Paul was writing— was Sappho, a talented musician on the island of Lesbos who sang love poems to both men and women. (We get the word *lesbian* from Sappho the Lesbian, though Sappho was bi.) It is bizarre to suppose that if condemning same-gender relationships was important to Paul, he nevertheless didn't write about it at length in any of his letters to the Greek churches—even though these letters *do* include extensive sermons on sexual immorality (1 Corinthians 5) and chastity (1 Corinthians 7).

Even if we *were* to accept the passing mention of *arsenokoites* later in that letter as being a reference to men who occupy the "top" position in anal intercourse, the term is gender-specific. That is, the term doesn't apply to women, despite the modern, homophobic use of this word to justify a comprehensive condemnation of our LGBTQ+ neighbors. The women of Corinth and Ephesus and Galatia, who would have known Sappho's love songs, encountered no passage in any apostolic letter to their churches that advised against love between women.

OFTEN WE READ INTO THE BIBLE WHAT WE EXPECT TO FIND

When we take our tissue-paper construction of a biblical pretext for condemning our LGBTQ+ neighbors, we are taking something Jesus never mentioned and that it's unlikely Paul condemned, and using that to support the torture and ostracization that is leading so many of our youth to take their lives rather than suffer another day. It is a way of gambling with people's lives. And it requires that we forget much that we have been taught about who Jesus was and what God requires of us as Christians.

We read into the Bible the prejudices that we already hold and we search our biblical texts for confirmation of the very cultural fears that hold our hearts in slavery. Maybe it is easier to do this than it is to overcome our fears and to practice the radical, unconditional, reckless *agape* love that Christ teaches and exemplifies. "Perfect love casts out fear" (1 John 4:18), but perfect love requires action, not feeling, so it is a difficult thing to live. It is easier to cling to our cultural fears and prejudices (and to justify doing so by persuading ourselves that God shares them) than it is to throw open every window in our house and let the hurricane wind of the Spirit sweep through to rearrange all the carefully ordered furniture of our lives.

In this manner, we land ourselves in a situation where, because of our religious tradition, we find ourselves clinging tenaciously to beliefs that are *demonstrably false* and for which lack biblical backing. For example, in the twenty-first century, we know that sexual orientation is not a choice people make; we do not at some point of our lives *choose* which genders we will feel sexually attracted to. Science aside, we know this because if sexual orientation is a choice, it logically follows that *everyone's* sexual orientation must be a choice. I am heterosexual, but there was no moment in my life when I *chose* to find women more sexually attractive to me than men. That isn't a choice that I made; in the vernacular of our time, it is simply "how I am wired." My faith that God did not make a mistake when he made me and that he did not make a mistake when he made my neighbors is far stronger than my loyalty to my culture's prejudices.

When we cling to our cultural tradition and find it (inevitably) in conflict with Jesus's commandment to love one another, we then begin to propose bizarre and circumlocutive explanations for how we might reconcile the two. For example, we end up professing (without ever really considering its implications) that we will "hate the sin and love the sinner." It isn't possible to *love* one another—in the Greek sense of *agape*—while professing to "hate" a core facet of their identity and something they never chose, a part of who they are. We cannot do that *and* believe that God the Father loves us as we are, just the way he made us. These two positions are not compatible. Following Christ, I do not have the luxury of despising my neighbor, or anyone for whom Christ gave his life. The cruelty of homophobia has no place in the kingdom of heaven. We have a choice of what to *unforget*—what to hold nearest our heart, continually, like a love letter pressed to our skin. Like the Pharisees in the gospels, if I am continually unforgetting my *paradosis* (my cultural and religious tradition) and holding that near my heart, I will be continually forgetting the love of God. I will not be

265

holding Jesus's words and his story nearest to my heart, because something else is already there. I must be willing to reverse the priority of those two allegiances; I must be willing to forget my cultural prejudices and *unforget* the love of Christ.

The *agape* love that Jesus models for us is not a passive-aggressive love or a love that comes with prerequisites and conditions; it is a radical, transformative love. *Agape* is that word for love that for the early Christians also becomes the term for a feast where all believers gather to break bread together (Jude 1:12), regardless of who they are. (Though Jude does identify false teachers as "blemishes" on these feasts.) At an *agape*, anyone is welcome at your table, whether they are a tax collector, a prostitute, a leper, or a priest:

> Those who say, "I love God," and hate their brothers or sisters, are liars; for those who do not love a brother or sister whom they have seen, cannot love God whom they have not seen. The commandment we have from him is this: those who love God must love their brothers and sisters also.
>
> 1 JOHN 4:20-21

> This is my commandment, that you love one another as I have loved you. No one has greater love than this, to lay down one's life for one's friends. You are my friends if you do what I command you.
>
> JOHN 15:12-14

So there is our modern folly: even as the generation before us pulled one verse out of context, applying the Curse of Canaan to justify slavery (Genesis 9:25), our generation has done likewise to justify hatred toward our LGBTQ+ neighbors or to justify apathy while their rights are stripped from them. Not only is the pretext itself flimsy, but the writings of John teach us that the search for such a pretext and the long defense of it is itself the antithesis of practical Christianity. The *wrongness* of this is so blatant that we have now arrived at a culture where in some parts of America, if a man (whatever his sexual orientation) gave a funeral speech for his dear friend as lovingly as David did for Jonathan in the Bible—*I am distressed for you, my passionate beloved; you were sweet and sweet to my heart, and I loved you more than I would ever love a woman*—he would be at risk of being spat on, beaten, or lynched.

That is a telling measure of how *wrong* our culture has grown, how our lies about our siblings have festered inside and between us.

If you would like to explore this issue further, I recommend Matthew Vines' *God and the Gay Christian*. He makes an eloquent case for abandoning our appropriation of select verses to justify our cultural prejudices, offers an appeal to our compassion and love, and issues a call for us to act as the Body of Christ in our own time.

GENDER AND THE BIBLE

I would also suggest that our modern, binary concept of gender is not strictly biblical. The idea that men are men and women are women, that these are the only genders, and that these genders are both fixed in definition and mutually exclusive, is a Western idea more than it is a biblical one. The ancient Hebrew texts that have become our Old Testament predate it. This *ancientness* and non-Western-ness of our Bible is an important thing to unforget, because our contemporary attitudes about gender are costing lives.

As a Christian, I suspect that our contemporary attitudes about gender are also costing us the deeper relationship with God that is our inheritance and our birthright. After all, in the Bible, God is so often described in feminine terms and metaphors, as a hen sheltering her chicks and as a feminine presence, a *shekinah*, dwelling over the Mercy Seat on the Ark of the Covenant. Yet we have landed ourselves in a culture that is hostile to exploring *all* the characteristics of God that are in our Bible. We want only *some* of our God. We have become drunk on the idea of the masculinity of God, and so we miss out. We rarely allow ourselves to encounter the motherly God of Hosea 11:3-4 and Isaiah 66:13, the God who gives birth in Deuteronomy 32:18, the God who cries out in labor in Isaiah 42:14 or the God who nurses her babies in Isaiah 49:15, or the God that Clement of Alexandria, one of the early church fathers, spoke of when he said that Christians nurse at the breasts of God the Father. Though *father* is the metaphor for God that Jesus used most to express God's love for us, it is not the only metaphor he used; he spoke in Matthew 23:37 and Luke 13:34 of God the hen who gathers all her chicks beneath her wings.

So we miss out on a lot of God when we ascribe to God one essential gender. But there's also an even deeper disconnect here. The qualities our culture tends to describe as essential to one gender or another—the essential traits that we read as either "masculine" or "feminine"—don't match the qualities that are gendered and idealized in the biblical texts. For example, in the Bible, strong men were men who felt things strongly. They were men who wept. They wept in compassion, as Jesus did; in ecstasy, as David did; and in grief, as Job did. Women of esteem in many biblical texts are admired not (or not primarily) for beauty, softness, or what we would call "femininity," but for intelligence, bravery, business acumen, and generosity. Take a look at the qualities that Isaac's matchmaker sought in Rebekah in Genesis 24 or the qualities that are praised in Proverbs 31. In other passages, Dorcas is praised for her fearlessness, Shiprah and Puah for their unyielding commitment to justice and their fierce protection of the lives of the oppressed, Deborah for her boldness, Judith for her cunning, Esther for her courage, the Queen of Sheba for her desire for wisdom, Mary the sister of Martha for her love of learning, and so on.

In ancient Mediterranean cultures, gender was a spectrum or continuum rather than a pair of binary and opposing states. And gender was often more fluid for the ancients than it has been for the moderns. Men and women alike might be valorous, business-like, wise, foolish, or vicious. "A valorous woman, who can find?" the writer of Proverbs asks his son, counseling him to find a woman of valor to marry. One might as easily imagine a Hebrew mother asking her daughter, "A valorous man, who can find?" Valor is presented in Old Testament stories as rare and praiseworthy in all people. Abigail's valor wins David's respect, and Ruth's valor and kindness wins Boaz's.

Though the ancient Greeks began to describe various qualities as more natural to one gender or another, this was less common for the Hebrews. It is true that women were often treated as commodities in the ancient Middle East, but the commerce in women is described in ancient texts in biological terms (in which women are at times reduced to wombs that might be bartered, bought, or sold) and *not* in gendered terms (in which women are assumed to have essentially different personality, character, emotions, or intellect). That gender essentialism is much more modern.

Also, most Hebrew passages that describe human beings in sexually binary terms (such as the creation story in Genesis—"male and female, he created them") are descriptive rather than prescriptive. That is, they are more easily read as a description of what the Hebrew people *see* than as an prescription for what the Hebrew people should *be*. This is an important distinction.

It becomes especially so when we look to the earliest rabbinical commentaries on the Old Testament, the Mishna and the Talmud—texts in which early Jewish scholars fluent in Hebrew interpreted biblical passages, during the same centuries when early Christians were seeking a biblical canon. In these rabbinical writings, we find more than two genders described. In fact, we find six, and there are passages in the Mishna and the Talmud that refer to each: to *zachar* (male), *nekeivah* (female), *androgynos* (both; the word is a Hebrew borrowing from Greek), *tumtum* (indeterminate), *ay'lonit* (identified female at birth but developing 'male' characteristics at puberty), and *saris* (identified male at birth but developing 'female' characteristics at puberty).

If you would like to learn more about gender identity in Hebrew—in the language and culture that produced much of our Bible—see Charlotte Elisheva Fonrobert's article "Gender Identity in Halakhic Discourse," which can be found here:

https://jwa.org/encyclopedia/article/gender-identity-in-halakhic-discourse

Fonrobert acknowledges that some passages in the Mishna are intended to propose a gender duality as one basis for early Jewish law. But at the same time, Fonrobert notes the many examples in the text itself that deconstruct that duality. She concludes:

> The halakhic discourse on gender in its classic rabbinic form cannot be described as an ontological or teleological essentialism. It does not posit an essential masculinity or femininity, nor is there a fixed nature to men or women, ascribing a given ontological superiority to men on which their halakhic privilege is to be based.

CHARLOTTE ELISHEVA FONROBERT

Although the Mishna and the Talmud do attempt to identify distinct differences between men and women, the authors of these ancient texts were not as quick as we have been to fall into the trap of thinking that there are qualities and behaviors that are essentially and exclusively male and other qualities and behaviors that are essentially and exclusively female, because they could see evidence both in the biblical texts and in their own communities to suggest that this was not the case. They did not allow their assumptions about what and who people *should be* to conceal from them what and who people *are.* Rather than trying to force all people into either *zachar* or *nekeivah* regardless of the evidence of their own bodies and minds, the rabbis wanted to take people as they actually are. The references to *tumtum, ay'lonit,* and *saris* individuals bear witness to this. The writers of halakhic law wanted to answer real-world questions: Can an individual who is *saris* marry? (The answer the rabbis came up with: Yes, in marriages in which the goal of the marriage is not procreation. In halakhic law, there were other reasons one might marry, besides to produce children.) Unwilling to force reality to conform to cultural expectation, the rabbinical scholars proved more committed than we have been to loving God's creation in all of its diversity.

By contrast, our modern society is often more swiftly and immediately intolerant. Many of us would rather simply pretend that *androgynos, tumtum, ay'lonit,* and *saris* individuals do not exist. When we encounter them, we'd rather erase them by conforming them, in one manner or another, to one of the identities that is more acceptable to us. Those of us who fit cultural expectations about gender may be less aware of just how powerful and unreasoning (and unloving) this urge toward gender conformity in our culture is.

In many states in the U.S., we still undertake the practice of gender assignment surgery at birth; when a child is born intersex—with indeterminate, atypical, or hermaphroditic genitalia—some doctors perform surgery with or without parental consent to conform the child's body to the expectation of one sex or another. The child who is born not fitting into what we expect is *assigned* "male" or "female" on paper and then altered to more closely fit one of those two acceptable descriptions. This is still legal in the United States.

And although the Mishna, long centuries before modern medicine, responded to the lived reality of gender dysphoria (a state of distress when your gender identity and your physical body or assigned gender are in conflict)—we in our time often fail to acknowledge that reality that many of our youths experience after puberty. We are less aware than the writers of the Mishna were—this, despite our living in a religious culture that frequently claims to have inherited (or, more offensively, "superseded" or replaced) Hebrew tradition. Unlike our religious precursors, we have frequently refused to recognize in the faces of our transgender and intersex citizens *tzelem elohim*, the image of God. Instead, arrogantly, we insist that our neighbors conform to *our* image. And often the insistence is not only arrogant but violent. That may be the violence of surgical tools at birth, or abuse at puberty, or fists when a woman is followed into a bathroom and beaten up because someone thinks she looks a little too much like a man.

I wish I knew how to help my fellow Christians understand how sinful and idolatrous it is, to do this to our fellow children of God, to force them to look, to act, and to love *like us* (or like who we think we should be). As I haven't the words for it, I will quote an Anabaptist friend of mine who is often wiser than I. She says:

> Honestly I cannot understand why anyone thinks it is a sin to be transgender. Transgender is a biological condition. Something happened to alter the body and create an

273

"atypical" scenario. This happens all the time, in some form or another, to nearly every human alive. Sometimes the body can't produce eggs or sperm and the person is infertile. Sometimes the body can't produce insulin and the person is diabetic. Sometimes the brain can't regulate its chemical balance and the person has depression or anxiety. Often there are alterations—like intersex—that are not classified as illnesses, that are simply differences. Sometimes there is autism, or an alteration that allows the body to run very fast or to have an affinity with learning foreign languages, with being able to play music or sing very well. These are all "atypical" cases, some of which are culturally acceptable and some of which are not.

Our fear of the "atypical" is nothing new; we are not so distant yet from a recent era in which left-handed people were burned as witches or beaten until they wrote right-handedly instead. It is with a similar spirit that intersex and transgender citizens are marginalized and brutalized today.

I find a cruel irony in the historical fact that Christians, who were founded as a community of the atypical and the outcasts, have often become the ones defining the "type" and doing the outcasting—as that, to me, is the most unChristian activity imaginable.

You who are reading this, I just plead with you—let us stop. Let's stop. Are we wiser than God, that we know better than our Master how people should be made? Suppose the way God works seems foolish at first glance to us; are we not taught that the foolishness of God is wiser than the wisdom of men (1 Corinthians 1:25)? And we, who are called to love foolishly and recklessly, we who are to define ourselves by our foolish, reckless capacity for love—who are we to judge other adults for loving one another? God above, how arrogant we have become! Just who do we think we *are*?

11. SIN IS AN ACTIVITY, NOT A STATE OF BEING

WHAT THIS CHAPTER IS ABOUT

By regarding sin as a state of being rather than an action, we have arrived at a culture that is more concerned with whether someone is shamed or shameless than with whether they have committed a sin. The actual sins themselves lose all meaning for us, because what matters to us is whether someone is, or is not, a "sinner." This is a profound misunderstanding of the biblical concepts that we have translated using the word "sin," and it is an utterly destructive misunderstanding. In this chapter, we'll investigate it.

"We all fade like a leaf,
and our iniquities, like the wind, take us away."

ISAIAH

ONCE THERE WAS A KING who had previously been a shepherd and a singer. He liked to walk his roof at night under the stars and sing psalms, which were cries from his heart to the heart that beats in every atom of the universe, the heart of God. He was a lusty, sensual man who felt things very deeply—and a man whose great strength was that when he felt, he always acted before he had time to think or fear. If he saw an opportunity, he took it. If he saw a threat, he fought it. Only afterward would he get the shakes and kneel to pray—or write a new song until the shakes passed. In the heat of the moment, there was time for neither shakes nor hesitation.

He told the previous king this, when he was a boy. A giant was threatening their people, and not one soldier in the army was willing to meet the giant in single combat. David, who at that time had not achieved his full growth and still had peach fuzz on his cheeks, was visiting his brothers in the war-camp, bringing gifts from his father. Enraged after hearing the giant's taunting of his people and his God, David walked directly to the king's tent.

"I will fight your giant," he said.

The king—a tall man himself—gave David a hard, long look. "You? You're just a boy. That giant has been a warrior all his life. Kid, that giant will just step on you."

"You don't understand," David said with some heat. "I've fought 'giants' before. I watch my father's flocks while my brothers fight your battles. Once, a lion threatened my father's sheep. I didn't hesitate, I just grabbed up what was nearest at hand—a stick—and I *ran* at that lion with my stick and I took that lion down. Another time, there was a bear. And I grabbed up a rock and ran at that bear and I took that bear down. And I will take down that giant for you."

And he did. He strode down toward the river where the giant waited, scooping up stones for his sling on the way.

And with a prayer and with sheer unstoppable momentum, David sent one of those stones through the air and into the giant's brow. He didn't permit himself time to be afraid or second-guess until the thing was done.

And that is why we admire David, in this underdog-beats-Goliath story. David has boldness. He has pluck. He has charisma. The others in the story love him, too. The women of Israel compose songs in his praise:

> King Saul has killed his thousands,
> David his tens of thousands!

1 SAMUEL 18:7

Young men love David, too. Some travel across their land to join him later when he lives as an outlaw in the hills, so in love with him and loyal to him that they will perform extraordinary feats just to earn his praise or make him smile:

> David was then in the stronghold; and the garrison of the Philistines was then at Bethlehem. David said longingly, "O that someone would give me water to drink from the well of Bethlehem that is by the gate!" Then the Three broke through the camp of the Philistines, and drew water from the well of Bethlehem that was by the gate, and they brought it to David. But David would not drink of it; he poured it out to the Lord, and said, "My God forbid that I should do this. Can I drink the blood of these men? For at the risk of their lives they brought it."

1 CHRONICLES 11:16-19

Even Jonathan, the king's son, whose father wants David dead, adores him:

> For as he loved his own soul, he loved him.

1 SAMUEL 20:17

David, in his stories of giant-slaying, wilderness trial, and outlawry is like a Hebrew Robin Hood, a man of boldness and panache who adheres to his own code. A man who will admire a starlit sky, a lover's body, or a well-drawn-up battle formation with equal pleasure. A man of action, who dares much and hesitates little, a man who will one day be king.

But something happens to David on the way to the throne.

Grief happens—and bitterness. Jonathan and King Saul are slain in battle, and David is so distraught at the news that he has the messenger who brought it put to death. He spends years trying to locate, save, and shelter Jonathan's sons. The death of Jonathan—whether he was blood-brother, best friend, lover, or all of the above—haunts him.

Rage happens to him. Like the king who preceded him, David flies easily into a temper, more so as the years pass. A wealthy man slights him, and David marches on the man's farmland, intending to slaughter and loot all he finds; only the intervention of the farmer's wife, hurrying into his path with gifts and kind words, calms David and stalls the violence.

And *pride* happens to him. The boy everyone loved grows up to be the man who believes himself entitled to

279

everyone's love. Walking on the roof and singing to the stars, he sees on another rooftop a woman bathing, naked and attractive in the moonlight. Without hesitation or pause for thought, he has the woman brought to his bedchamber. Acting before he has time to fear or think had been his strength, but it is his terrible weakness, too. Perhaps he seduces Bathsheba, or rapes her; regardless of the details the writer doesn't share with us, it is impossible to ignore the entitlement and coercion implicit in a situation where a woman is dragged unexpectedly, in the middle of the night, into the bedchamber of her king and her husband's war-commander, her husband's boss.

It is a well-known story.

Bathsheba gets pregnant, and when David hears of it, he acts swiftly again, before permitting himself to think. He has her husband killed.

David's story is not a happy one; it is a story about sin, about actions having consequences. His coercion or assault on Bathsheba is the violent and unjust action that makes future injustices easier. And not just the murder of Bathsheba's husband, his friend—other crimes, too. He ignores an assault committed on his own daughter by his son, and his inaction precipitates a civil war and the slaughter of some branches of his family.

In the end, when David is old, the final consequences of his sins (for him) are visited upon him in the form of abject loneliness and a loss of agency. Loneliness, because though he is a king with many wives and concubines, none will consent to keep his old bones warm in his bed. He is unloved, and his staff search the kingdom for "a beautiful virgin" who will sleep in the king's bed, not because the king is still virile but to keep him from dying in his sleep of cold and abandonment:

> King David was old and advanced in years; and although they covered him with clothes, he could not get warm. So his servants said to him, "Let a young virgin be sought for my lord the king, and let her wait on the king, and be his attendant; let her lie in your bosom, so that my lord the king may be warm." So they searched for a beautiful girl throughout all the territory of Israel, and found Abishag the Shunammite, and brought her to the king. The girl was very beautiful. She became the king's attendant and served him, but the king did not know her sexually.
>
> 2 KINGS 1:1-4

And he suffers a loss of agency; on his deathbed he is maneuvered by Bathsheba into confirming her son as his heir. He acts out of his guilt for what he has done to her and his sense of unfulfilled obligation to her, to take some small part of this and make it right. Entering his bedchamber, Bathsheba finds him with Abishag there, and bows. You can almost read David's guilt as he says simply and without preamble, "What do you wish?"

And her response is just as direct: "My lord, you swore to me by God that my son would succeed you; but now another of your sons is claiming the throne."

"As I swore, so will I do this day," the king promises (2 Kings 1:16, 17, 30).

And when David is at the point of death, he speaks last with Bathsheba's son, Solomon, his appointed heir. "I am about to go the way of all flesh," he says, and with Solomon listening, David recounts tales of unpaid debts:

of revenge unsatisfied or injustices uncorrected (2 Kings 2:1-9). It is as if the old man is saying, "I have left a mess for you. You will need to clean it up, as I no longer can. Be strong, be brave, follow God, and be wiser and more faithful than I was."

David dies in power and privilege and with every comfort his treasury can afford, and he leaves behind him a fortified and strong country and a legacy of some of the world's greatest religious poetry. Yet he dies all but alone, with only Abishag beside him and with a son to instruct who likely has, at best, ambivalent feelings toward him. And his last words are to plead that his son will atone for his sins once he has gone, and do what he can to make things right.

WHAT IS "SIN"?

Let's talk about "sin." Sin is an English word we have used to translate various separate (though related) concepts in the Bible. There is *hata*, to miss the mark, as when a spearman or an archer fails to strike the target—and *hamartia*, which is the Greek version of *hata*. There is *avon*, which means both "injustice" and the penalty for it; we sometimes translate this in English as "iniquity," an older variation on the English word "inequity." And there is *pesha*, oathbreaking. These are all activities that we have at times translated as "sin": to miss the mark or fall short; to commit an injustice; to transgress a covenant or break a promise.

There are ways that we talk about "sin" in our culture, however, that are unbiblical. Part of the reason for this is that we frequently confuse "sin" and "abomination." Misunderstanding both, we talk of sin as if it is a state of being rather than an action. Because of this confusion, there are things that are never referred to in the Bible as sinful but that some modern readers do regard as sinful. These things may be *toebah* ("abomination," "forbidden," "taboo") for the tribe of Levi, but they are only *pesha* ("oathbreaking") if Levites do them. Eating shellfish is one example; anal sex is another. These are *toebah*, but they are not *hata* or *avon*. We confuse taboo and sin.

On the other hand, in our time we fail to label acts of injustice (*avon*) consistently as sinful acts. Different bus seats for "whites" and "coloreds" in the 1950s, and prohibiting homosexual couples in the 1990s under DOMA from marrying or visiting one another in critical care in the hospital are both examples of *avon* (injustice), yet it was rare to see white Christians in the 1950s or straight Christians in the 1990s speaking of these injustices as "sinful."

Due to our culture's disproportionate focus on venial or carnal sins and to the belief that chastity and promiscuity are rival and binary states of being rather than sets of actions and choices, we have come to regard the soul as also having two binary states: sinful and sinless. It's an unbiblical idea, and I am hard pressed to come up with a situation in which such an idea might prove useful rather than destructive. Ironically, this idea takes us to a place where sin becomes regarded not as an action that has consequences (as it is for Paul, when he writes, "the wages of sin are death") but instead a state in which people either exist or don't. In this way of thinking, certain categories of people can be described as "sinners"—or as "living" in sin," rather than simply *doing* sins. This in turn makes it easier to separate women into categories like *good women* and *whores*, or to speak of "hating the sin and loving the sinner," which is problematic both because this is usually used when referring to something that isn't *hata* in the Bible and because it is oxymoronic to speak of "loving the sinner." There are no "sinners" as a category of human being in New Testament ethics, except in the words of the Pharisees; there are just people—and people commit sins.

THE DIFFERENCE BETWEEN SHAME AND GUILT

Psalm 51 is attributed to David, and the occasion is the aftermath of his assault on Bathsheba and his murder of her husband. It is the most famous prayer of contrition in the Bible, and in it, all three Hebrew words for sin appear:

> For I know my transgressions (*pesha'ay*),
> and my sin (*hatta*) is ever before me.
>
> Hide your face from my sins (*hatta'ay*),
> and blot out all my iniquities (*awonotay*).
> Create in me a clean heart, O God,
> and put a new and right spirit within me.

PSALM 51:3, 9-10

David has committed *pesha* by breaking his vows to God. He has committed *hata* by falling short of what is expected of a king and of a man who serves God. And he has committed *avon* by his violent abuses of power, by taking advantage of Bathsheba and having her husband murdered. Now, in his guilt, he prays, yearning that his injustices might somehow be blotted out, made as if they had never occurred, and that he might be given a "clean heart" and a "new and right spirit." The prayer is not just *Take away what I have done and its consequences* but also *Help me do otherwise.*

When David prays Psalm 51, his concern is not with shame but with guilt. Shame is about what you *are*, and guilt is about what you have *done*. Shame is futile and defeating; guilt can be useful if it drives a change in action. Our disaster in modern America is that we have maintained a culture that is concerned with shame rather than guilt. Women are shamed for their sexuality, and LGBTQ+ people for their identity and their desires. Asexual people are shamed for their perceived lack of desire. Men who have incurred tremendous guilt are elected or appointed nonetheless to high office, where they perform feats of rhetoric to avoid any imputation not of guilt but of shame. If an official is accused of assault, some are more concerned with whether he will be shamed, his reputation besmeared, than with whether he might have guilt.

That is the world we occupy today: one in which sin is seen as a binary state of being that incurs shame, rather than an action that incurs guilt. Sin has become for us like a switch you flip. Either you are *sinful and shamed*, or you are *virtuous and shameless*. We don't speak of whether we are committing sins and injustices, but of whether we are sinners. In the same way, it is customary in our culture to believe that either you are or are not a racist; we don't speak of whether someone is doing racist things or supportive of or benefiting from systemic racism, but with whether they "are" a racist. The question is removed from the world of acts and consequences, and becomes one of whether someone is shamed or shameless. In such a culture, "sin" no longer has any real meaning, because your appearance and reputation become more important than your actions and their impact. "My sin is ever before me," David sings in his abiding horror at what he has done. But in our culture, apology is rare and genuine confession even rarer. Public apologies are written to save face, not to say, "I know my transgressions; my sin is ever before me."

In our time, it is undocumented students who speak of broken promises (*pesha*), and it is black athletes who call out injustices (*avon*), while some of our religious leaders are more concerned with what is *toebah* (taboo) and *bosheth* (shameful), than they are with what is *avon* (unjust), *pesha* (promise-breaking) or *hata* (falling short). Despite talking frequently *about* sin, they are more concerned with shame than they are with sin.

THE SIN OF CAIN

There is another way in which the Bible talks about sin, and which fascinates me. The Hebrew word *hata* first appears in the story of Cain and Abel:

> The Lord said to Cain, "Why are you angry, and why has your countenance fallen? If you do well, will you not be

accepted? And if you do not do well, sin (*hattah*) is lurking at the door; its desire is for you, but you must master it."

GENESIS 4:6-7

It is a fascinating passage, as *hata* gets imagined as a sort of creature who might inhabit your life just as you might inhabit a house. Here's a bit of rabbinical commentary on the passage:

> Once admitted, it makes itself master of the house. The primary punishment for sin is that it makes another sin more likely. We acquire the habit of behaving in a certain way.

ETZ HAYIM

Hata is lurking in wait; it craves and desires to inhabit you. You must master it, or it will master you. Cain's addictions are pride and anger. He feels entitled to God's favor (and to his parents', one might suppose if one were doing a psychoanalytical reading of the text), and this breeds anger at his brother, whose actions are "accepted" by God. The anger inhabits Cain, driving his actions, until he kills his brother. When confronted by God afterward, he cries out, "my *avon* is greater than I can bear!" (Genesis 4:13)—a phrase that we butcher in translation, because in Hebrew it means simultaneously "my unjust act is greater than I can bear," "my guilt is greater than I can bear," and "my punishment is greater than I can bear," but in translation we're forced to pick just one.

Sin has inhabited Cain; it has become his habit. It has wrecked his house. Paul defines sin in similar terms in the letter to the Romans:

287

I do not understand my own actions. For I do not do what I want, but I do the very thing I hate. Now if I do what I do not want, I agree that the law is good. But in fact it is no longer I that do it, but sin that dwells within me. For I know that nothing good dwells within me, that is, in my flesh. I can will what is right, but I cannot do it. For I do not do the good I want, but the evil I do not want is what I do. Now if I do what I do not want, it is no longer I that do it, but sin that dwells within me.

ROMANS 7:15-20

Note that sin is not a state of being here, but a set of actions that are repeated until they become a habit, until these actions inhabit and dwell inside you, to such an extent that this repeated activity messes with your identity: "it is no longer I." Sinning, we relinquish our self-control, and so our sins rob us of our agency. We become driven by our appetites and fears, and our acts of injustice or predation—our *iniquities*—sweep away our selfhood like a bitter wind:

"We all fade like a leaf,
and our iniquities, like the wind, take us away."

ISAIAH 64:6

This biblical idea of sin—and particularly injustice—as an addictive and self-annihilating set of behaviors is intriguing, and not talked about often enough, I think.

CANCER AND CURE

One of the most popular evangelical metaphors for sin is that it is a cancer (and Christ is the cure). But the way the Bible describes sin is not much like a cancer at all; it is more like either an addiction or a compulsive surrender of agency, a reduction of ourselves to merely animal instincts and appetites. However, taking a look at the likely biblical sources of the "cancer" metaphor can help us to examine more closely where our culture's attitudes toward wrongdoing have gone, well, *wrong*.

I think the idea of 'sin as cancer' is partly inspired by two passages in the New Testament. One is an analogy Jesus shared, and the other is a suggestion of Paul's in his first letter to the church in Corinth. In a sermon on resurrection, Paul writes,

> For since death came through a human being, the resurrection of the dead has also come through a human being; for as all die in Adam, so all will be made alive in Christ.

1 CORINTHIANS 15:21-22

In Pauline theology, Adam was the first man to sin—and the first man to die. This passage has led many theologians to posit that the predilection to sin is something that is passed from parent to child, down all the generations of humanity from Adam to the present, like a genetic trait. By the Middle Ages, this became codified as a doctrine of "original sin." But this is not the only possible or even the likeliest interpretation of Paul's remark about how death entered the world. As Danielle Shroyer reminds us eloquently in her book *Original Blessing*, nowhere in the Bible is the doctrine of "original sin" laid out. Paul's words don't imply a genetic predisposition for sin (Paul had never heard of genetics, and makes no mention of sin as something hereditary) but rather *repetition*: that ever since Adam's sin, no human being had proven able to stop from sinning, until Jesus did. Until Jesus, people may have tried not to sin, but they kept missing the mark—they kept "falling short of the glory of God." Sin, for Paul, is not a disease, but a repeated behavioral failing.

Even Augustine—the fourth-century theologian who is often credited with first formulating what we now know as the doctrine of original sin—apparently struggled with the question of what it would mean if sin were a state of being, what the implications for Christian ethics might be. Uncertain of the answer, he never completed that doctrine; he simply posited it as a possibility for other theologians, his peers, to respond to. Though the church of later centuries used Augustine's writings as the foundation for statements of doctrine and creed, Augustine himself wanted a discourse rather than a doctrine. He had a difficult question to ask and he hoped people would discuss it and wrestle with it.

The second passage that inspires the "cancer" metaphor is Jesus' retort to the Pharisees when they accuse him of dining with sinners:

> When Jesus heard this, he said to them, "Those who are well have no need of a physician, but those who are sick; I have come to call not the righteous but sinners."

MARK 2:17

Jesus' retort is barbed. Throughout the gospels, he is continually provoking the Pharisees to consider that they may not be as "healthy" as they think. In fact, they may prove to be "whitewashed tombs," appearing clean on the outside but filled with decay inside (Matthew 23:27). He challenges them to consider honestly whether they truly are the *dikaios*, the "righteous" or "just." Jesus has come to save *them*, too, remember. He is not suggesting a dichotomy of healthy saints versus sickly sinners; he is *challenging* such a dichotomy that already exists in this first-century society and that he finds problematic and destructive. Because there are not groups of people who sin and groups of people who don't, and there are not groups of people who are loved by God and groups of people who aren't. In Jesus's teaching, we all sin and we are all loved by God.

Sin in the Bible is neither a cancer nor a hereditary condition; it is more likely a habit, one that is hard to kick, impossible without help. And the New Testament's proposed "cure" is not a transactional proclamation of belief in the Son of the One God, but instead, *metanoia*: a day-by-day commitment to new behavior, achieved by loving and emulating Jesus and made possible by accepting God's love, grace, and forgiveness—that is, by accepting that God loves us whatever our failings. That he loves us so much that he sent his Son to show us the way and to bring us home at any cost. That God's reckless faith in *us* is great enough to move mountains. That he believes we can do this, that we can one day, as a community, live lovingly and without sin, and that he will do a good work in us and change us until we *can* do it.

12. OUR UNDERSTANDING OF IDOLATRY IS SIMPLISTIC

WHAT THIS CHAPTER IS ABOUT

The Bible proposes that you can tell God apart from idols because God feeds us, giving recklessly of himself so that *we* might be full. An idol, on the other hand, demands that *we* feed *it*, leaving us empty. In our time, today, we have many idols. We are often taught that "idolatry" means commitment to some other religion than our own. In fact, it is a Greek word for service given to an idol. Frequently we forget to look for the idols near at home, the idols we serve, the idols to which we sacrifice our time, our integrity, our relationships, and our humanity.

"Now in Babylon you will see gods made of silver and gold and wood, which people carry on their shoulders, and which cause the heathen to fear. So beware of becoming at all like the foreigners or of letting fear for these gods possess you when you see the multitude before and behind them worshipping them… They light more lamps for [these gods] than they do for themselves, though their gods can see none of them… [These gods] cannot restore sight to the blind; they cannot rescue one who is in distress. They cannot take pity on a widow or do good to an orphan… Why then must anyone think that they are gods, or call them gods?"

THE LETTER OF JEREMIAH (BARUCH 6)

IDOLATRY IS ALL ABOUT *HUNGER*. When you hear and respond to the whisper of the gods—seductive and sweet—who is feeding whom? Do you feed the gods, offering up a pleasing sacrifice, or does God feed *you*? Do you pour wine on the ground as a libation to the immortal ones, or does God pour living water into *your* mouth? Do you give up even your children in your service to the idol you worship—or does God give *his* Son as bread to fill your mouth and the mouths of your loved ones?

Because I wrote *The Zombie Bible*, reimagining biblical tales as episodes in humanity's long struggle against hunger and the hungry dead, I often get asked if Jesus was "a zombie." I reply that the zombie is a parody of Christ, an inverted mirror. Zombies rise from the dead and feed *on* you; Jesus rises and feeds *you*—his own body and blood, bread and wine. Our idols are like zombies. They are inverted mirrors of the divine. They are shaped like gods, but they have been hollowed out, emptied, and they are hungry. They will devour and consume you, as Chemosh Baal consumes children on the hill, in the Old Testament book of Jeremiah:

> The people have forsaken me, and have profaned this place by making offerings in it to other gods whom neither

they nor their ancestors nor the kings of Judah have known, and because they have filled this place with the blood of the innocent, and gone on building the high places of Baal to burn their children in the fire as burnt offerings to Baal, which I did not command or decree, nor did it enter my mind...

JEREMIAH 19:4-6

I have always found myself moved and troubled by Jeremiah's story. Like Cassandra of Troy, cursed by the god Apollo to see the future but be believed by no one, Jeremiah walks the streets of ancient Jerusalem before its fall, pleading with the economically well-to-do, the religiously content, and the politically complacent. *Look at our city*, he demands. *One child is sacrificed to the flames on the hill, while another starves in the street while just indoors, on the other side of a wall, an affluent woman with well-fed children bakes cakes to Astarte, and sings so that she will not hear the screams of another woman's child.*

I set Jeremiah's complaints against injustice and idolatry (which he saw as a root cause of injustice) to fiction in my novel *Death has Come up into Our Windows*. I wanted to try and put that prophet's heart and his words of fire on the page for a modern reader. Here is a quick scene from it:

His unease with seductive, heathen deities was hot in his chest. Gazing at the smoke on the hill's summit, Yirmiyahu almost thought he could hear, faint in the day's heat, the calling of those hungry gods and goddesses whom his People had not brought with them out of the desert long ago but had found waiting for them in this land. Deities who spread their arms wide and moaned: *Come to me, I will give you wealth or security or love, or what you desire, only feed me, feed me. I am so hungry; don't you want to feed me?*

Sometimes the cries of those other gods, who had established no abiding Covenant with the People, rose from a faint moan on the hill to a shriek of urgent, demanding need; at those times he would look away from the summit, shivering even in the day heat as the merchants chattered and argued around him. And all the while, Yirmiyahu's God murmured from behind the veil in her Temple, *I am here. If you want me, you must be faithful to me, and you must nourish my children. You must work hard to provide for them. Then I will let you take me in your arms and I will delight you and nourish you.* A God of Covenant for a People of the Covenant, a divine spouse and not only a divine lover. That is how the *navi* saw it.

It would be an easy thing, perhaps, to keep his eyes from straying to that hill. To not ask what sacrifices Chemosh received up there. Yet Yirmiyahu couldn't stop looking. The sight of that haze gnawed at him. Of all the People's lovers, he *feared* Chemosh. Chemosh was a god apart. Astarte's love was playful and vitalizing; Baal's was stern and demanding; Dagon's was tempestuous, overwhelming, and fickle as the sea in which he swam with his fish; but Chemosh—that was a god who would beat his lovers and batter them. And Chemosh would only grin darkly in the knowledge that such treatment would just convince his worshippers all the more of his power and his strength to provide for them, keep them, and shield them: that the more he beat his worshippers, the more they would fall to the earth, kiss his feet, and beg for the privilege of feeding him.

DEATH HAS COME UP INTO OUR WINDOWS

Later in the novel, Yirmiyahu (Jeremiah) recalls the story of the *akedah*, the Binding of Isaac:

Long ago his own ancestors had sacrificed their firstborn at altars, even as other peoples in the farther parts of the land still did. But one of his People's oldest stories told of the Akedah, the binding of the firstborn, when God had placed her hand at Abraham's chest and stopped him from drawing his knife across his son's throat. When Yirmiyahu had been a small boy, his father had told the tale with horror and panache, and young Yirmiyahu had shivered to think of the upraised hand, the flash of the knife, the cry of the boy.

Abraham had taught this to all his children, and they to their children: We do not feed God, God feeds us. God is sufficient to feed herself and us.

DEATH HAS COME UP INTO OUR WINDOWS

God feeds *us*. In the final chapter of the last canonical gospel to be written, the Gospel of John, Jesus meets his disciples after his Resurrection on the shores of the sea of Galilee. Together, they cook fish over a small fire. "Simon," he asks one of his disciples, "do you love me?"

"You know I do, master," Simon replies.

"Feed my lambs," Jesus says.

And a little while later, he asks again, "Simon Peter, do you love me?"

"I do!"

"Feed my sheep."

And again a third time. Because Simon had earlier denied his responsibilities to Jesus, publicly, three times, he must now accept that mantle of responsibility, of discipleship, of love three times. Also, the message is important enough to repeat. To do the work of God in the world is to feed his children.

Idols—which sometimes look *like* God to us—require that we feed our children to *them*. For Jeremiah thousands of years ago, an idol looked like a statue of Chemosh above a flaming pit, where a living sacrifice could be rolled into the flames. Today's idols are not so blatant, nor are they named Chemosh. Yet still they drive us to feed and feed and *feed* them until we have nothing left to give and we are rendered as empty as they. We becomes zombies of ourselves, shambling through the motions of our lives, nourishing no one—neither ourselves nor others.

In the book of Baruch (which is excluded from many American Protestant Bibles but canonical in most other Bibles), there is a letter from Jeremiah to those of his people who have been taken from their fallen city and led away captive to Babylon. In Babylon, Jeremiah warns the exiles, the false gods provide for no orphans and comfort no widows, and what provision and comfort the people themselves might give, they devote to the gods instead. The people there "light more lamps for these gods than they do for themselves."

That is the nature of idolatry. In pouring oneself into feeding the appetite of a false god, one finds it easier over time to neglect every other commitment—to God and to each other. The two "greatest commandments" in the Bible are to love God and to love one another. Idolatry is the breaking of both. That is why false gods, for the ancient Hebrews, are to be avoided. They destroy community.

Today, in our time, who are *our* false, seductive gods?

We may not *call* them gods—yet we worship them, revere them, *feed* them, and define our identities *by* them.

THE GODS OF ROME AND THE GODS OF AMERICA

Babylon is far in our past. Rome is nearer, because in the West we have imitated and improved upon many of Rome's institutions, its systems of law and government, its cherished values, and its attitudes toward religion. Consider the gods of Rome.

For the Romans, gods were not supernatural beings with their own lives and affairs, as they were for the Greeks. Roman deities were impersonal forces that could be manipulated by a precise combination of ritual acts and ritual recitation. These gods were sometimes personified for the sake of poetry or entertainment, but Rome's gods were always more forces than people—and for that very reason, they were followed with more desperation and discipline than you see in other ancient cultures. A Roman ritual had to be performed *exactly* right. One mistake, and you had to start over from the beginning. In her *Masters of Rome* series, Colleen McCullough tells a story about a Roman dictator (Lucius Cornelius Sulla) who hated his senatorial colleagues so passionately that he appointed a pontifex maximus (high priest) with a stutter.

The gods that mattered in day to day life included Fama or *fame*; Fortuna or *fortune and a chance at prosperity*; Cupid or *lucky dating*; and Janus, the god who oversaw doorways and opportunities. And beneath all of these, more important than any of them, was Family Tradition, embodied by the *di parentes*, the divine ancestors of your family line. Before leaving for work, an ancient Roman honored the god Janus at the door. In a moment of crisis, an ancient Roman hurried to the tombs of his fathers (typically a mausoleum adjacent to the home, for an upper-class Roman) with an offering and a request for their blessing and advice.

Today, our understanding of idolatry has become so simplistic that those of us who are Christian and who say we care about it have often stopped recognizing our own idolatry. Idolatry does not only occur in a temple; nor are all temples called by that name. America today has a pantheon of impersonal "gods" in a similar manner to Rome. Hard Work promises you prosperity in return for loyal service. Fame promises you value and immortality (at least for a few minutes or a day). Within the church, we have even made a god out of Tradition, and we recite his praises in many sermons—just *follow all the rules, be pure, live by this moral standard, follow this specific political agenda*—and you will be fully justified. The pearly gates will swing wide for you. And let's not even talk about the idolatrous relationship we have with our national flag, to which we give an actual, literal pledge of allegiance—and honoring which, some insist, is more important than preserving the lives of our African American citizens. We often attach the name of Jesus or the name "God" to these false gods that we worship, as though Prosperity and Patriotism are wearing Jesus costumes. And people sacrifice human lives to them—frequently the most vulnerable among us, even as in the days of old, the days of Moab and the god Chemosh.

Most gods are not evil in of themselves—hard work, tradition, patriotism, these are not bad things—but they become evil *when* and *because* we make them gods: driving forces in our lives to which we commit and sacrifice; ideals enshrined and celebrated in our media; and symbols to which we sacrifice our relationships and in whose name we trample the needs of other people. When we make these things into false gods, when we put our service to one of these things first, before all else, when we allow one of these things to define our identity—that is the essence of *eidololatria* (idolatry), "service to an idol." It is that kind of idolatry that Jesus warns of when he teaches, "You cannot serve both God and Wealth" (Matthew 6:21). And it is this kind of *eidololatria* that Paul tells first-century Christians to *flee*—and not just flee, but flee vigorously. "*Pheugete!*" he urges them (1 Cor 10:14). We get our English word "fugitive" from that verb, by way of the Latin *fugere*. Rather than serve these idols one moment more, Paul urges, go on the run from them!

When we serve an idol, we drink from the cup of *lethe*. We forget who we are, what we have been promised, and who we have promised to be. Rather than imitating the life of Christ, we rely on the idol to determine our dreams and desires and to govern our identity and our labor. Serving the idol, we accept a lie about who we are and what gives us value. Having accepted the lie, having forgotten what is true, we stop unforgetting other things, too—like loving others. Serving money and avarice, we might come to consider everything and everyone in our lives as possessions, and people become mere objects in an economy that we are always trying to game; we deny their autonomy, their agency, their ownership of their bodies because they become *things* that we must *have*. Serving fame, people become opposition or means to an end, tools to use and discard. Serving the American Way, abstract symbols and slogans and flags command our loyalty more than the lives of our fellow Americans. Like the people of Babylon who lit more lamps for their gods than for themselves, we light lamps about our monuments while some of our people starve and shiver in the dark.

This is why a "lie" was considered such a terrible thing among first-century Christians: to accept a lie about who we are is to put on chains. Idolatry is a form of slavery in which we celebrate our slavery even as we hate it. Many early church martyrs gave up their lives rather than tell a lie about who they were, rather than publicly *forget* who they were and the story they were called as witnesses to. In fact *martyros* is just the Greek word for "witness": the one who tells the story, who "bears witness" to how God has changed their life and the life of their community. These people felt so powerfully that there was a "more excellent way" to live—a way of love—that they refused to forget it. They refused to accept or speak any lie in replacement of it. They had seen what *eidololatria* does to a community, how it divides a community into the haves and the have-nots, the eaters and the eaten, and they would not be a part of it; they would rather burn.

13. THE TRAP OF "SUBMISSION" TO AUTHORITY

WHAT THIS CHAPTER IS ABOUT

Verses from the Bible have been used and abused to convince Christians to stand idly by while atrocities are permitted—during the Spanish Inquisition, in the Third Reich, and on many occasions right here at home. Yet the early Christians, and many since, were disobedient to authorities—and died for it. It's time to unforget our heritage.

"We must obey God rather than men."

SIMON PETER

"WE MUST OBEY GOD rather than men," Simon Peter tells the religious authorities (Acts 5:29). Because I have recently heard my fellow Christians speaking of the need to *submit to authority*—and often in an explicitly political context—I wish to take a moment to unforget the stories of our family in Christ who came before us. I want us to unforget the disobedient ones, the defiant ones, the gentle ones, those who spoke truth to power and suffered for it, those who by their example show us the way. Not only Peter imprisoned by religious authorities for a long dark night before an angel broke his chains, but so many others over the long centuries: like Paul and Silas, who sang hymns from their cell in Philippi; like William Tyndale, who was burned at the stake by religious authorities with the Bible he had dared to translate into English hung about his neck; like Dietrich Bonhoeffer, who died in a Nazi concentration camp, and like Corrie ten Boom, who survived one, and like all the many people in the Third Reich who hid Jewish families behind their walls or in their cellars; like Martin Luther King, Jr., writing to his fellow ministers from Birmingham Jail; like so many unnamed Christians, unwilling to recant their faith, who died as human torches, as lamps to light the Emperor Nero Claudius Caesar Augustus Germanicus's private gardens; like Catherine of Siena, who in 1374 insisted on remaining in her hometown to nurse those struck down by the plague, by day and by night, no more obedient to the demands of sleep than she had been to authorities who wished to evacuate the healthy; like the unnumbered thousands of women in the Roman Empire who defied the *lex Julia*, remained unmarried, and led and served their communities as "holy virgins," and who sometimes were tortured or died for that choice; like Martin Luther, who nailed nearly a hundred disagreements to a church door; like Harriet Tubman, who smuggled fugitive slaves over the underground railroad to Canada; like the many Christian suffragettes who voted illegally in the 1920s, stating boldly that God had made them in her image just as God made men in his, that they possessed no less equal and inalienable rights in our Republic than men did; like

Gladys Aylward, a British maid who insisted on traveling alone, unauthorized, as a missionary to China, and who later saved the lives of one hundred orphaned children during World War II, leading the children over the mountains to safety while she was wounded; and like my own friend K, who was jailed and abused in ways that would have broken me, had it *been* me. K is a white man who took action against apartheid in South Africa and became branded by white authorities as a "race traitor."

All these people chose to "obey God rather than men." They *submitted*—that is, they "were sent out on a mission," which is the Latin sense of that word—but they did not "submit" *to earthly authorities*. In the stories the earliest Christians told of him, Jesus himself was relentlessly disobedient to the religious regulations of the Pharisees as well as to the cultural expectations and codes of his time— and he proved unwilling to submit to that one final and allegedly irrefutable earthly authority, which is death itself. The Resurrection was the ultimate act of civil disobedience to which early Christians looked for their example and their hope. To live in Christ and die to one's life in the world—that was what Paul taught. To take up the cross like a criminal and follow him—that was what Jesus taught. And to obey God rather than men—that was what Peter taught. And that is what many early Christians tried to live. Sometimes, to be *paracletes* for each other, standing for and with each other, we have to raise a ruckus.

If we do not—if we instead permit ourselves to forget that in many times and in many places our very religion itself has been illegal or that following Christ often requires going "out on a limb" for others, if we can forget that so thoroughly that we then find ourselves counseling each other to "submit to authority"—then we will have fallen short of the example and expectation of our founders, our ancestors and siblings in the faith. In Greek, we will have sinned. (Remember that "sin" in Greek is *hamartia*, "falling short").

This forgetting is what Mordecai accuses Hadassah of, in the book of Esther. Hadassah wears Persian clothes and has a Persian name (Esther) and is wedded to the Persian king. Materially, she is comfortable and safe. She is at risk of forgetting that she is a Jew. When Mordecai asks her to plead on behalf of the Jews to the king her husband—though to do so will mean breaking Persian law and might well mean her own death—he pleads with her to remember who she is:

> Do not think that in the king's palace you will escape any more than all the other Jews, if you keep silence at such a time as this ... Who knows? Perhaps you have come to royal dignity for just such a time as this."
>
> ESTHER 4:14

What will Hadassah do? Will she remain comfortably obedient to the authority that governs both her nation and her household? Or will she speak up for her people? Will she risk causing a ruckus?

She chooses the second. "If I perish, I perish," she says.

ROMANS 13

While en route to protest the separation of children from asylum-seeking parents at the US border in 2018, an activist friend wrote me a note asking me what I thought of the US attorney general's recent remarks to the press. In those remarks, the attorney general quoted Romans 13 to insist on respect for authorities, specifically in regard to letting our elected officials do as they please with the children of immigrants seeking asylum. I told my friend I could easily give an earful on that topic. Interpretations of the opening verses of Romans 13 are controversial, and there is a *lot* written on them.

It is troubling to me when I hear federal officials mouthing biblical verses to support government policies, whether those policies be kind or cruel. The United States is not and I hope to God will never be a theocracy. Many of our founders fought and bled and died for the right to live in a country that would *not* be governed according to one faction's particular interpretation of any religious text. I mean that: our predecessors fled Europe, fought wars, and *died* for this. So when our federal government starts quoting Scripture to dispel dissent, I get angry. This is still the United States of America, not the Republic of Gilead (the repressive government in Margaret Atwood's novel *A Handmaid's Tale*), and our people bled to keep it so; I wish more of citizens would remember it.

We are seeing a crisis in many American churches. Some voices in the church urge us to take a stand in defense of our neighbors or against actions and policies that are incompatible with Christ, such as the forcible separation of asylum-seeking families on our border. Other voices urge us to fulfill our Christian duties by tendering both "respect" and "submission" to church and state authorities. These voices frequently cite Romans 13:1-5 as their bulwark against protest or civil disobedience.

These five verses are so often taken by themselves as if they're a standalone manifesto and are then deployed to silence dissent—as if Paul is advocating *against* civil disobedience rather than advocating *for* caution. But if you read the rest of the letter—and, for that matter, the account of Paul's life in Acts—you may realize that the idea of Paul preaching against civil disobedience is ridiculous. Paul is literally under house arrest for civil disobedience while writing some of his letters. Again and again in the book of Acts, Paul ends up arrested by the authorities for choosing civil disobedience when disobedience is necessary. I want to take a quick look at Romans 13 together, making three points—one about Paul's context, one about his argument, and one about the type of authority he is referring to. I think this will be useful; the way verses from Romans 13 get ripped out of context is symptomatic of the way we too often try to jam the square peg of a biblical passage into the round hole of our contemporary tradition or our political or cultural ideologies.

1. Paul's Context

First, remember that chapter and verse numbers in our Bibles are arbitrary—an innovation from a few centuries back. And because the ancient manuscripts of the New Testament predate the invention of modern punctuation, punctuating a Koine Greek sentence is itself often an interpretive choice. If you want to read the opening verses of Romans 13 seriously, you need to read the section before it and the section after it, rather than just pluck part of a Greek text out and treat it like a standalone manifesto.

It's embedded in the middle of an argument about how the first-century Roman church might conduct itself while beset with both internal division and oppression from external authorities. Many scholars believe that the passage is a response to a dispute in the early church over how to handle taxation under Nero. You can read a quick paraphrase of some of the different takes on the historical and rhetorical context here:

www.directionjournal.org/issues/gen/art_849_.html

This article is not at all comprehensive but it will give a starting point and it comes with a list of references.

The short-short version is that some in the early Roman church were calling for the radical act of refusing to pay taxes—an issue that Paul addresses directly in Romans 13:6-7. In context, Paul is cautioning the church to pay its taxes and not provoke an oppressive government. Such provocation will lead to punishment (*krima*) from that government. "Those who resist will incur judgment" (13:2), because the agents of that government "bear a sword" (13:5). Readers of the King James Bible may get the wrong idea here and think that *God* will punish those who resist governing authorities, because the KJV translates *krima* as "damnation," and in today's vernacular we read "damnation" as a moral condemnation (with a presumed verdict of eternal hellfire); we have forgotten the original meaning of the word, which was simply a judgment delivered (*deemed* or *damned*) in court. Paul is counseling the Roman church to avoid a situation where their members (some of whom lack the protections of

Roman citizenship, but all of whom are required by Roman law to pay their taxes) are hauled into the courts for refusing to pay taxes and are then fined, enslaved, or otherwise penalized.

This is important.

There is no evidence that the first five verses of Romans 13 were intended by their author to be read as a universal creed for unconditional obedience to state authorities. Paul is responding in a personal letter to a specific and local issue about taxation in Rome. He is advocating not stirring things up by withholding taxes—an act of rebellion that he judges to be without efficacy or purpose. In this, he echoes (and is likely guided by) Jesus' answer to the Pharisees, when those religious authorities asked the rabbi whether to pay taxes to Rome: "Render to Caesar what is Caesar's, and to God what is God's."

2. Paul's Argument

Second, just because Paul is saying in Romans 13 that refusing to pay taxes to Caesar is not a battle worth picking does not mean he believes *no* battles are worth picking.

Consider the verses that follow later in that chapter— the ones the US attorney general didn't bother to quote, even though they provide Paul's summation of his case:

> "Owe no one anything, except to love one another; for the one who loves another has fulfilled the law ... Love does no wrong to a neighbor; therefore, love is the fulfilling of the law."

ROMANS 13:8, 10

Paul is making the argument for obeying taxation law within the larger context of making sure nothing is obstructing the church from its principal work, which is loving one another. Getting in a financial dispute with the Emperor and getting members of your community fined, enslaved (as *poenae servae*, penal slaves), or killed would definitely get in the way of that. Perhaps a bit wryly, Paul contends that the only other real impact that refusing to pay taxes is likely to have is that the tax collectors won't get paid and won't have food on the table (Romans 13: 6-7). Whatever the good *intent* of those Christians who want to refuse to pay taxes as a form of resistance, the *impact* will be that they'll get tried and convicted, and their neighbors who are tasked with the collection of taxes will go hungry. "Love does no wrong to a neighbor," Paul urges. If refusing to pay taxes to Nero is a fruitless resistance that will only result in collateral damage toward one's neighbors, then Paul suggests that it is not the most effective way to love one's neighbors.

The obvious corollary to this is that there may be other cases where loving one's neighbor *requires* civil disobedience. When loving one's neighbor and doing no wrong to them requires that you disobey or protest unjust laws, Paul is very much in support of doing so. Loving each other comes *first*. In that, the law of God is fulfilled (Romans 13:10).

The letters in the New Testament are frequently unequivocal in advising first-century churches to shelter the orphan, the widow, and the immigrant. In fact, the apostle James writes that it is in such action that "clean and untainted religion" consists (James 1:27). So for officials in our time to take a fragment of Paul's argument out of context and insist that to us it means, "Shut up and let your government put children in concentration camps"—when the early church was *specifically* tasked with providing sanctuary and refuge for immigrants and orphans—is abhorrent. That's not Paul. That's not Peter either (*he* told the powers that be that we who follow Christ "must obey God rather than man"). And that's definitely not Jesus.

For a Christian, the first directive is always to love one another as selflessly as God loves us, and *that* is the criterion that must drive our decisions to obey or disobey earthly authorities. That is why Dietrich Bonhoeffer cited Paul and Peter in his resistance to Hitler's exportation of the Jews to camps in Poland, and why Martin Luther King, Jr. quoted Paul in support of civil disobedience in his *Letter from Birmingham Jail.* That's an apt reference here, because this warping of a few lines of text to mean the exact *opposite* of the writer's apparent argument is not just something that happens to Paul. We see the same move when federal officials, pastors, or pundits quote the "I Have a Dream Speech" to suggest that Martin Luther King, Jr.—of all people!—would have urged today's citizens not to protest in the street or march on the capital. A moment's reflection on our history has to reveal how absurd that is, since Martin Luther King, Jr. marched on the capital himself. In the same way, it is absurd to adopt the words of Paul—a man frequently arrested and jailed for civil disobedience—to counsel today's Christians against civil disobedience while their government is engaged in atrocities against our neighbors.

This kind of rhetorical gymnastics to justify blind obedience to a federal government that is carrying out atrocities is worthier of the Third Reich than of the nation that we have frequently insisted the United States is or could become. And it is insulting to our intelligence, our conscience, and our shared humanity.

3. The Type of Authority Paul is Referring To

The Greek word translated "authorities" in Roman 13 is *exousia*, which is literally "powers"—those who have ability and force. The *exousia* refer to the oppressive leaders of Rome: Nero and those appointed by Nero. Now, Paul may believe that Nero was "deployed" (*tasso*) in his position by an act of God, but that is manifestly not the case with the elected officials of the United States of America. Our president and our attorney general were not appointed by prophets of God or by visible acts of God. Rather, our president was elected by ourselves and our representatives (the Electoral College), and the attorney general was nominated by our elected president and confirmed by our elected Congress. These officials are therefore answerable to us in a way that Nero was not answerable to the first-century Christians in Rome.

When our attorney general quotes Romans 13, he is suggesting that we should obey our elected officials in the same way and for the same reasons that we would obey an emperor or dictator—the same way that we would obey the *exousia*, those who rule by force. That is an appalling thought. "Don't resist" means something very different when the Empire (or at the federal official) is saying it than when the radical (Paul) is saying it.

In Chapter 9, I warned against the risk of naïve adherence to traditional interpretations and doctrines endorsed by a modern generations of religious authorities. I cautioned that in clinging too tightly to the teachings of men we might lose sight of the heart of God, that a slavish fidelity to the prejudices and traditions of our culture might cause us to miss the call to the adventure, to the adventure of encountering the Word of God.

An additional, similar risk is that the more we train ourselves to naïvely follow religious authorities, the more we are training ourselves to naïvely follow *all* temporal authorities. Christianity began as a religion of people practicing civil disobedience, but today some Christians interpret their duties to Christ as including obedience to the state. And that in turn leads us to the risk of reading and interpreting our Bible in the ways that government authorities tell us to. History has taught us often how dangerous that is.

WHEN RELENTLESS LOVE MEANS RELENTLESS DISOBEDIENCE

I confess that a version of my religion that can permit the cries of children penned at the border and make excuses for it is not a religion I desire any part of. That is Christianity violated, Christianity with its heart torn out of its body. That is a Christianity with no Christ in it. Merely a corpse of my religion, sent shambling like a zombie across our contentious political landscape. For myself, I desire no religion that has no Christ in it. It is Christ, not religion, that brought me here—his story, his words, his sacrifice, his *love*. Excise that living being from this religion, and all you have left is an emptied and ruinous house, a desecrated structure with no heat in the winter and no roof to provide shade in the August heat. A house we crouch in to shiver or sweat and die. Christ, by his example—which in the gospel he lived even to the point of death on the cross, even to the point of shattering the law of mortality and striding out of the tomb into the morning air—teaches us that relentless love can require relentless disobedience.

When an authority figure beings Bible-quoting in order to quell dissent or dissuade action, that is a purely a distraction and silencing tactic. It is meant to get citizens who are practicing Christians to be complacent or slow to act. It is an abuser's tactic. But this is not a time to be slow in acting. This is a time when children are being concentrated in camps within our borders, and it is our duty to stop it. It is our duty as citizens to whom our elected representatives answer. For Christians, it is our duty as imitators of Christ and lovers of our neighbors. It is our duty as human beings.

There are a lot of gray areas in religion, politics, and human action. This isn't one.

For the love of God, the love of your neighbor, and the love of your country—if you happen to be reading this book in the United States prior to the resolution of our border crisis, if asylum seekers are still being separated from their children and detained indefinitely on our border in defiance of international human rights conventions, please do not let your religious commitment be blind obedience to obeying the *exousia*. Instead, let your commitment be fearless love. We are the sanctuary-givers. It's why we *have* "sanctuaries" in our churches. So I plead with you: give sanctuary. Do all you can. Get informed about the situation, and be *loud* until our federal authorities cease this inhumane, cruel, and ungodly practice of kidnapping children from asylum-seeking parents. Unforget who walked in Jesus's footsteps before us, and what examples those dissidents who loved Christ have provided us.

14. WHAT "TURNING THE OTHER CHEEK" REALLY MEANS

WHAT THIS CHAPTER IS ABOUT

Continuing our discussion of civil disobedience from the previous chapter, I want to talk a moment about "turning the other cheek," a concept from the Sermon on the Mount that has puzzled many modern readers. In the first century, it was likely advice on nonviolent resistance and loving insistence on the shared humanity of oppressed and oppressor. The context is worth knowing.

"You have heard that it was said, 'An eye for an eye and a tooth for a tooth.' But I say to you, Do not resist an evildoer. But if anyone strikes you on the right cheek, turn the other also; and if anyone wants to sue you and take your coat, give your cloak as well; and if anyone forces you to go one mile, go also the second mile ... You have heard that it was said, 'You shall love your neighbor and hate your enemy.' But I say to you, Love your enemies and pray for those who persecute you, so that you may be children of your Father in heaven; for he makes his sun rise on the evil and on the good, and sends rain on the righteous and on the unrighteous."

JESUS

THIS IS HOW IT WORKS. In first-century Palestine, a Roman citizen could strike a Jew across the face because Romans regarded non-Romans as categorically inferior. They would therefore backhand, as they would a slave. To strike with your open palm would be to acknowledge the other as an equal. "Turning the other cheek" toward the Roman provided a means of nonviolent resistance: to force the oppressor into a choice of either not striking a second time or striking open-handed, in a way that acknowledges the other as an equal, as one who might call you to account for the violence or be justified in striking back. It is similar in concept to Gandhi's *ahimsa* (which it also partially informed); *ahimsa* is about maneuvering the oppressor into a situation in which they have to meet you eye to eye and acknowledge your shared humanity.

So, too, with the other examples Jesus gives in the Sermon on the Mount. The law allowed a Roman citizen to commandeer a non-citizen's labor, but limited the duration of that labor. For example, a Roman could require a first-century Jew to carry their gear for them for one Roman mile. "Go also a second mile," Jesus advises. This would engineer a situation in which the oppressed individual who has already carried the Roman's gear *goes on* carrying it while the Roman pleads, "Wait! Wait! Give that back, please!" because the Roman has no desire to be fined under his own law for *exceeding* the privileges the law gives him.

"You have heard that it was said, 'An eye for an eye and a tooth for a tooth' ... but I say to you, Love your enemies and pray for those who persecute you," Jesus teaches. The context is that both Jesus and his original listeners are members of an oppressed nation whose people are divided on whether to pursue armed revolt or appeasement. Jesus offers a third path: rather than slaughtering Romans in the back alleys (like the *sicarii*, of whom Judas Iscariot is one) or forming an armed rebellion (like Simon the Zealot pleads with him to do), and rather than appeasing the Romans (the course favored by the majority of the priesthood), instead, engage in activities that provoke the Romans to recognize you as fellow human beings, activities that force their retreat out of shame. And pray for your persecutors—that in seeing *your* humanity, they will recover their own. It was this teaching that Gandhi found compelling and that Martin Luther King, Jr. adopted as a basis for his own practice of nonviolent action.

"Turning the other cheek" isn't *meekness* as we understand it. Even meekness in the Sermon on the Mount isn't meekness. The Greek word used in "Blessed are the meek" is *hoi praeis*, which means "the trained" or "the domesticated" It is the word used in the ancient world for a magnificent war horse or for an expertly trained hound. *Praeia* is used to describe an animal that has been trained to a particular purpose and is able to follow that purpose unwaveringly, choosing fidelity to that purpose over surrender to its fears or satisfaction of its appetites. Such concepts of meekness (*praeia*) and self-restraint (*egkrateia*) recur throughout Jesus's Sermon on the Mount. Do you remember how, in Chapter 2, we considered the passage in which Jesus advises young men that it is their job to exercise self-control rather than lust after or stalk a woman? Giving in to one's erotic hunger may not be a good way to love other human beings, Jesus warns. "Turning the other cheek" is another example of Jesus talking about restraint—this time, in the context of not lashing out violently and unthinkingly at one who is humiliating or wounding you. Again, what is at issue is how to love other human beings, how to recognize, communicate, and act on our shared humanity. If we remain enslaved to our appetites, then our appetites, unchecked, might provoke us to behave as predators toward others, like the man lusting after a woman who does not welcome his attention. And if we remain enslaved to our *fears*, then our fears, unchecked, might provoke us to behave as prey toward others. Responding like prey to another's injustice or violence, we either break or we retaliate in kind. In either case, we risk our own humanity.

Paul strikes a similar note in his letter to the church of the Galatians:

> For freedom Christ has set us free ... Stand firm, therefore, and do not submit again to a yoke of slavery. the fruit of the Spirit is love, joy, peace, patience, kindness, generosity, faithfulness, gentleness, and self-control. There is no law against such things. And those who belong to Christ Jesus have crucified the flesh with its passions and desires. If we live by the Spirit, let us also be guided by the Spirit.

GALATIANS 5:1, 22-25

Freed from our appetites and fears and guided by the Spirit in the practice of love and self-control, we choose actions that are not motivated by fear or hate, but instead by the desire to relate to others as fellow human beings.

And we pray for those others, that they will recover their humanity and recognize ours. Rather than either cower or strike back, we face the man who struck us, and we say, *Roman, you who struck me, we two are children of one Father. I grieve for you, that you have so forgotten the face of your Father and your own sonship that you would strike your brother. I love you, brother, even now.*

That is what it means to turn the other cheek.

TWO CAUTIONARY NOTES

I want to offer two quick warnings, lest we take "turn the other cheek" out of its context and try to apply it universally to *all* contexts. First, while nonviolent insistence can be a loving and effective tactic for resisting an oppressor who can be brought to recognize your humanity, on the other hand, if the oppressor does *not* recognize your humanity, then no amount of turning the other cheek will provoke a human response. Turning the other cheek does not work in Auschwitz. Mohatma Gandhi drew a lot of criticism from Jewish voices when he suggested that the Jews should not have resisted the Nazis with violence, as occurred in the Warsaw ghetto as elsewhere; Gandhi was speaking as a man who had certainly endured great privation, but who had never stood naked in the snow in Dachau. The British soldiers in occupied India and the Roman citizens in occupied Palestine had cultural concepts of shared humanity that could be appealed to. Many of the most fanatical Nazis no longer did; it was something Hitler and Goebbels had taken great care to strip from them. When the oppressor *does not know* that the oppressed is human, other methods of resistance may be required.

Second, as we saw in Chapter 13, we also risk taking New Testament teachings severely out of context when we place them in the mouths of those in power. In the Sermon on the Mount, one member of an oppressed people is speaking to other members of that people about how to respond to one's enemies in a way that empowers us to honor God and love others. This is *not* advice that is being handed to first-century Hebrews by agents of Caesar. It's not advice being handed to them by Roman citizens, either. "Don't forcefully resist your enemies" would mean something very different if it were the "enemy" saying it! And if Christians who are more privileged ever find themselves quoting these words of Christ to less privileged members of the community with the intent of delaying or discouraging action, that is a context in which words of life get twisted into words of oppression. That is more like the Roman citizens telling the Jews to shut up than like Jesus telling his countrymen how to respond to the Romans. Beware.

If you are curious to dig into the first-century context more deeply, I recommend Walter Wink's book *Engaging the Powers: Discernment and Resistance in a World of Domination.*

15. HUMANITY DOES NOT RULE IN "DOMINION" OVER THE EARTH

WHAT THIS CHAPTER IS ABOUT

Dominion is not a Greek idea. It is not a Hebrew idea. There are two narratives in Genesis describing humanity's relationship to the physical environment, and neither is quite what we expect.

———————

"You shall not defile the land in which you live, in which I also dwell."

NUMBERS

"DOMINION" TROUBLES ME. Dominionism, both in its attitudes toward the environment and toward civil affairs, strikes me as a theology that is extraordinarily self-serving and anachronistic, a doctrine that doesn't even pretend to engage with the original texts in their original languages. Recently, a friend asked me about it, writing me this note:

What is the biblical context of "dominion?" I see it described two ways by Christians: 1) The animal world is subservient to Humanity, and we are to dominate and manage animals as we see fit, and 2) We are the caretakers of the animal kingdom, and it is our responsibility to assure their safety and future. Is there a specific answer here?

I replied: "Well, there are two answers."

But before we get to that, consider that word "dominion" for a moment. It's not an idea from Genesis; it's an idea that comes out of late-antiquity Roman theology. It's from the Latin, and it has to do with order and empire, with arranging the world as if the world is a house (a *domus*) and Man is the master (the *dominus*) of the house. However, even in Latin, "dominion" doesn't really mean what we take it to mean in English. We see "dominion" and think of *domination* or command, but a Roman would have thought of *responsibility*.

A Roman man who controls the *domus* has absolute responsibility for everyone in the house and for everything that occurs in it; the proverbial buck stops with him, and he is the only member of the household who is legally accountable to the state. That is why, in ancient Rome, the *dominus* of the house is anxious about keeping the women of the house under control; he must account for their behavior to the Roman government. When Jerome translated the Bible into Latin in the late fourth century, he struggled to find Latin terms that could correspond to concepts in the original biblical texts. Translating through the lens of late-antiquity theology and ethics, he chose a Latin word suggestive of a man's responsibility to his *domus* likely because it was the best option he could find to translate the concept of profound responsibility to both earth and community that one finds in the Old Testament.

323

Spiderman knows that "with great power comes great responsibility," and Jesus teaches that leaders must be servants first, but in English we strip all sense of responsibility from the word "dominion," choosing instead to interpret it as *power*. As we saw in Chapter 2, this is similar to what we have done with the word "submission." To the Romans, being sent out *sub missio*, "under a mission," suggested quite a different emphasis than the word suggests to us; in modern English, we tend to read "submission" as a synonym for "obedience."

So even if "dominion" was in the Bible, we still aren't getting it right. However, dominion does not appear in the Bible—neither in its English nor its Latin sense. So what *is* in the Hebrew, if not "dominion"? To explore this, it's important to know that here are two creation-of-humanity accounts recorded in the written book of Genesis, one that appears in Genesis 1 and one in Genesis 2 in our Bibles. Biblical scholars refer to these, traditionally, as the Elohist and Jahwist/Yahwist accounts, referring to the fact that in the Genesis 1 account, God is referred to as *Elohim*, and in the Genesis 2 account, God is referred to by the tetragrammaton that Christians print in English as YHWH and that Jews don't print at all. The two accounts are opposed in a number of ways. One of the many points of departure between the two is that they propose opposite visions for humanity's connection with the earth and its inhabitants. Let's look at each.

NARRATIVE 1: HUMANITY AS PLUNDERERS

In the Elohist account, humanity, blessed to multiply and fill the earth, is also set to "force," "assault," or "subdue" (*kabash*) the earth (Genesis 1:28). In later texts such as the books of Nehemiah and Esther, this verb *kabash* is used for rape. It's the same word used when the Persian king finds Haman clutching Hadassah's knees and the king demands in fury, "Will you rape my wife while I am in the house?!" In the Elohist account, God places humans on the loose, blesses them with fertility, and leaves them to overwhelm the earth.

The word we translate "have dominion over" in English also appears in this passage. That verb is *radah*, which means "trample." It doesn't really suggest imperial order or authority (benign or otherwise); it literally means to tread someone underfoot. When it appears in Old Testament texts more figuratively, it means to enslave—as the Egyptians do with the Children of Israel.

The imagery used in Genesis 1:28—probably the older of the two accounts, borrowing from the oral tradition of a once-nomadic people—is of humans as raiders who will swarm fruitfully over the earth and plunder and use it.

NARRATIVE 2: HUMANITY AS SERVANTS AND KEEPERS

In the Jahwist account, God places humans in a garden and instructs them to "serve and preserve" the earth (Genesis 2:15).

We sometimes translate the instruction as "keep and tend," or, more loosely, as "till and cultivate." The Hebrew here is *abad* ("work" or "serve") and *shamar* ("preserve" or "protect"). *Shamar* is to keep, to guard, to defend; it is the same word used when Cain demands of God, "Am I my brother's keeper?" For both Adam in Genesis 2 and for his son Cain in Genesis 4, *shamar* is humanity's duty—both to the land and to each other. In this narrative, humanity's first responsibility is literally "to serve and protect"—not as a police force but as citizens of a garden earth.

IN EITHER CASE, "DOMINION" IS OUT

Both accounts exist, but there is no option in the original Hebrew to take refuge in a prettied-up idea of "dominion," of humanity governing the land and its inhabitants as we might imagine governing a Roman house. In Hebrew, humans will either be plunderers or servants of the earth, either enslavers or keepers; there are no Empire-friendly euphemisms employed in Genesis.

If one is to choose between humanity as ravagers of the land or humanity as defenders and workers of the land, it's worth noting that the Torah chooses the second. The rest of the instructions in the Law of Moses related to the land and its non-human inhabitants are founded on *shamar*. Although many tales in the Old Testament do represent the ancient Hebrews as plunderers seizing territory, the 613 *mishvot* in the laws of Moses do not refer back to the Genesis 1:28 language of subduing the earth and its creatures. In the Torah, humans bear responsibility to the earth, and their treatment of the earth and of each other is inextricably tied. Throughout the books of Moses, violence and especially murder defile the earth; when Abel is slain by Cain, his blood "is crying out" to God from the soil that his murder has polluted. As you treat the land, so you treat each other; as you treat each other, so you treat the land.

The books of Moses provide extensive instructions to the Hebrews to care for and preserve the land, including the provision of a "sabbath for the land" (Leviticus 25:4). That sabbath is a year of rest from cultivation that serves both to prevent dust bowls and to remind those who keep the law that the land is ultimately God's and not ours. In today's national state of Israel, the government funds extensive projects to reforest the land, to reverse the widespread deforestation conducted under the Ottoman Empire, which had let in the desert and dried out a once lush and fertile area. In that country, *shamar* is a national priority. In my own country, I have heard some of my fellow Christians contend that we need not act as good stewards of the ecosystems we inhabit or from which we draw resources because we live in "dominion" over the earth. In effect, these neighbors of mine are advocating that we operate as plunderers, trampling and raping the earth (*kabash*). If evidence is presented that we are in fact doing widespread damage to our ecosystems, this is widely denied in some quarters. It is as if we are suggesting that the earth will just have to lie there and take it, and that the earth is probably enjoying the rape anyway. But because the language of rape and plunder is uncomfortable, we have prettied it up as "subdue and have dominion over."

But if we read the *second* account of the creation of humanity, we find a very different role and duty to which

327

we might be called. Throughout the Torah, the people of Israel are cautioned that if they do violence and injustice on the land or if they fail to preserve its cleanness and fertility, the land will cry out to God that it has been violated, and they will be driven from it:

> You shall not pollute the land in which you live; for blood pollutes the land, and no expiation can be made for the land, for the blood that is shed in it, except by the blood of the one who shed it. You shall not defile the land in which you live, in which I also dwell; for I the Lord dwell among the Israelites.
>
> NUMBERS 35:33-34

> And the Lord said, "What have you done? Listen; your brother's blood is crying out to me from the ground! And now you are cursed from the ground, which has opened its mouth to receive your brother's blood from your hand. When you till the ground, it will no longer yield to you its strength; you will be a fugitive and a wanderer on the earth."
>
> GENESIS 4:10-12

The sin of Cain is twofold: murder of a fellow human being, yes, but also pollution of the land with defiling blood. What if we took these passages seriously? What if we regarded the earth not as "that which we have dominion over and can use," but as "the dwelling place where God lives among us," a place that must be tended and preserved and kept beautiful and healthy because it is where a Holy God desires to live with us?

16. What "Sparing the Rod" Doesn't Mean

What This Chapter is About

In this brief chapter, I want to note a proverb that has often been both misquoted and taken out of context to justify beating children. Let's take a good look at what got lost in translation.

"Those who spare the rod hate their children,
but those who love them are diligent to discipline them."

PROVERBS

On the topic of authority and power, I know that a few of my fellow Christians still justify corporal punishment for children using a religious proverb that is horribly misunderstood: "Spare the rod, spoil the child." I do not think that popular abridgement of Proverbs 13:24 means what we frequently assume it means. It is an agrarian and pastoral metaphor. I grew up on a farm, and I would like to comment on it.

I usually hear "spare the rod, spoil the child" glossed as an instruction to spank or beat children, to deliver corporal punishment rather than allow our children to misbehave, go astray, or grow up spoiled or entitled. But in an agrarian context, this interpretation makes absolutely no sense at all. The *shebet* (rod) referred to here is a shepherd's implement, and *musar* (discipline) refers not to punishment but to correction.

In this ancient proverb, a parent is being compared to a shepherd. But here's the thing. A good shepherd *doesn't beat* the sheep. Punishment isn't what the rod is for. The shepherd uses the *shebet* to tap a shoulder or nudge the flank, to push the sheep away from danger and into the right direction. If a farmer were to *beat* the sheep, they might wound the animal, or damage the animal psychologically so that the animal would never come near them again. That would be the most wasteful, foolish, and cruel farmer! "Don't spare the rod" *doesn't mean beat the child!*

17. CONVERSION THROUGH FEAR IS AS UNBIBLICAL AS IT IS ABUSIVE

WHAT THIS CHAPTER IS ABOUT

Some Bible Belt churches teach evangelism as a rapid-fire delivery of four verses, starting with "The wages of sin are death" and "All have fallen short of the glory of God" (Romans 6:23, 3:23). It's a commercial approach to sharing the gospel: Manufacture discontent or fear in the listener, then sell the idea that your product will alleviate the fear you have created. It is the same logic that drives television commercials. If you don't want to lonely, buy this perfume or this body spray. If you don't want to be seen as un-masculine, buy this exceptionally manly vehicle. But there is no account in the New Testament of Christians evangelizing in this way, or of treating the gospel as a commodity to sell. They were more concerned with "casting out fear" than with creating it. In this chapter, we will look at the roots of evangelism by fear and contrast it with the evangelism that the earliest apostles practiced.

"There is no fear in love, but perfect love casts out fear; for fear has to do with punishment, and whoever fears has not reached perfection in love."

THE FIRST LETTER OF JOHN

331

THE FEAR OF HELL IS NOT AN INCENTIVE to begin an intimate relationship with one's Savior—for much the same reason that avoiding being beaten is not an incentive to submit to an intimate relationship with a lover. Not only does this notion of conversion by fear defy common sense; it is profoundly unbiblical.

It is also very American (though not exclusively American). In the 1600s, Puritan brimstone preacher Jonathan Edwards delivered a famous sermon that still echoes in our sermons today, like a tortured ghost rattling its chains across the centuries. The sermon was titled *Sinners in the Hands of an Angry God.* I will give you a quick taste of it, if you'll forgive me. It's likely that even if you have never read Jonathan Edwards, you will find the rhetoric familiar:

> The bow of God's wrath is bent, and the arrow made ready on the string, and justice bends the arrow at your heart, and strains the bow, and it is nothing but the mere pleasure of God, and that of an angry God, without any promise or obligation at all, that keeps the arrow one moment from being made drunk with your blood.

> JONATHAN EDWARDS

I might argue, of course, that in Christian metaphysics, there is indeed such a promise, and that Jesus himself is that incarnated promise of the reckless love of God, and by his existence, we know that there is *not* an arrow bent toward your heart.

But in case that quote from Jonathan Edwards isn't troubling enough, try this one:

The God that holds you over the pit of hell, much as one holds a spider or some loathsome insect over the fire, abhors you, and is dreadfully provoked. His wrath towards you burns like fire; he looks upon you as worthy of nothing else but to be cast into the fire. He is of purer eyes than to bear you in his sight; you are ten thousand times as abominable in his eyes as the most hateful, venomous serpent is in ours.

You have offended him infinitely more than ever a stubborn rebel did his prince, and yet it is nothing but his hand that holds you from falling into the fire every moment. It is to be ascribed to nothing else that you did not got to hell the last night; that you were suffered to awake again in this world, after you closed your eyes to sleep. And there is no other reason to be given why you have not dropped into hell since you arose in the morning, but that God's hand has held you up. There is no other reason to be given why you have not gone to hell since you have sat here in the house of God provoking his pure eye by your sinful, wicked manner of attending his solemn worship. Yea, there is nothing else that is to be given as a reason why you do not *this very moment* drop down into hell.

JONATHAN EDWARDS

Behold the human being, held dangling and loathed like an unwanted spider over the pit of destruction!

Doesn't that give you the willies?

Did you know that Jonathan Edwards never delivered that sermon, *Sinners in the Hands of an Angry God*, in quite the way we usually imagine? He never thumped his Bible against the pulpit or shouted at his congregation. What he actually did was more unnerving: he would lean over his

333

notes and speak in a rasp barely above a whisper, so that those attending service had to lean toward him and *strain* to hear him speak. The entire church was hushed. And as for Jonathan, in the softest, thinnest voice, he would tell you something like this: "God holds you over the fire as a loathsome insect because you, sinner, you disgust him, and at any moment, even now, even *now*, he might drop you into the flames of hell…"

It was reported at the time that some people screamed and fainted during that sermon.

Now that—that is *not* how we share the good news. "You're going to hell" was *never* how the early church opened the story. (In fact, in the next chapter, we'll take a moment to consider that in the first century, they *had* no hell.) Do you know how first-century Christians greeted their fellow human beings? *Chaire*! they cried. "Rejoice!" A word separated by only one letter from the word for grace. Rejoice! *That* is how they said hello. That is how they began their story.

Remember the shepherds in Luke, tending their flocks by night? An angel appears before them, on fire with the presence of God, and in the Bible this is a terrifying thing. Angels are not pretty babies with feathery wings, in the Bible. When they appear fresh from the glory of God and without any earthly disguise, when they *want* to be recognized, they have six wings and a thousand eyes and they arrive in wind and fire. The earth shakes. The sky tears open. The shepherds tremble. And the first thing the angel says to them is: "Fear not."

Don't be afraid.

That is always the first thing an angel of heaven says upon arriving.

Don't be afraid; I bring you good news.

When Jesus is about to perform a miracle, he says, "Don't be afraid; this little girl is not dead, she is only sleeping. I will wake her." When he walks across the water and the disciples moan with fear because they think they are witnessing the approach of an evil spirit, he says, "Don't be afraid."

We perhaps get confused because of the emphasis the Bible puts on the fear of God. The Hebrew word used for fear in those verses has the same root as the word for Torah, "instruction." Fear of God refers specifically to reverential and committed observance of the Law of Moses and its instructions on how to treat others. As we saw in Chapter 3, that fear of God that we encounter in the Old Testament comes up especially when the children of Israel are being told not to worship idols, and not to deliver injustice to the orphan, the widow, and the stranger in the land. Abraham fears he may find himself among those who have no fear of God and who will be cruel toward the immigrant and the vulnerable, and David sings in the Psalms of the terror of finding oneself beset on all sides by enemies who do not fear God.

There is also the Letter to the Philippians with its reference to fear and trembling:

> Therefore, my beloved, just as you have always obeyed me, not only in my presence, but much more now in my absence, work out your own salvation with fear and trembling; for it is God who is at work in you, enabling you both to will and to work for his good pleasure.

PHILIPPIANS 2:12

335

But this is a passage about living one's faith, not about evangelism. And indeed, "it is a fearful thing to fall into the hands of the living God" (Hebrews 10:31), to be required to live with relentless love and to do justice, to open oneself to being completely changed, and to follow God's call across the desert like Abraham or across the water like Peter, or to step into a king's throne room to speak truth to power like Hadassah (Esther). So yes, working out one's faith is an experience of trembling with both joy and fear; it is part of the work of trying to live a radical and "more excellent way" of "faith, hope, and love" from within an unjust society (1 Corinthians 12:31, 13:13).

But the Bible never describes the delivery of the *gospel* as an incitement to fear. Consider the joy of the 3,000 converts at Pentecost in Acts 2, the first members of the first Christian church, who gathered to break bread together *en agalliasei kai aphelotēti kardias*. We translate this into English so tamely as "with glad and generous hearts" (Acts 2:46), but *agalliasis* means "wild joy" or "ecstatic delight." It is a compound of the words *agan* ("much") + *hállomai* ("to gush up" like bubbling water). *Agalliasis* is a joy that is like living water gushing up inside you, overflowing.

It is not with terror that the early church was called together and the first converts were made, but with *agalliasis*. The delivery of the gospel is not a stoking of fear but a sharing of extreme joy. *We walked with God,* the early apostles witness. *He ate meals with us. He healed the sick. We saw him rise from the tomb! He told us that he loves us and that there's room for everyone in his house. For everyone—slaves and free citizens, women and men, Jews and Greeks alike, all of us. He told us that nothing is more important than loving one another. And he said he would come back to walk with us again. We have such joy! Listen, this is the story.*

"Don't be afraid," the angel says to the shepherds on the night of Christ's birth, "for look! *Euangelizomai hymin charan megalēn!*" (I bring you excellent news of great joy!). Even today, the two most fundamental Christian sacraments are baptism (an enactment of joyous rebirth and resurrection into what Paul calls "newness of life") and communion or eucharist (a Greek word meaning "thanksgiving"). These sacraments that have persisted since the days of the early church are expressions of joy. And the apostle Peter writes to the early churches advising their members to be always ready to give a reason for "the hope that is in you" (1 Peter 3:15)—because his expectation was that Christians would live and speak so joyously that people, seeing it, would want to ask *why*. And Luke reports that Paul and Silas "sang praises" at midnight in a jail cell (Acts 16:25), because neither chains nor concrete nor cold stone could contain the joy in their hearts. Is it any wonder that the early church's metaphor for paradise is a wedding feast? Or that Jesus's first miracle was to change water into wine to gladden the guests at a wedding? Or that God—in the story of the prodigal father, the proud elder brother, and the reckless younger brother—throws a feast with these words:

> But we had to celebrate and rejoice, because this brother of yours was dead and has come to life; he was lost and has been found.
>
> LUKE 11:32

Or that Paul's instruction to the church at Philippi is:

> Rejoice in the Lord always; again I will say, Rejoice.

PHILIPPIANS 4:4

For the early apostles, the Way was a way of "newness of life" (Romans 6:4) and "joy unspeakable" (1 Peter 1:8), joy that outweighed any cost.

Fear sells—but our commission as Christians is not to "sell" the good news but to "give freely" (Matthew 10:8) and joyously.

18. THE FIRST-CENTURY CHURCH DIDN'T HAVE A LITERAL HELL

WHAT THIS CHAPTER IS ABOUT

The "fear" narrative that we took issue with in the previous chapter is rendered perhaps inevitable by a belief in the existence of an eternal penitentiary. But the early apostles had no such concept of hell as we do, nor did they require one to spread the good story that we all have an inheritance in heaven and that unforgetting the promises of God can set us free (from sin, from idolatry, from death and from the death-in-life of having our lives defined and our futures circumscribed by our past behaviors or by the hierarchies and cultural expectations of the Greco-Roman world). Hell as we know it is a post-biblical blending of Greek and Norse myth and medieval folklore, and it is far more useful for inspiring fear and controlling people than it is for inspiring joy and setting people free.

———————

"Do not let your hearts be troubled. Trust in God, trust also in me. In my Father's house there are many rooms."

JESUS

———————

WE ALL KNOW THE STORY. It's as common a tale in our time as the river of Lethe (forgetting) was in the time of the ancient Greeks. It goes like this: You die, and either you have acknowledged the One God or you have not. If not, you are cast forever, irretrievably, into a pit of eternal fire and obscene tortures. Depending on who is telling the tale, there may be further lurid details. Perhaps demonic gaolers with their fangs and pitchforks, or fallen angels hurrying back and forth on their errands to tempt the world and gather souls for their master to devour. Whatever the specifics, there in hell you remain, time without end, in eternal pain, with the shrieking of the damned forever in your ears. Or perhaps it is your own screams you hear.

If, being confronted with this medieval horror-tale, you dare to point out that an eternal torture-chamber is incompatible with the idea of a loving God who has redeemed his children, some well-meaning (or ill-meaning) person will recite you the platitude that crimes have to be paid for. Why they should be paid for with torture and suffering is never quite explained. Nor why a God who forgives all, extending to all the free gift of love and life abundant, and who atones by his own action for all the world's ills, should at the same time require our personal and eternal atonement after death, nor why infinite reparation is required for a finite lifetime of sin. Hell has claimed such a powerful hold on the medieval and modern imagination that the paradoxes in the story are permitted to pass without comment. We are rather obsessed with hell, in ways that would not have made any sense to the writers in the early church, who talked a lot about heaven and about behaving as citizens of heaven, but very little about hell.

Our word *hell* is Germanic and it originally meant a concealed or covered place; it is distantly related to our English word *cellar*, and it is closely related to our word *hall*; in Old Norse mythology, *Valhalla* is the "hall of the slain," where those who die glorious deaths in battle go, and *Niflhel* or simply *Hel* is the "hall of mist," the fogworld at the bottom of the universe among the roots of the World Tree, where those who lived forgettable lives go to be forgotten. When King James' seventeenth-century committee of translators brought the Bible to English, they used "hell" to translate a whole array of disparate ideas and metaphors.

These concepts vary from *sheol* (the grave) to *hades* (the oblivion that awaits beyond Lethe or Forgetting) to *gehenna*—a Greek transliteration of *ge ben hinnom*, "the valley of the son of Hinnom." In the Old Testament, the valley of Hinnom is a location near Jerusalem where the prophet Jeremiah reported to his horror that child sacrifices occurred—where the living firstborn were tossed into fiery pits to appease the god Chemosh. In the sermons of Jesus, this becomes a convenient metaphor, where the god who devours with fire is no longer Chemosh but Lust. *Gehenna* now becomes a sacrificial pit into which men cast their bodies and souls when they fail to keep themselves from stalking and harassing women (Matthew 18:9; Mark 9:43). The valley of unholy sacrifice is now, poetically, a place where men are sacrificed by their own unholy actions. Jesus suggests, hyperbolically: If you really can't keep from pursuing her or assaulting her (*have some self-control, man! you're not a child*), then it would be better to sacrifice your own eye by plucking it out, rather than sacrifice your whole being in *gehenna*, throwing yourself to the flames as madly as the ancients threw their children. Then there is *to skotos to exōteron*, the metaphorical "outer darkness" referred to in Jesus's sermons, where people weep and wail in anguish because their unloving choices and actions have separated them from their neighbors and from God. But none of these phrases appear to suggest an eternal otherworld prison. Outside of poetry and parable, when the writers of the New Testament speak of the dead, they speak of those "who have fallen asleep," who now await the awakening that will be the resurrection at the end of time.

There are two exceptions in the New Testament where the dead are not simply sleeping and awaiting the final healing of the world. The first of these is when Christ tells the thief on the cross, "Amen, this day you will be with me in paradise" (Luke 23:43). The second is when Jesus relates the parable about the rich man and Lazarus. The rich man, having spent his life spurning and mistreating the poor, thirsts after death in a parched desert, a wasteland of heat, and he pleads for someone who is with "Abraham far away" to bring him a drop of water to drink (Luke 16:23-24). But that is a parable, a fable, no more to be read literally than Jesus' other parables in which God has a vineyard or is to be found sitting in a Hebrew court. They are metaphors.

The closing passages of the prophetic book of Apocalypse (or Revelation) do mention *limne pur*, a "lake of fire" where the devil burns and where the dead after judgment suffer "the second death"—but it is left ambiguous in the text whether the human dead perish or are also held in torment (Revelation 20:14-15), and in any case this is embedded in a poetic vision that speaks in the language of symbol and allegory, not in actual depictions of actual places. Elsewhere, the apostle Peter makes brief mention of rebel angels chained in the Greek "Tartaros" to await a day of judgment, but makes no mention of human beings there (2 Peter 2:4). Tartaros and "the lake of fire" are clearly different concepts—one a holding cell for rebellious supernatural beings, the other a "second death" at the end of earthly time, but those are the closest the New Testament comes to ideas we might recognize as "hell." In the original languages each of these poetic passages presents a different concept. *Sheol, gehenna, tartaros, limne pur, to skotos to exōteron*, and *hades* are not equivalent to each other. Later generations, reading in Latin, tried to reconcile all these verses into one picture of an abode of the damned, rather clumsily, but the first-century churches did not have a consistent or systematic cosmology—nor did they see a need for one.

Hell as a defined piece of psychic post-mortal real estate is largely an invention of the Middle Ages. There are a *few* precursors. For example, in his *De Spectaculis*, a third-century treatise condemning Rome's entertainment industry, Tertullian fantasized about "the dissolving flame" and "fiery billows" of judgment. Drawing heavily on Plato for his imagery and concept of the afterlife, bitter old Tertullian imagined a day when philosophers, actors, and athletes would all burn. Awfully, he reveled in "seeing and exulting in such things as these...in the picturings of imagination." But at the time only the churches of north Africa paid any attention to Tertullian's idea; the other major churches taught quite differently about the nature of eternal life and "universal salvation." In the fourth century, Augustine proposed a possible doctrine of hell, but it wasn't until long after his death, as church authorities became more centralized, that some of Augustine's views on hell became widely accepted as orthodoxy.

During the Middle Ages, while theologians went hunting in their Bibles for scriptural support for the penitentiary of the damned, the popular folklore of the eternal prison began rolling downhill toward our time like a snowball or a katamari, picking up fresh bits of horrific imagery everywhere it went—imagery often adapted or stolen from pagan legend. There was a cave at Lough Derg where young Irish men once spent the night, testing their mettle as they endured the shrieks and moans of hostile beings beneath the earth (as the wind whistled and howled through crevices and cracks in the stone). During the Middle Ages, this cave becomes a site where medieval monks and pilgrims journey into the earth to hear a foretaste of the agony of the damned. (At least until indignant Protestants destroy the abbey at the site and fill in the cave during the sixteenth century.) Hell was originally underground. The Latin word *infernum* meant "the low place." We get the word *inferno* from that, but the connection of "inferno" with "fire" is a later development. In Dante Alighieri's fourteenth-century *Divine Comedy*, the "inferno" is not a place of fire but an underworld. In fact, the further down you go in Dante's inferno, the *colder* it gets—until at last, at the very bottom, you find the devil himself frozen for eternity in solid ice below the waist.

The idea of hell proved so compelling that during the European Middle Ages it cross-contaminated the folklore of other Abrahamic religions. Jews living in Diaspora picked up on the local folklore, so that even today there is a kaddish or prayer for the relief of the dead, even though Jewish teaching does not include a penitentiary for the damned. And the Qu'ran, commenting on the Jewish Tanakh and the Christian New Testament, picked up on the Christian idea of hellfire and translated the Greek *gehenna* to Arabic as *jahannam*, a place of everlasting flame. But today, no one else in the world talks about hell with the same vigor and passion that some Christian sects do. Hellfire remains "our" unfortunate invention—a cultural artifact that the Bible predates but that we choose to regard as biblical.

If you are interested in tracking how the mythology and lore of hell and purgatory developed and for what reasons, I recommend Stephen Greenblatt's study *Hamlet in Purgatory*. It is a fascinating read. One of the things you will discover (one of the surprising things, if you have never thought about it before) is how this lore fueled most philanthropic and charitable activity in Europe during the Middle Ages:

> Sermons and images trained people to imagine in vivid detail the miseries of suffering souls, and the church then offered ways to transform empathic identification into generous action. Many of these ways involved religious rituals, but they also included alms to the poor, subsidized education, hospitals for the sick, assistance in giving the indigent a proper burial. A Middle English poem "The Relief of Souls in Purgatory," in a fifteenth-century devotional compilation is accompanied by a drawing showing souls being pulled out of the purgatorial flames in a bucket. The bucket is drawn by a thick rope that passes through a pulley at the entrance of Heaven and then back

down to the earth where it is pulled by a group of priests saying Mass at an altar... The rope continues past the altar and reaches an individual, evidently a layman, who is giving alms to two poor people, one of whom has an artificial leg.

STEPHEN GREENBLATT

In the Middle Ages—unlike in our modern era—the concept of a post-mortal penitentiary at least had a social function. The more terrifying a vision you could imagine of hell, the more you didn't want your relatives to be there. If your relatives had not been good people but hadn't been terrible people either, or if they had died unbaptized, perhaps they persisted not in hell but in purgatory, a limbo state that over the medieval centuries came to possess terrifying punishments of its own. The difference with purgatory was that it was a place of purgation, not damnation; once purged of its sin, the soul could proceed to heaven where it belonged. And if you had lost someone you loved, you could help them along because the prayers of the saints move angels to bring aid to those in purgatory. If you were rich and missing someone you loved, and you were frightened that they may be in pain in the afterlife, perhaps for centuries, then you might use your funds to establish a hospital whose patients would pray for the soul of your lost relative. Or an orphanage where the children would pray for your beloved. Or a chapel or school where hymns would be sung in your beloved's name. In this way, your philanthropy would lift the one you loved out of torment and provide for the needs of the disadvantaged here on earth. (Needless to say, the church would get a cut, too.)

People yearned for connection with their dead; Irish and Anglo-Saxon mothers buried stillborn children and infants under the eaves of churches, and some historians think this was because they hoped the rain (angels' tears) would fall on the graves, baptizing and cleansing the souls of the lost babies, easing their passage out of purgatory into heaven. The belief in purgatory, however ghoulish it might appear to us today, did give people in Europe a means of communion with their departed loved ones:

> ...the border between this world and the afterlife was not irrevocably closed... The living could have an ongoing relationship with one important segment of the dead, and not simply a relationship constituted by memory. There were things the living could do for the dead... The whole social and economic importance of Purgatory in Catholic Europe rested on the belief that prayers, fasts, almsgiving, and masses constituted a valuable commodity—"suffrages," as they were termed—that could in effect be purchased, directly or indirectly, on behalf of specific dead persons... it was possible for individuals after death to receive help from others, just as living debtors languishing in prison could have their debts paid by their friends.

STEPHEN GREENBLATT

During the Protestant Reformation, many churches abolished the doctrine of purgatory as post-biblical and heretical. When Henry VIII declared himself head of the English church and looked for ways to confiscate church funds for crown use, he seized on the reformers' criticisms of purgatory, and he abolished all charitable institutions in

England that benefited from "alms for the dead." His Chantries Act closed 2,374 chantries and chapels, 110 hospitals, and 90 nonprofit colleges. More famous for imprisoning his second wife in a tower and then executing her, Henry VIII was evidently unsure enough of his conscience that despite having closed the institutions of purgatory, he left in his will "one thousand marks of the lawful money of England" to go to the poor in hopes they would pray for the purgation of his soul.

Today, few Christians remember purgatory, unless they are reading Dante. On All Hallows' Eve (Halloween night), church bells no longer ring until dawn while entire communities hold vigil to pray for the souls of the beloved dead. Purgatory is fading slowly from memory—but unaccountably, we have kept hellfire. I suppose hell is sadly too useful an idea to be easily abandoned. But where the fantasy of purgatory was socially "useful" in funding schools, orphanages, and hospitals, the only purpose a fantasy of hell serves in our world today is as a nightmare story we can tell about life after death to frighten people to an altar call or into adhering to a moral code, like a bogeyman tale to scare children into cleaning their room or going to bed on time.

But like purgatory, hellfire is *also* a post-biblical idea, and even largely a post-Roman idea. It is possible to construct a tissue-paper chain of biblical passages (drawn indiscriminately and without context from poetry, parables, a book of prophecy) and try to use them to validate the idea of hell—as medieval writers did, reading their Bibles only in translation (in Latin), even as we do ours (in English). But rather than attempt to squeeze disparate verses forcibly into a dogma we already hold, we could take the adventure and see what we discover as we travel through the strange texts of the Bible. The writers of the New Testament spoke often about death and resurrection. But when the apostles wrote of eternal life, it was not in fear of hell (or even with mention of a hell) but in wild joy:

> Listen, I will tell you a mystery! We will not all die, but we will all be changed, in a moment, in the twinkling of an eye, at the last trumpet. For the trumpet will sound, and the dead will be raised imperishable, and we will be changed. For this perishable body must put on imperishability, and this mortal body must put on immortality. When this perishable body puts on imperishability, and this mortal body puts on immortality, then the saying that is written will be fulfilled:
>
> > "Death has been swallowed up in victory.
> > Where, O death, is your victory?
> > Where, O death, is your sting?"
>
> 1 CORINTHIANS 15:51-55

In that letter, Paul speaks at length of resurrection and of the imperishable life that awaits. What is to come is *exciting*. For Paul and his colleagues, the good news isn't "we will not all go to hell"; the good news is "we will not all *die*." That there is an imperishable inheritance in God's house that begins this moment and then doesn't *end*. Nowhere in that does Paul mention a hell-prison after death. Certainly there is no evidence that Paul or any of the other New Testament writers conceived of anyone they knew residing in a penitentiary of eternal torment. Too busy celebrating, the earliest Christians didn't know anything about our "hell" and they hadn't time to invent one. They had drunk the wine of heaven, and they wished to invite us all to that wedding at which every glass of water is changed into wine and where we ourselves are God's cherished bride.

19. GOD'S LOVE HAS NO CONDITIONS

WHAT THIS CHAPTER IS ABOUT

In much contemporary Christian thinking, we have confused cause and effect. We have mistaken the gift of grace for an economic exchange, a bartering of repentance in exchange for love and abundant life. But the New Testament teaches that grace comes first—a gift without strings attached. *Metanoia* (the changing of our minds and hearts) is the living out of our gratitude at the gift of love—love so profound that receiving it *changes* us.

"We love because he first loved us."

THE FIRST LETTER OF JOHN

THIS IS THE BIG ONE. What the New Testament proposes and what filled the early church with such ebullient joy is *not* that we need to be saved, but that we are *already* saved, every one of us. Every one of us is already profoundly loved and accepted by God. When the

351

prodigal son returns home, his father runs out weeping to embrace him because he has already long since forgiven him. In fact, the son's transgressions were never even marked down in the father's ledger. That is the God we love and who loves us. It is possible to willfully stand outside the house refusing to go in—like the elder brother, haughtily sure of himself and the value of his deeds and not caring to love either his brother or his father. He loves only what he might get *from* his father. So at the end of the story, he is still standing outside the door, unwilling to go into the feast. But he is not barred from it. He might enter at any moment. He need only let go his pride and resentment at his younger brother, and relinquish his belief that his father's love is something that can be earned or unearned.

In Chapter 4, we saw that in John of Patmos's vision—recorded in the book of Revelation at the end of the Bible—the gates of paradise stand wide open at all hours, all twelve of them:

> Its gates will never be shut by day—and there will be no night there. People will bring into it the glory and the honor of the nations.

REVELATION 21:25-26

In John's vision, there *are* people standing outside—idolaters and murderers and "everyone who loves and practices a lie," and others—but in his vision, they stand outside by choice, because the gates are forever open. Figuratively, John records that these people have only to "wash their clothes" in the river outside the gates and come in to the wedding feast. If they desire it—if that wedding and union has become the deepest desire of their hearts.

Inside the city, "the Spirit and the bride" (the bride here is a figure for *us*) say together:

And let everyone who is thirsty come.
Let anyone who wishes take the water of life as a gift.

REVELATION 22:17

This story of the wedding in paradise is suggestive of several things. First, that those who follow God—those who are the "bride"—are not gatekeepers! Second, that we mortal beings who arrive at the wedding arrive in a state of glory and overwhelming love; we are the bride. Third, that the water of life—water sweet as wine, which we drink at the wedding instead of the sluggish water of Lethe (the water of forgetting)—is a free gift. So many passages on salvation in the New Testament have to do with the gift or *charis* (grace), with the gift of life. And it is a *gift*. "Freely you have received," Jesus tells his disciples; "now freely give" (Matthew 10:8).

As Derrida writes in *The Gift of Death*, a gift is not an exchange. Grace is not an exchange—it is something that *is not paid for*, a gift that shatters the rigid and moralistic economies of our world. If we had to repent—or do anything at all—in order to be saved, it would not be grace. It would not be a gift. It would not be God.

What we call repentance is a response to the gift, not a prerequisite or a payment for it. *Hēmeis agapōmen hoti autos prōtos ēgapēsen hēmas:* "We love because he first loved us" (1 John 4:19). Repentance—whether we mean by it

353

"returning" (Hebrew *teshuvah,* "turning back") or "changing mind" (Greek *metanoia*)—is not something we do *in order to be* loved and accepted, but something we do in gratitude for having been loved and accepted already.

The question is not whether we will be saved—because we are already given refuge, we are already *sos.* The question is what we will *do,* having been saved. Offered adoption into the Father's house as co-heirs with Christ, will we be moved to live in ways that make our Father proud of his children? Will we, knowing ourselves loved, love others? Will we extend that refuge, unconditionally, to others? The question is: How does the profound realization of how loved we are change how we live our lives? What would it mean to live a life of faithing? What would you do differently today, if the deepest knowledge you carried in your heart was that God loves and adores you? How moved we might be to make God proud of us (though God is already). How moved we might be to clothe, feed, and love our siblings, to stand up for them when they are hurt, to carry them when they are broken, to defend them when they might be brutalized or slain. Love is not something you *feel* toward your fellow human beings, it is something you *do.*

What if our waking thought each morning was, *Today, help me love as deeply and recklessly as I am loved.*

What if that *agape* love beat in our heart, in the pulse of our blood, what if it could be heard behind every sentence that escaped our mouths? In a world populated by such loved and loving citizens of heaven, I would not fear for my daughter in her wheelchair or for my friend who is trans or for my neighbors praying in their mosque. What room would any of us have in our hearts for fear, if we lived such lives of love? If we drank living water until it bubbled up inside us in an *agallíasis,* an upwelling of extreme joy?

I yearn for such a wedding-day world. I crave it.

"Clothe yourselves with compassion," Paul writes to the church at Colossae. What would it be like if, when we encounter someone, the impulse to examine their status or their sin and judge where they are in relation to God or to us never crossed our mind? What would it be like if when we meet one another, the only thing blazing in our hearts—like a fire kindled there by the Paraclete—was compassion? Living in *that* world would truly be the greatest adventure.

AFTERWORD AND ADVENT: MAKING THE GOOD STORY A TRUE STORY, AN UNFORGOTTEN STORY

As I WRITE THIS, IT IS ADVENT—and I love Advent. I love the idea of awaiting a child's birth, of holding our breath in wonder at the arrival of a baby, and at the renewal of our faith that something new *can* come into this world. This old, weary world where the winter nights are long, where there is suffering and tears. My Jewish friends have a Pesach (Passover) tradition whereby they leave one chair empty at the table and pour an extra cup of wine and open the door for Elijah—because you never know when Elijah might walk in. Each time a baby is born, you don't know, but that baby could grow up to change the world, to save people, to bring peace. Each baby's arrival might be the impossible Event that changes forever what *is* possible.

I like to think that Advent can convey a similar idea to Christians. In remembering the arrival of one baby, we might rediscover our joy and wonder at the arrival of every baby. In celebrating a night that changed the world, we might celebrate the possibility that the world can change again. Advent is the yearning for the coming of the Event—the desire for the unexpected and impossible. It is when we hear so clearly the invitation to *advent*ure, to imagine a world made new. It is a holy season that looks both back and forward, and both outward to the world and inward to the hearth. And so I love Advent. I light the candles. I sing the songs. I hug my children. And I await the coming of the Christ child and the baby's giggle that is both God's giggle and ours. To me, it is a season of hope.

At the same time, some of my Christian neighbors get riled in and by this season. I hear the same grumbling every year about a supposed "war on Christmas," even though every year the Christmas trees go up, the candles get lit, I get days off work, and I sing *Veni Veni Emmanuel* and *O Holy Night* with others of my faith without any interruption or intervention to keep me from doing so. And I try to find gentle ways to remind my community that just because some of our neighbors celebrate Chanukah or just because my wife burns a Yule log and puts up a pentagram beside the wreath, or just because a cashier wishes them "Happy Holidays," it doesn't mean that there is a war on Christmas or a persecution against those observing a Christmas holiday.

There was, once. Some time ago.

There *was* a legal "war" on Christmas, four centuries back. The history of it (and the historical irony) is fascinating. At various times during the seventeenth century, many Puritan and Calvinist communities—including London, England and Salem, Massachusetts—banned the observance of Christmas. The holiday was considered either too Catholic or too Pagan (many Puritans regarded those two adjectives as essentially synonyms). Within the municipal limits of those communities, it was illegal to celebrate Christmas. (In fact,

Massachusetts did not officially recognize Christmas until 1856.) In Salem, Christmas and All Hallows and May Day and all the old festivals were seen as unfit for Christians because they were witches' holidays, and we surely remember what Salem did to witches. In London, on one memorable occasion, Ben Jonson put on a masque (titled *Christmas His Masque*) for the king and his court during the monarch's visit to the city, to invite or incite the king's intervention. At the start of the play, Father Christmas is led out in chains by the London Guard, to plead his case before the king. Yes, he dresses fancy and gives gifts and decorates trees, but Father Christmas insists that "he's as Protestant as any," and the poor orphan children of London should be allowed to see him this December, surely?

That is one of many historical ironies that have popped up over the course of this book: it was originally the Calvinists who wanted to do away with Christmas, the theological ancestors of those very people who today shout loudest about a presumed "war on Christmas."

Father Christmas being led on stage in chains to plead with the king—that was only four centuries ago. The wheel of history rotates rapidly, but our memories are so short, and so few of us know much of our history or know it well. When we speak naively of the war on Christmas or of the meaning of Christmas in our own time, we often focus on the trappings of the holiday and miss the import of its story. We forget that it is a story about the arrival and shelter of strangers in the night—not only Mary and Joseph, but the arrival of strange angelic beings in the heavens, a strange baby on earth, and strange men from faraway lands bearing strange gifts. The more concerned we become with defending what we *expect* to see, the more we lose the opportunity to encounter the Advent story as a story of the impossible and *unexpected*. What would happen if instead we approached the story of Advent as an invitation to adventure—as it was to those the angel spoke to, or to the magi seeing a new star in the sky. What if we made daring choices about what this story might *mean* translated into our time? What if we chose *not* to tame the Christ story but to unleash it, to permit the Christ story to be wild as a lion, wild as Aslan in Narnia, shaking apart our culture with its roar, upending all the carefully ordered and disciplined furniture of our lives and remaking our hearts?

I plead with my friends in the faith: Let's shift our attention this year away from the war on Christmas and from the various other frivolous persecutions we claim to be undergoing—and focus instead on living in imitation of Christ. Which is to be less concerned with the supremacy of our faith and more concerned with the love and succor of our neighbors and with the sharing of a story of great hope. In the United States, white middle-class Christians in most sects are not the *persecuted* but among those benefiting, knowingly or unknowingly, from the actions of *persecutors*. It is time for us to stand once again with those who are truly persecuted—with the refugees, the fugitives, the unhomed.

Putting Christ into Christmas means telling a story of a family seeking refuge. The traditional way we tell the Christmas story is a tale of *refuge denied*—of a traveling family who find no room at the inn and have to hunker down in a stable the very night that Mary goes into labor.

The Greek text of Luke 2 suggests something different, though just as relevant: a tale of *refuge given*, where Joseph and Mary arrive unexpectedly, possibly at the house of distant relatives or at a house of an affluent and hospitable local family, and find that the *kataluma* (the upper room or guest room in a private residence) is already full. Rather than turn away a traveler and distant relation who is nine months pregnant and showing signs of going into labor, the family who lives in the house permits Mary and Joseph to bed down with them, in the straw on the main floor where (in a first-century Judean home) the family and their livestock customarily sleep. In both versions—our traditional folk retelling of the story and the original Greek text—the question is the same, though the answers differ: Will people far from home find shelter?

In the Greek text, Mary and Joseph do find shelter in Bethlehem—but that shelter is later broken by the threat of violence from King Herod, the power-mad and paranoid monarch who decrees the death of all male toddlers and babies in Bethlehem. To preserve the life of their child, Jesus's family has to depart in haste to a foreign country where they have neither family nor citizenship, where they must seek refuge and the mercy of strangers. And the miracle in the story is that Mary's baby then grows up to be a man who extends refuge unconditionally to all.

But the authorities in Egypt have no way of knowing this. They don't know that God has come visiting or that Mary's baby carries the hope of the world. They have only the question: Will they give shelter to these hungry parents and their children who have arrived at their border, fleeing the violence in their homeland, with little more than the clothes on their backs and perhaps as-yet untested skills and labor to offer? And in our cherished Christmas story, Egypt answers, *Yes. You can.*

You can stay here and be safe and work here. You've come a long way. Now come inside, feed your child, be warm.

There is a powerful story hidden in plain sight there, though we rarely remark on it. In the account of the Exodus, Jesus's ancestors fled violence and mistreatment in Egypt to seek homes elsewhere. In the gospel of Matthew, Jesus's family flees their own homeland *back* to Egypt, returning to the land of their ancient enemies, to find welcome and safety there in the most unexpected of places. It is a refugee's story, through and through: That the safest of homes can be torn away. But it is also a story that a nation that has been cruel can still choose to be kind.

To give refuge, whether in Bethlehem or Egypt or North America. To see a pregnant woman and her husband show up unexpectedly at your door, exhausted and weary from a difficult and dangerous journey. Or to see parents and toddlers show up at your border, terrified, fleeing the slaughter of innocents—and to respond to them with compassion. We can put Christ back into Christmas by telling and living *that* story.

Our faith has the potential to be transformative—for our community, not only for our individual selves. The story of Christ welcoming everyone to the father's table, feeding everyone, getting everyone in safe under one roof, is what sent Paul and Barnabas and Sister Apphia and others traveling across a world to share a story that was often illegal to tell. We today who say we follow Christ, if we unforget that story, if we *live* that story, if we *faith* it, if we open our homes and our hearts, if we stand fearlessly beside and with and *for* those who are suffering around us, those who are so often invisible to us—and if we make them more visible by standing with them, by hearing their story and passing it on and *insisting* that others hear it too, by making a place at the table—if we do that, then the promise of transformation, of communal salvation and refuge that burns inside the story of the gospel will be more than just a pile of pretty sayings or a bit of spectacle on Sunday mornings. The Christmas story is not just handfuls of dainties or toys stuffed into stockings above a fireplace. The Christmas story today is happening at our border; it is a story of families who need homes and safety and hope. It is the story of a woman pregnant and needing a roof tonight. It is the story of a family seeking asylum because the powers that rule in their homeland have vowed to slaughter their children. Shall we welcome and shelter them, as Jesus's family was sheltered, as Jesus bid us shelter others? Shall we be paracletes again? Can this be our *kairos*, "the right moment," which can be *any* moment to those who believe the impossible can occur, who trust that God can touch the world? Can this day, this week, this year be the occasion that breaks the march-step of time and tradition, overturning it like a moneychanger's table? Can this be the moment when we—moved by the Christ story and touched by a glimpse of eternity like the shepherds gazing up at a midnight sky full of light—rewrite everything we thought we knew and understood about our past and imagine possibilities for our future (as human beings, as co-heirs with Christ, as members of one family) that just a moment before would have appeared impossible?

At this moment, shall we answer Jesus's call to adventure—to the most reckless adventure of all, the adventure Advent is *for*? The adventure of seeing one another, loving one other, suffering with and for one other, bearing one another's burdens, consoling the grieving, feeding the hungry, bringing the stranger in from the winter cold to our hearth? Shall we live on this broken earth like citizens of heaven, like beloved and adopted children of our Father, and make him proud at how we treat one another? Shall we make our most cherished story a true story again, a story that we will not forget? For,

> *Truly he taught us to love one another*
> *For his law is love and his gospel is peace;*
> *Chains shall he break, for the slave he is our brother*
> *And in his name all oppression shall cease.*
>
> *Long lay the world in sin and error pining*
> *Till he appeared and the soul felt its worth*
> *A thrill of hope—the weary world rejoices*
> *For yonder breaks a new and glorious morn.*
> *Fall on your knees—Oh, hear the angel voices*
> *O night divine*
> *O night when Christ was born*

Grace and peace be with you, my friends, my fellow readers and adventurers.

STANT LITORE
ADVENT 2018

IF THIS BOOK MOVES YOU

PLEASE SHARE IT. GOOD STORIES deserve to be shared and unforgotten. Buy copies for your friends, your family. You can also write to me at zombiebible@gmail.com and let me know what you thought. The reason I wrote this book at all was because people wrote to me asking for these stories. I would love to hear from you.

My work on this book—and on my novels, too—has been funded by the generous support of my Patreon members. If you would like to join them, help support my work, and see previews of what I am working on next, you can do that here:

WWW.PATREON.COM/STANTLITORE

May your life always be full of good stories, may your ears always be open to the stories of others, and may you continually unforget that which is most important to your heart.

STANT LITORE

ACKNOWLEDGMENTS

NO ONE makes it through writing a book alone. My helpers have been innumerable, but I will mention a few here especially. My thanks to Father Schlatter and Professor Roberta Payne, who each vastly improved my Latin when I was a young graduate student; to Luke, who teased me about writing Hildegard von Bingen hymns in the snow outside a Jesuit chapel on campus, so that naturally I kept doing it; to Andrew Hallam for discussions of poststructuralism and theology and to Isidore Nettleship for discussions of the Torah and Talmud; to Tim Grade, pastor of Platt Park Church, who kept me humble while I wrote this book; to Susie Grade, pastor, who empowered me and moved me often with her own teachings; to Kim Klimek, associate professor of medieval history at Metropolitan State University of Denver, who read an early manuscript of this book with careful attention and shared with me the story of Abelard and the oratory he named Paraclete; to Todd Bergman, pastor of the United Methodist Church in Mooreland, Oklahoma—and a fellow science fiction fan—who kept me encouraged; to Charlie Dodrill, whose monastic and Orthodox spirituality often informed me, whose music brought me joy, and whose reckless love for both the text and his community helped me unforget many things; to Kim Keane, who promised to buy copies for all her friends; to Rhiannon Frater, who cheered me often with witty Old Testament memes, whenever I doubted that I would ever finish this book; to the many people who wrote me letters, emails, or long social media messages over the past year because something I had written moved them, made them cry, or made them laugh after long grief—it is for each of you that I wrote this book; to all my Patreon members, without whose support this book would not exist; and, above all, to Jessica my wife for her love and her laughter, and to my children River, Inara, and Círdan—you three are the best story Jessica and I have written together. You are our best and bravest and truest story, and I am excited for the adventure of all the chapters in your story that we have yet to read.

ABOUT THE AUTHOR

STANT LITORE is the author of the nonfiction titles *Lives of Unstoppable Hope, Write Characters Your Readers Won't Forget, Write Worlds Your Readers Won't Forget,* and the fiction titles *Ansible, The Zombie Bible, Nyota's Tyrannosaur,* and *Dante's Heart.* Best known for his weird fiction, alternate history, and science fiction, he holds a Ph.D. in English from the University of Denver (as Daniel Fusch) and has served as a developmental editor for Westmarch Publishing. His fiction has been acclaimed by NPR, has served as the topic for scholarly work in *Relegere* and *Weird Fiction Review,* and he has been hailed as "SF's premier poet of loneliness." He is fascinated by ancient languages, history, and religious studies. He lives in Colorado with his wife and three children and is working on his next book.

MORE BOOKS
FROM STANT LITORE

Lives of

Unstoppable

HOPE

STANT LITORE

LIVES OF UNSTOPPABLE HOPE: LIVING THE BEATITUDES

"I HAVE LEARNED THAT HOPE, which I had thought small and delicate like a moth in the night, can be hard as steel, a blade in your hand."

Dark nights waiting by his daughter Inara's hospital bed and a long journey through the Beatitudes in Koine Greek challenged everything Stant Litore thought he knew about being "blessed" and "poor in spirit," and what it might mean to live a life of unstoppable hope.

In this deeply personal and insightful study, Litore invites you into that journey, too.

https://www.amazon.com/dp/B00X4UYW2A

THE ZOMBIE BIBLE

BIBLE

SILVER EDITION

STANT LITORE

Death Has Come Up Into Our Windows

STANT LITORE

What Our Eyes Have Witnessed

STANT LITORE

Strangers in the Land

STANT LITORE

No Lasting Burial

STANT LITORE

I Will Hold My Death Close

STANT LITORE

THE ZOMBIE BIBLE

DEATH HAS COME UP INTO OUR WINDOWS
the story of Jeremiah, the weeping prophet

WHAT OUR EYES HAVE WITNESSED
the story of the martyrdom of Polycarp

STRANGERS IN THE LAND
the story of Deborah and Jael

NO LASTING BURIAL
the story of Jesus

I WILL HOLD MY DEATH CLOSE
the story of Jepthah's daughter

Each volume retells a biblical tale as an episode in humanity's enduring struggle against hunger—and the hungry dead.

"Litore's vibrant writing rips the lid off of the King James version and reveals to us a world of intense human hopes, dreams and pathos. You've never seen anything like this before." —Richard Ellis Preston, Jr., author of *Romulus Buckle and the City of the Founders*

STANT LITORE

NYOTA'S
TYRANNOSAUR

NYOTA'S TYRANNOSAUR

MEET NYOTA MADAKI AND HER TYRANNOSAUR.
FIGHTING FOR SURVIVAL IN THE FAR FUTURE.

Stranded inside the world where massive dinosaurs are grown for the arenas, Nyota will face many perils—the hunger of nocturnal predators, the crash of starvation, and the devouring rot of a bioweapon unleashed inside the tyrannosaur world while war in space rages just outside.

But Nyota is ready. Inhabited by entire ecosystems of nanites, trained for strength and speed and elegance, capable of feats that would leave others broken on the forest floor, Nyota can handle anything. Anything, that is, except the sudden rush of forgotten memories into her heart. Anything but the realization of who she really is.

Luckily she won't have to face that alone. Not with this tyrannosaur egg hatching beside her.

https://www.amazon.com/dp/B07FQ76J2Q

"Stant Litore turns a concept that would be clunky, camp, or just plain weird in other hands into something as natural as feeling the stretch of your own muscles when you move." —O.E. Tearmann, author of The Hands We're Given (Aces High, Jokers Wild)

Made in the USA
Middletown, DE
18 April 2019